Farstraers

Voyages and Homecomings

Jocelyn Rendall

Farstraers

Voyages and Homecomings

Jocelyn Rendall

Drawings by Crispin Worthington

First published in 2021 by Errival,
Holland, Papa Westray KW17 2BU

Copyright © Jocelyn Rendall, 2021

ISBN   978-1-7398497-0-2

Design by Ross Jamieson
Front cover: illustration Crispin Worthington/Photography Rebecca Marr
Back cover: image Orkney Library and Archive

Typeset in Palatino and Monotype Corsiva
Printed by Think Digital Books
www.thinkdigitalbooks.co.uk

Contents

Foreword

When Jocelyn Rendall is not working on the farm that she and her husband Neil run on Papa Westray, she can often be found in Orkney's excellent Library and Archive in Kirkwall. A meticulous researcher and elegant prose writer, Jocelyn has a sharp eye for a telling detail, no matter how small or insignificant looking; yet she never loses touch with the bigger picture in which the gems are set. This is borne out in her last book, *Steering the Stone Ships*, her masterly account of church and people in Orkney over fourteen centuries. Readers who have enjoyed Jocelyn's painstaking, but never dull, writing have been looking forward to what might come next from her pen; her latest book will not disappoint.

FARSTRAERS: Voyages and Homecomings is a stunning book, one which fills a significant gap in Orkney's historiography. Right from the start, the author explains that, while the word farstraers can be found in an Orkney document of 1658, it does not seem to surface anywhere else; nevertheless she successfully persuades the shy but intriguing word to do a lot of heavy lifting throughout the text of a book that talks about wandering and adventurous Orcadians over several centuries. The reader will be introduced to alleged witches, salty sea captains, rogues, rebels, pioneers, an Orkney Nabob, Edinburgh scandals and even a Westray ghost story. The raw material comes from vivid letters written by Orcadians in different parts of the world and from different generations, all mined from what the author calls "the treasure house of the Orkney Archives". Enhancing the stories she has woven round these letters, are the beautiful illustrations she has gathered from collections on both sides of the Atlantic and Crispin Worthington's delightful drawings. I can say with confidence that there can be no finer guide to these ancient and more modern Orkney treasures than the indefatigable Jocelyn Rendall, a congenial, witty and wise companion.

RON FERGUSON

Acknowledgements

Farstraers would never have left home port, let alone reached its destination, if it were not for the kind friends who have helped me at every stage of a long journey to chart a course, navigate through historical minefields and literary doldrums and finally steer the book into publication.

Anne Mitchell, undertaking the herculean task of cataloguing the immense archive of Balfour papers in the Kirkwall Library and Archive, introduced me to this family and their remarkable correspondence. Some of their letters, such as Marcus Calder's wonderful account of James Stewart's reappearance in Westray five years after his death, were first discovered by Anne. Her discoveries, enthusiasm, insights and advice have been invaluable and it is impossible to thank her enough.

I cannot imagine *Farstraers* without Crispin Worthington's wonderful maps and drawings. Both Crispin and Charlotte took great trouble in researching maps, sailing distances, types of ship and costumes appropriate to the date of the illustrations I requested; I can only say a huge Thank You to them both and hope that the text lives up to the drawings.

I am very grateful to Catharine Niven and Michael McGhee for proof-reading, to Ross Jamieson for turning a much-altered manuscript into a book, and to Mark Edmonds for steering it into print.

The cover was design-by-committee: thank you Rebecca Marr, Crispin, Mark, Ross and Anne.

Most of the stories in this book had their beginnings in the Kirkwall Library. I would like to thank David Mackie and Lucy Gibbon for permission to quote from and reproduce documents and photographs in the Archive, and all the staff for being unfailingly helpful.

Morag MacInnes kindly gave me permission to quote from her poem *Alias Isobel*. The following also gave me permission to reproduce paintings, photographs and manuscripts in their collections: Aberdeen City and Aberdeenshire Archives, DeLille Diament, the Hudson's Bay Company Archive, Kirkwall Museums, the Leith family, Library and Archives Canada, Mary Evans Picture Library, National Army Museum, National Maritime Museum, National Museums of Scotland, National Trust, North Wind Picture Archives, the Royal Collection, Stromness Museum, Victoria and Albert Museum.

From the beginning, Ron Ferguson has generously given me his time, advice and encouragement. I am deeply grateful to him for writing the foreword to *Farstraers*, but even more, to him and to Cristine, for their much-valued love and support. Finally, my thanks to Neil, who had to live with the farstraers for a very long time.

Papa Westray 2021

List of Illustrations

Unless otherwise stated, photographs used in this book are by the author and maps and drawings are by Crispin Worthington. Jocelyn Rendall and Crispin Worthington retain the copyright on these images.

The following abbreviation for credits is used:
OLA   reproduced courtesy of Orkney Library and Archive.

Bay Company, signed A.H. Hider (1870-1952), (Photograph by Rebecca Marr © Stromness Museum).
7.11   Map of Assiniboia 1817.
7.12   Fort Garry, a Hudson's Bay trading post on the Red River, early 1800s, hand-coloured woodcut after black-and-white woodcut in J.Winsor, ed., *Narrative and Critical History of America* published Boston 1888 (North Wind Picture Archives GCAN2A-00034).
7.13   Birch-bark canoes in rapids on the Red River, hand-coloured woodcut after black-and-white woodcut in R. Brown, *The Countries of the World: Being a Popular Description of the Various Continents, Islands, Rivers, Seas, and Peoples of the Globe,* published London n. d. (North Wind Picture Archives BUSN2A-00101).
8.1   Map of India.
8.2   John Balfour 1750-1842, probably painted in Edinburgh 1771-72, photograph by D. Shearer of the painting formerly in Balfour Castle (OLA).
8.3   Fort St George on the Coromandel Coast Belonging to the East India Company of England, coloured engraving by Jan Van Ryne 1754 (National Maritime Museum, Greenwich, London).
8.4   Gold star pagoda with a figure of Vishnu on one face and a star on the other, minted in Madras 1740-1807 (Classical Numismatic Group, Inc., Wikimedia Commons).
8.5   The battle of Pollilur in 1780 with Tipu Sultan defeating the British troops, copy of a mural painted on Tipu's palace at Seringapatam, gouache on paper (Mary Evans/© Otto Money, photography by AIC Photographic Services).
8.6   Balfour Castle in Shapinsay, designed by David Bryce for David Balfour 1847 (Purplebaron, Wikimedia Commons).
8.7   Tipu's Tiger, an automaton created for Tipu Sultan; carved and painted wood representing a tiger savaging a European, late 18th century (Victoria and Albert Museum).
8.8   Duleep Singh, oil on canvas by Franz Xaver Winterhalter, signed and dated 1854, Osborne House (Royal Collection Trust/© Her Majesty Queen Elizabeth II 2020).
8.9   Family tree of the Burroughs and Traill families.
8.10   Captain Frederick William Burroughs, photogaph (OLA).
8.11   The 93rd Highlanders Storming of the Secundra Bagh 16 November 1857, watercolour by Orlando Norie (Image courtesy of the National Army Museum, London).
8.12   The Taj Mahal, Agra, built by Shah Jehan as a mausoleum for his wife Mumtaz Mahal 1632.
8.13   The Qutub Minar in Delhi.
8.14   Fort Attock on the River Indus, photograph by Maj. M.C. Holmes 1919 (Image courtesy of the National Army Museum, London).
8.15   Trumland House, Rousay, designed by David Bryce for General and Mrs Burroughs.
8.16   Houses on a canal, Srinagar, Kashmir, engraving by Alfred Koechlin-Schwartz 1858 (Mary Evans Picture Library).
9.1   St Mary's, the old North parish kirk in Pierowall, Westray.
9.2   James Stewart of Brough, oil on canvas by John Watson Gordon (1788-1864), (Orkney Museums).

A Note on Spelling

The spelling of personal and place names is rarely consistent in 18th- and 19th-century documents, sometimes varying within a single letter. The Balfour estate in Westray, for example, is written as Trenaby, Trenabie and Trenabay. I have aimed to use the spelling most commonly used in my sources, which is not always the same as on modern maps, so Charlestown rather than Charleston, and Archangel not Arkhangelsk.

Introduction

In August 1658 Patrick Craigie, Baillie of the Burgh of Kirkwall, sailed across the Pentland Firth and set out for Edinburgh. Behind him lay islands looted and plundered and oppressed by seven years of military occupation by Cromwell's troops. Ahead of him lay more than 300 miles of treacherous roads, mountains, firths and ferries. His saddlebags were stuffed with the lengthy pages of the commission given to him by the Magistrates and Town Council of Kirkwall. He was to plead with the Council of State for redress of Orkney's grievances. That achieved, he was to obtain warrants *against all unfrie men, and specialle against farstraers that is dispersit alongst the hail countrie, and islands.* Farstraers. The word jumped out at me, I could not find it in any dictionary but it fell into a gap where a word was needed. The magistrates were using it in a negative sense, for lawbreakers, but *those who strayed far* exactly described so many Orkney people of past centuries who strayed far and wide geographically, the thousands who, out of economic necessity, had literally *dispersit* all over the world. There were also those, usually women, who far-strayed metaphorically, forced by circumstances outside their usual feminine roles or social norms, or pushed out of society because they were perceived to stray beyond the bounds of knowledge or practice acceptable to the Kirk.

Our ephemera of emails and digital photographs is unlikely to survive for future historians. We are more fortunate. Many of our predecessors not only wrote long letters to their family and friends but hoarded those they received, generation after generation, and an astonishing number ended in the safe haven of the Orkney Archives. To hold one is to have a magic link to people living 150 years, even 250 years ago, to read the stories of their lives as they told them in their own words, to engage with them as individuals.

1

The main sources for the stories written in this book are letters written between the mid 18th and mid 19th centuries. Some were written in Orkney to friends and relations on the islands, many more were written from abroad to families at home. Few personal letters survive from earlier times, but even when people did not or could not write, dialogues quoted in contemporary records can bring them to life. With these as my starting points, and with the aid of diaries, biographies and the invaluable *Statistical Accounts*, I have tried to paint the historical backdrop to the writers' and speakers' words and put some flesh on the bare bones of their names. Sometimes their stories are entertaining, sometimes tragic, sometimes they raise uncomfortable issues, such as the persecution of women as witches or the involvement of Scots in the slave trade; issues still to be fully confronted not just in Orkney but in all parts of Scotland.

The letters draw us into a time constantly overshadowed by threats of war or famine, of political upheaval or economic disaster, of families separated by thousands of miles before the telegraph or steamboat could materially alter the pace of travel and the transmission of news. They gather together a cross-section of Orkney society: lairds and their ladies and servants, farmers and factors and ships' captains, ministers and soldiers, lawyers and labourers and children. Many of these made no significant mark on Orkney history and their names were virtually unknown outside the islands, yet their stories make one realise just how remarkable the lives of many 'ordinary' Orcadians were.

Orkney is a relatively small community and wherever you go you can be sure of seeing familiar faces. To mentally wander through the streets of the past is exactly the same experience. In their letters, you cannot help but bump into Balfours or Baikies or Mansons or their friends and innumerable relations at every corner. The same individuals are encountered again and again (wearing different hats for different occasions, just as they would today), so they become as familiar as one's contemporaries. We recognise that, underneath unfamiliar clothes and modes of speech, they are just like us. Many of them are linked by a network of kinship or business or friendship and the same web links the chapters in this book.

Orcadians wrote home to their families from all over the known world and their stories bring into poignant focus the extent of the Orkney diaspora. The islands the writers grew up in – and fled from – were very different places to what they are now. They were seen as a dead-end of drastic poverty where it was essential for the boys of a family to leave as soon as possible to make a living elsewhere. Even the 'gentry' were constantly worrying about their debts and shortage of cash. Their wealth was in their ship-borne cargoes, always vulnerable to shipwreck or capture by enemy shipping; their harvests which so often failed. Although the land was fertile, frequent cycles of bad weather devastated crops and, throughout the 16th, 17th and 18th centuries, famine reappeared at regular intervals. Even in the 19th century, deaths from starvation during the bad years were averted only because famine relief was more organised and there were more opportunities for emigration.

The sea offered the fishing, near home or in the seas off Iceland, or the freezing hardship of the whaling ships in the Davis Straits. The discovery of arctic furs, and the incomparable advantages of beaver hides for making gentlemen's hats, launched the Hudson's Bay Company which lured generations of Orkney men to the Nor'Wast. Soldiering and the navy provided other options. In the 18th century Britain was almost continually at war and in the 19th century perpetually expanding and defending the frontiers of empire. Ships and regiments demanded men for crew and cannon fodder. The manpower required to crew the Royal Navy almost trebled in the 1700s, and a few harrowing letters that found their way to Orkney carry tales of men pressed and then captured by enemy shipping, languishing in French or Spanish prisons. Others, recruited with promises of the King's shilling, died in distant and incomprehensible conflicts, failing to keep the American colonies British, or to dictate the politics of Afghanistan.

Parents were desperate to find their sons employment out of the islands. Boys left home at 15 or 16 or even younger and went wherever an uncle or family friend found them a 'situation'. They went to sea on merchant ships and men-of-war, to sugar plantations in the West Indies, trading companies in Boston and East India Company desks in Madras. Their letters are often unhappy; they are homesick, sick or just frustrated at what a very long way they are from making a fortune and being able to come home. Often they are exasperatingly uninformative; dutiful teenage bulletins of health and enquiries after relatives at home that leave the interesting questions unanswered. I imagine Orkney mothers scanning them with frustration. The writers' lives are often tragically short. Robert Mowat returned home from the Caribbean with empty pockets and broken health, having failed to make any money in four years of misery and fever. He died soon after reaching Orkney, aged 21. Sometimes a single letter sets one off on a trail of an extraordinary adventure: servant lad Baikie Harvey sailed from Kirkwall in 1775 with a shipload of poor emigrants who hoped to find a better life in Georgia and instead found themselves fleeing massacres by natives and attacked by both rebels and loyalists in the American Revolution. Harvey was shot in a skirmish aged 20.

The correspondence is of course one-sided, and has huge gaps where letters never arrived or were lost, but it can be a key to open a door just a chink and let us peer through to see something of Orkney in the past, and also of the world seen through Orkney eyes two or three hundred years ago. The letters from India or Jamaica, Hudson Bay[1] or Georgia have been read and re-read and read again by the *Honoured Parents* to whom they are addressed, passed around the grandparents, cousins, neighbours to whom the young writer has offered his *best respects*, and at last put safely away and treasured. It is always a source of wonder that something so fragile as a flimsy piece of paper has survived for so long, but it is a miracle that they reached Orkney in the first place.

The great majority of the many thousands who left the islands to make a living overseas sailed into a black hole as far as history is concerned. For those who could write, there were few opportunities to send letters home. When John Balfour went to India in 1770 there were only two boats a year sailing from Madras to Britain and, once they reached a British port, it would be several more weeks of travel by coach and ship again by Leith or Aberdeen before mail reached the Northern Isles. Ships sailed to the Hudson's Bay Company posts on the east coast of North America once a year with supplies and mail and took at least six weeks to return; when the Company expanded to the west coast, the journey to or from Vancouver took six months. Letters had to escape shipwreck, piracy and enemy shipping on their way home. Their writers would have been astonished to know that their correspondence would survive them by two or even three hundred years to become treasured archives, waiting for someone to open and reread them, sympathise with the writers' misfortunes, thrill at their adventures, admire their achievements or laugh at their gossip.

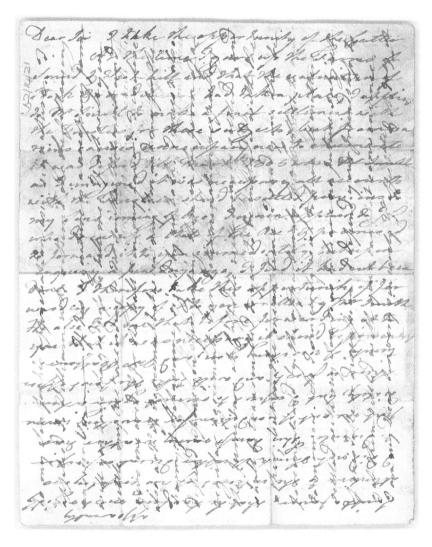

Introduction 1
Draft letter from Frances Balfour (OLA D2/14/21)

A postal service theoretically existed in Britain from 1635 when Charles I opened up his 'Royal Mail' for public use. Twenty years later, Oliver Cromwell established the General Post Office, but this service, with rates based on distance and the number of sheets of paper used, was prohibitively expensive for most people, who just relied on someone with horse or carriage or ship travelling in the right direction. Coffee-houses often acted as collection centres for mail; Thomas Balfour of Huip, for example, addressed his letters from the 'Exchange Coffee House Edinburgh' when he was away from home on business. Even those who used the GPO economised by using a single sheet of paper which was folded over, addressed and sealed with wax; an envelope would have counted as an extra page. (Envelopes only started to come into use when the pre-paid postage stamp was invented in 1840, and the introduction of a uniform penny post for postage within the British Isles made writing letters affordable to all.) Reading the letters is often a difficult decoding exercise: the ink is faded, the thin sheets torn at the edges, some of the writers have maddeningly illegible handwriting and some have saved costly paper and postage by writing both across the page and up it.

The poor and illiterate of course did not write letters, but the words of even the poorest and most marginalised in the community were captured in records of Kirk meetings and of criminal trials. These are not nearly as dry and formal as they sound: dialogues, however lengthy, were recorded verbatim and so often present a lively picture of the personalities, passions and prejudices of the speakers. These documents can take us further back in time than family letters and provide an insight into daily life in 17th-century Orkney, into beliefs and controversies and ways of thought long forgotten. Perhaps the most fascinating, and saddest, documents concern the accusations of witchcraft which brought a number of men and women to their trial in St Magnus Cathedral and to the stake on Kirkwall's Gallowhill. In the records of the trials we hear the victims speak, and they become not statistics but individuals in a tragic story.

It is in their letters, however, that people become most alive and real, sometimes their personalities almost jumping out of the page, and occasionally one hits epistolary gold. For sheer drama it is hard to beat Sandy Watt's wonderful description of his harrowing sea journey to the Caribbean, his sentences punctuated only by howling winds and crashing masts. A certain Captain Burroughs wrote long letters to David Balfour, full of observant details of the scenery, the architecture, and the customs of an India that he relished and loved to describe. A paragraph of Marion Balfour's society gossip can whirl one in a second to an 18th-century Edinburgh drawing-room, bonneted heads bent giggling over their teacups, while Peggy Balfour's breathless account of being presented at Court is sheer delight. Letters from women tend to be much more revealing about family life, more personal and, often, far more entertaining than those of their menfolk.

Of all the remarkable collections of correspondence in the Orkney Archives, that of the Balfour family must weigh in as the richest and most extraordinary. The Balfours of Trenaby were a family of indefatigable letter-writers and hoarders of their personal and business letters, estate papers and accounts. Some 50,000 documents spanning almost 400 years of Balfours from the mid 16th century until the early 20th came to the Kirkwall Library bundled in what often seem random gatherings of letters from different authors written at different times. So far less than half the enormous collection has been catalogued in detail, letter by letter. This has the frustrating drawback that half a story may come to light but the other half remains inaccessible. Nonetheless, these letters brilliantly bring to life not only the extended family and their contemporaries but also throw a spotlight on national politics and the international events which were the concerns of the day.

John Balfour wrote from India at the time the East India Company was turning itself from a trading company into an aggressively imperialistic power. Lord Ligonier, Frances Balfour's brother, sent distressing news of the defeat of British troops in the American Revolution and her son William Balfour wrote home about the naval engagements with the French. In their letters, long-dead Balfours and their friends recount the ups and downs of their family life, their views on everything from turnip cultivation to the likelihood of a French invasion, from Mughal architecture in India to a narrow escape from shipwreck. There is news of famine and fashion, schooling and smuggling, tabloid-style gossip about scandals in the royal family and rumours of a landing by Napoleon. You can read about the slave trade and the price of kelp, follow Orcadians from the snows of Hudson Bay to the wilds of the North-West Frontier of India, and meet all the passion, bitchiness, affection, loyalties and infidelities one might expect of any family in any age. Anyone who enjoyed *Downton Abbey* would find similar dynastic dramas in the pages of the Balfour letters.[2]

The stories that emerged from all these sources fell roughly into the sections in which I have divided this book, starting in the turbulent years of the 17th and early 18th centuries which were harrowed by famine, religious and political conflict and chronic insecurity. Some of the divisions are geographical, reflecting the far-flung long-term destinations from which Orkney men wrote home.

Most of the letters I have read were written by men and describe a man's world, but often they are written to the much-loved and respected matriarchs who are holding everything together at home. Such huge numbers of men working overseas meant a disproportionate number of females in the islands – in some parishes there were twice as many women as men – so it is appropriate that space is given to the many remarkable women who were left in charge of their households, farms and businesses and estates, forced to 'stray far' from traditional expectations of a woman's role in order to provide for their families. I found plenty of young farstraers too. There were lairds' sons, like the Balfour boys, taken from the North Isles to prep school in London aged nine and ten and despatched into the army and navy in wartime when they were barely into their teens, and, at the other end of the social scale, unaccompanied paupers joining emigrant ships at the age of ten.

Finally, there is a marvellous ghost story from Westray, about the laird who 'strayed' from the other side of the grave ...

Introduction 2
Letter from Elizabeth Balfour to her son Thomas, 3/9/1795. Obviously Thomas ignored the injunction to burn this when you have read it! *(OLA D2/6/8)*

Introduction Notes

1   The bay named after Sir Henry Hudson, who mapped the coastline in 1610/11,
     is Hudson Bay. However, the Company which was to have such a significant
     impact on Orkney's history is the Hudson's Bay Company.
2   The Balfour Archive was housed in Balfour Castle on Shapinsay until the last of
     the Balfour family died without heirs in 1961 and the castle was sold to Tadeusz
     Zawadski. The 57 boxes containing the archive, (some seven hundredweight of
     documents) were then rescued by Orkney Library archivist Euan MacGillivray
     for the Orkney Library and Archive.

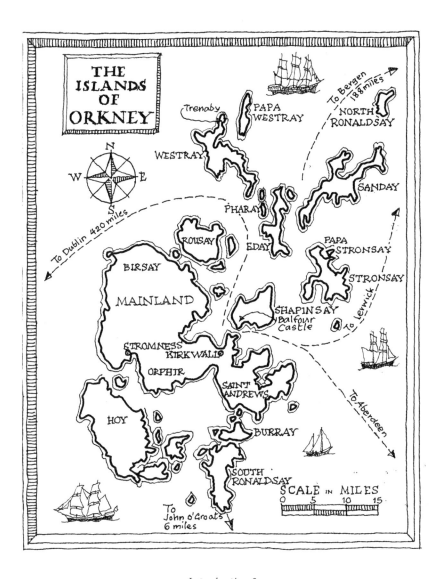

Introduction 3

11

CHAPTER 1

Witches, Politics and Power

Prologue

To open a window on the 17th century is to look upon a grim period in Orkney history, when long spells of harsh weather brought frequent famines and religious and political upheaval troubled the whole country. It was a time of chronic insecurity among both rich and poor and in contemporary records we hear the voices of a deeply divided, frightened and angry people, uninhibited in the violence of their quarrels.

The reformed Kirk of Scotland tightened its grip on society. Many of the old traditions and folk-beliefs that had co-existed comfortably with the pre-Reformation Church were now denounced as 'papist' – at best – or even diabolical. Men and women whose skills – real or imaginary – were seen as 'farstraying' outside the bounds of ordinary knowledge were accused of witchcraft by jealous or spiteful neighbours, interrogated by their parish Kirk Session and then the Presbytery before being referred to a secular court. Some were brutally punished, some burnt at the stake on Kirkwall's Gallowhill. To us it is very evident that, rather than 'straying' from social norms, the 'witches' were pushed to the margins of society, victims of a misogynistic and punitive Kirk and a people desperate to find scapegoats for their distresses.

The Kirk Sessions and Presbyteries were of course composed of men drawn from the landed and property-owning class who attempted to enforce 'godly behaviour' upon their social inferiors. The Kirk was obsessed with sexuality and it is evident that women were targeted in the crackdown on immorality. Those who had 'farstrayed' morally (considering their number, they could hardly be regarded as straying out of normal behaviour) could expect rebuke and punishment. However, the ungodly by no means always submitted quietly to being rebuked. In fact, the minutes of Kirk meetings shed some entertaining light on the far from docile attitude of Orkney women towards authority!

While the poor struggled with endemic poverty and hunger, the 'gentry' – the lairds and ministers – quarrelled fiercely amongst themselves as they *struggled to keep a safe footing on what had become the very slippery floor of national politics. The mid decades of the 17th century brought the tide of civil war to Orkney: Cromwell's troops garrisoned Kirkwall, the islands lay under military occupation. Controversy raged between the different factions and those in positions of power balanced nervously on knife-edges of uncertainty lest they should lose wealth, status, even their lives with the next pendulum-swing of politics. Not a position for maintaining one's mental equilibrium.*

The political instability continued well into the 18th century, only settling after the thorough suppression of the Jacobite rebellions. Rivalry between the supporters of King and Covenant, of Episcopacy and Presbyterianism, of Hanoverians and Jacobites dominated Orkney life at both ends of the social scale and led to violent collisions of passions and prejudices.

Famine and Flames

On the 7th of July 1624 fifteen Orkney men gathered in the south transept of St Magnus Cathedral in Kirkwall. They were all landowners and 'big men' of the county, called to an assize presided over by Sir John Scottiscraig, *knight, justiciar and sheriff-principal of Orkney and Shetland.* They had assembled to convict a witch. *Entered Marable Couper ... accused of committing the devilish and abominable crime of superstition, witchcraft and sorcery.*[1]

These assizes are often called witchcraft trials but it is soon obvious that they are not 'trials' in the modern sense of the word at all. The evidence for the prosecution is heard but there is no defence, no interrogation of witnesses, no weighing of evidence, no right of appeal and definitely no pussy-footing around with 'innocent until proved guilty'. Marable denied most of the charges that were read out but that did her little good; she had a reputation as a witch and that was quite enough for the assize to condemn her to be *tane by the lockman* [jailer], *hir hands bund, and be carried to the head of the Loan, the place of execution, and their knet to ane staik, wiried to the death* [tied to a stake, strangled to death] *and brunt in ashes.*[2] The verdict was inevitable from the beginning.

Marable was just one of some 80 people accused of witchcraft in Orkney between the last years of the 16th and the first years of the 18th century,[3] at least 15 of whom met Marable's fate of being *wiried* and burnt.[4] At first sight, the transcripts of the trials, dense with legal jargon and heavily cluttered with dog-Latin, remove the principal characters into a remote and inaccessible past. Yet they do provide a rare chance at least to catch a glimpse of the daily lives of these people, of the economy of their little farms, their possessions – or lack of them – and their beliefs. In the depositions one can hear snatches of the kind of gossip one might have overheard in Birsay or Rendall or Rousay while fetching water from the well or leading one's cow to pasture; it is even possible to hear something of the individual personalities of the speakers. Gradually they emerge out of the shadows as real people.

The daughter of Mr Couper, Marable was married to John Spence. They had at least one son, Robbie, and they lived in a house in the settlement Northside in Birsay parish where their descendants were still living in the 20th century. She was not the 'old hag' of fairy stories but a woman young enough to be 'in childbed' at the time of some of the quarrels with her neighbours, and quarrelling with Marable was perilous. She had a fearsome reputation for having the power to inflict fatal sickness on her enemies and to lift it again if she chose. She had a sense of humour and a taste for practical jokes – unappreciated by their victims – which were solemnly recorded at her trial. When Oliver Garacoat, the gullible Session Clerk, came to her house to summon her to face the Session, she was lying in bed and claimed she could not possibly come because her neighbour, *Alexander Philip's wife*, had quarrelled with her and *tramped out her guts, and ye let him see as it had been your guts, lying beside you, most fearful to look to ...* A note in the margin reads: *Marable confessed it was the guts of a lamb!*[5]

As in the rest of Scotland, the majority of the Orkney population subsisted off the land, a cluster of households like Northside living closely together and sharing an insecure joint-tenancy of a township. A few cattle provided milk, butter to pay the rent, traction for the plough and occasional income. Small, undrained, overworked strips of arable ground grew oats and bere,[6] the grain ground into meal or brewed into ale for human consumption and the straw fed to the livestock. Methods of agriculture were primitive. 'Improvements' like drainage, enclosures and fodder crops for winter feed were still far in the future. (Two hundred years after Marable's time, cattle were being carried out of byres in the spring because they were too weak from starvation to stand.) In winter families shared their small, earth-floored, windowless dwellings with their livestock. Cramped together in insanitary conditions as they were, disease was endemic among both animals and humans and mortality high. The desperately inefficient farms could not produce a surplus that would enable a family to survive a bad season and in the 1600s bad seasons were all too frequent. The

'Little Ice Age' brought cycles of savage weather (one of the worst was in the 1620s) that caused widespread distress.[7] Malnutrition and even death from starvation were not uncommon in Orkney and Shetland. The frequent guests in every home were hunger and despair.

The gravity of the situation is well documented. In 1615 a Kirkwall statute forbade anyone to recruit young men to go away to the fishing off Iceland or elsewhere, *forasmuch as the lands are laid lay* [ley, fallow] *and waste by the frequent death of the labourers of the ground these years bygone, through the great scarcity, famine and dearth of the land.*[8] A few years after Marable's trial, the bishops of Orkney and Caithness wrote to the Privy Council for help because *multitudes die in the open fields and there is none to burie thame ... The ground yields thame no cornes and the sea affords no fishes unto them as formerlie it wount to doe ... Some devoure sea ware; some eate dogges; some steale foules. Of nine in a familie seven at once died ... Manie are redacted to that extremity that they are forced to steale and thereafter are execute; and some have desperatelie run in the sea and drowned thamselffis.*[9]

It seems astonishing that the population had the resilience to survive at all. In the 1680s *an universal sterility prevailed in Orkney, when people died in hundreds; the lands were laid waste for want of strength both of man and beast, and no seed; many of the best places were totally relinquished ...*[10] The 1690s, 'King William's Years' were no better, and cycles of appalling weather continued to bring serious hardship in the next century.

Reading these contemporary accounts, the shrill denunciations in the records sound less like bitchiness and grumpiness and more like the screams of people driven to the edge of endurance. The close proximity of neighbours (likely to be bad-tempered and edgy from hunger and anxiety) must have often strained relationships to breaking point. The fields were not enclosed, the livestock were tethered – or supposed to be tethered – during the summer months to keep them out of the growing crops; in the winter they wandered freely. There was plenty of opportunity to be irritated by the neighbour who was habitually hanging round your door begging and borrowing, whose cow or sheep strayed into your patch of oats or your precious scrap of hayfield, or whose wandering calf ate your kerchief drying on the dyke. The little farms depended on a good deal of sharing, men and women worked at major tasks like the harvest together. Anyone who would not pull his or her weight would quickly become unpopular and there was plenty of opportunity for jealousy as well: if one woman was churning good butter and her neighbour none at all, if one cow produced a good calf but next door's calf died, if one man's rig produced 20 sheaves of corn and another's only two.

What had Marable actually done? Her accusers were her neighbours, chiefly the Mowats who had had a run of misfortune with their cattle. *Four years ago, David Mowat in Banks, and his wife Margaret had three newly-calved cows, but Margaret had no profit from them* [she could not make any butter] ... *At the following Candlemas Margaret met with you at your own door and after many hard words she struck you because of the loss she had had of her cows. The following years they had three cows, but one died when she calved, the second calved a calf but she never gave any milk, and the third cow for four years past never took bull. And at the following Beltane she had one cow and two young cattle that died. You* [Marable] *did these things through your witchcraft and devilry ... Which, rank witch, you cannot deny.*

Those charges are typical of the great majority of accusations against witches, not just in Orkney but all over rural Europe or Africa, or anywhere that cows were a household's most precious but vulnerable commodity. There was no understanding of disease and no recognition that *anything* could happen by accident; if the milk of the starved cow was so thin that it would not churn into butter, it was because a witch *had taken away the profit*, if a beast sickened or fell over the cliff, the cause was a curse or spell. There was absolutely no other explanation. The short answer to what had Marable done? She had fallen foul of a neighbour.

It seems that Marable was a frequent but unwelcome visitor around the Mowats' byre and barn. It was winter, the sheaves of oats and bere were in the barn ready to be threshed and the grain then ground into meal. Margaret reported that, one day, she and her servant could not turn their quern at all, and when they did manage to grind, their meal was *like dust,* but it turned back into good meal again when Marable was reproached for bewitching it. Due to the wet climate, corn had to be artificially dried before it could be milled into meal and drying kilns were usually built in or onto one end of the barn, the heat from a slow fire lit in the barn being led through a flue to heat and dry the grain. The fire needed to be attended to constantly for eight or ten hours and, inevitably, it sometimes got out of control. The last straw for the Mowats was the calamity of their kiln catching fire ... *you came to David's house, and after much quarrelling, he struck you and pushed you to the door, and you swore that he would repent of that stroke. Four days later, having put six meills of oats on his kiln to dry, the kiln went on fire; the grain that he was able to save he took to Alexander Ingsay's kiln, and it likewise went on fire and burnt, by your witchcraft.*[11]

Figure 1.1
Barn and corn-drying kiln, Birsay.

At this point, one can feel some sympathy for the Mowats. As a family with at least three cows and employing one or two servants, they were better off than most of the tenants in Northside, but the loss of their cattle and their hard-won grain would still have been catastrophic. Even today, modern veterinary science can often find no cause for sudden deaths of cattle and somehow inexplicable misfortune seems harder to bear than when one can understand the cause. It seems to be a constant of the human condition that we need to find someone or something to blame for apparently randomly afflicted tragedy. The Mowats were totally typical of their age in blaming witchcraft. No-one in 17th-century Scotland, from the poorest to the best educated, had any doubt at all that witches existed, and the Old Testament injunction: *thou shalt not suffer a witch to live*[12] provided an unequivocal justification for their removal.

Witch-hunts almost invariably coincided with times of crisis. The Reformation fractured northern Europe along religious lines and the medieval illusion of a 'united Christendom' collapsed to reveal a fragmented world of chronic insecurity. Trials and burnings of witches became almost commonplace on the Continent by the late 15th century, and chronicles of that time make the connection between adversity and persecution explicit. *In that year, because of the bad weather, people began to grumble loudly against female witches.*[13] Harvest failure and hunger stoked fires fanned by religious and political instability, and all those factors were present in Orkney in the 1600s.

The new National Kirk which came into being in Scotland in 1560, out of the chaos of civil war and the disintegration of Queen Mary's reign, had not only a centralized authority but a power at grass-roots level which had never existed before. While many people in rural areas probably had little understanding of the new theology, their daily lives were definitely changed by the new bureaucracy which placed even the remotest part of Scotland under the jurisdiction of the Church courts: the hierarchy of General Assembly, Synod, Presbytery and Kirk Session.

Behind the Church courts, and enforcing their authority, was the power of the 'godly State', interpreting and imposing the will of God. Christina Larner, the foremost historian of witch-craft in Scotland in recent years, pointed out that it is a characteristic of new regimes in search of legitimacy that they demand a high level of conformity in behaviour as well as in belief. 20th-century states such as China, Cuba and Iran were as repressive as 17th-century Scotland towards sexuality, drunkenness and festivals. Kirk Sessions kept their congregations under as close a scrutiny as the Stasi,[14] private lives ceased to be private and sinners were punished with public rebuke, fines or humiliating rites of repentance. The intention was to encourage 'godliness' but the effect was to encourage people to spy on and denounce a disliked neighbour. This was the background to the process by which the Mowats rid themselves of Marable Couper.

Clearly, the charms and spells that were cited in witchcraft trial records were cultural heritage that had been handed down through the centuries. Fairies, hobgoblins, giants and trows were stowaways from the pagan past who had co-existed comfortably alongside hazy notions of Christianity for generations. Belief in them was universal, among the educated as well as the illiterate, and it was commonly accepted that some people at least had the power to engage with them for their own ends, either good or evil. The pre-Reformation Church had little impact on this underworld and its own rituals fostered belief in invisible ranks of beings who took an intimate interest in the dealings of humans and could be influenced by the repetition of certain formulae of words or small payments. However, increasingly, the Protestant Kirk saw magic and superstition not as mere ignorance but as a diabolical conspiracy between the powers of darkness and their human servants against Christianity.

In 1563 the Scottish Parliament passed the *Act anent Witchcraftis.* It was actually quite sceptical in its wording: it was not only practising witchcraft but deceiving people by *claiming* to have supernatural powers, or consulting witches, that became capital offences. The witches who ended up on Gallowhill were not condemned on a first accusation. The Sessions and Presbytery dealt severely with the first reports of any *charmers, consulters, and abusers* to set an example and deter others. For *abusing the people* by claiming magical powers, Inga

Figure 1.2
The Kirk kept their congregation's private lives under close scrutiny. Sinners were made to do public penance, standing in a sackcloth 'repentance gown', or sitting on the 'repentance stool' during Sunday service. (Image © National Museums of Scotland)

Flett in Shapinsay was sentenced to *satisfy in the vilest habit of penitentiarie*,[15] sackcloth, and as these garments were in constant use by a succession of individuals they were probably vile indeed. Katherine Grieve and Marion Richart – who were seen sitting in a ruined house evidently chatting with the Devil – were placed in the stocks in Sanday.[16] Harsher measures were resorted to if these 'cautionary' punishments failed to deter the culprits.

The Church courts were not criminal courts and anyone suspected of serious crimes such as murder, infanticide or witchcraft had to be handed over to the civil magistrates and the terrible sentences passed on the 'witches' have to be seen in the context of a society which exacted severe penalties for what we would consider petty crimes. In the case of witchcraft, the magistrates could apply to the Privy Council for a commission which authorized them to convene an ad hoc court with powers to try and sentence. Marable had been tried once already, eight years before her final trial and execution. She was one of five women and two men who were tried for witchcraft in Orkney in June 1616 and sentenced to banishment from their parish. This was hardly a soft option. A few years earlier, Jonet Drever in the island of Westray had been condemned to be scourged from one end of the town to the other and then banished, never to return, under pain of death. Sometimes branding on the face with a hot iron accompanied a sentence of banishment, so that there was no possibility of the witch returning home undetected. Katherine Grieve, who was charged with using charms by the Sanday Kirk Session in 1633, 'escaped' with branding and the threat that, if she was seen haunting suspected places or using charms in the future, she would be burnt forthwith.

In fact, banishment was little better than a death sentence, as the reputation of a witch ensured that he or she would be equally unwelcome everywhere else. By law, beggars and vagabonds were obliged to stay in their own parish, and if they turned up homeless in another parish they would be arrested and beaten out of it. In the unlikely event of anyone supporting them, they would be severely punished too. Kirkwall statutes forbade anyone to *grant hospitality to such persons, under pain of 40 shillings Scots ...* [and] *the joggs*[17] – an iron collar on a short chain stapled to the kirk wall or mercat [market] cross. The high proportion of witches who are described as beggars highlights the chronic poverty of the time which forced many to become vagabonds, wanderers, farstraers.

Orkney witches were still being hounded from parish to parish at the end of the 17th century. In 1698 the Kirk Session of Wick minuted that: *Being informed likewise that sorcery and witchcraft abound so much in the parish – that sorcerors banished out of Orkney lurke there – they recommend seriously to the heritors and magistrate to banish all such out of the town and country.*[18]

Lord Advocate George Mackenzie in Edinburgh, (known as 'the bloody Mackenzie' for his harsh verdicts), wrote of examining a woman who told him *she had not confest because she was guilty, but being a poor creature, who wrought* [begged] *for her meat, and being defam'ed for a witch she knew she would starve, for no person thereafter would either give her meat or lodging, and that all men would beat her, and hound Dogs at her, and that therefore she desired to be out of the World.*[19] To be banished must have been rather like being a refugee getting into a leaking, overcrowded boat because the alternative was to be killed, but every time you tried to land you were pushed back into the sea to drown.

So, despite the risks, Marable had returned to Northside – she had a home and a husband and a son there after all – but this put her in contempt of court. More immediately, it threw her in the path of her old enemy, Margaret Corston, who denounced her again. Three years ago, *she* [Margaret] *fell sick and was ill for four months and could get no cure at home or when she was taken to Kirkwall.*[20] *When she came home again and was passing your house* [Marable's] *... you were standing at your door, and Margaret quarrelled with you and called you a banished witch, and said that if she died, she would blame her death on you. You said to her that she might have reproved you quietly if she had anything to say to you, and you took her into your house, and took a birstane stone* [brimstone, burnt stone] *and put it in the fire, and heated a drink of ale with it and gave her to drink. Whereby, as by your witchcraft you caused the sickness, so by the same devilry she got her health.*[21]

Even after four hundred years, one can hear the different personalities of the two women in their voices: Margaret's shrill shriek *Banished witch!* and Marable's calm reply. Our immediate reaction is to ask: if Margaret *really* believed that Marable was a witch, what on earth was she doing going into her house and drinking her ale? However, no-one in the court asked that question. They were not there to assess evidence, but to convict.

Figure 1.3
Marable Couper and others accused of witchcraft were led down the south aisle of the cathedral to be tried before a court assembled in the south transept. From there it was a quick exit into the horrible dungeon 'Marwick's Hole'.

Most of the Orkney trials took place, as Marable's did, in St Magnus Cathedral. Being arrested and bundled off to Kirkwall must have been a traumatic experience in itself: many of the 'witches' were from country parishes or even the North Isles and had probably never been to the town or among strangers before. Before their trial they were incarcerated in 'Marwick's Hole', a totally dark bottle-dungeon formed in a space between the walls of the south transept and the choir. From here they were dragged out – frozen with cold, filthy, half-starved, blinded by the daylight and absolutely terrified – to face the grim line-up of the court. No wonder that when Annie Taylor from Sanday was interrogated *she denied not but said she was uncouth* [ignorant] *and wist not what to say*.[22] In the state of fear and confusion they were in, it would have been easy to persuade them to say whatever the court wanted to hear.

We know from Marable's two trials that she had been the target of accusations by her neighbours for a number of years. In many witchcraft cases, the charges refer to incidents that happened as far back as ten or fifteen years before the trial, or even more. Jonet Drever, who was burnt in 1615, was accused of conversing with the Westray fairies *26 years* earlier. We would question how accurate people's memory was after that time. It is as if the accusations are made with the benefit of hindsight, only after the witch had had considerable time to build up a reputation as a *common and notorious witch*.

Execution probably happened very quickly after the judgement or 'doom' had been given. Sometimes it was the same day, or just a few days later to give time to prepare the bonfire: to gather together loads of peat from the hill and some large driftwood logs dragged from the shore, a bucket of tar to ensure a spectacular blaze. This was not just an execution. It was both a warning and a demonstration of the power of the Kirk in its battle against the Devil. It was not just a condemnation to a horrible death in a fire, but a condemnation to suffering in eternal fire, for without a body there was no possibility of resurrection.[23] There was little room for God's mercy in 17th-century theology.

We do not have a contemporary description of the burnings in Kirkwall but the costs of burning witches survive in the financial accounts of the Burgh of Aberdeen for the years 1596-97 (when there was a major witch-hunt in the area), and this chillingly banal document is fuel enough for the imagination. For one fire we find: *Item, for 16 loads of peats £1 15s; for 4 loads of fir 16s; for 1 oil barrel 10s; 1 tar barrel 6s 8d; 3 fathoms of rope 3s; for the stake, carrying and setting it up 13s 4d; for carrying the peats, coals, and barrels to the hill 8s.* Then there were the costs of carrying four railings *to withstand the press of the people* trying to get a closer view of the spectacle: 8s 8d, and of a new halberd for Thomas Dickson because his was broken trying to keep order among the crowd, and of the fee for John Justice, the hangman: 6s 8d for every execution.[24]

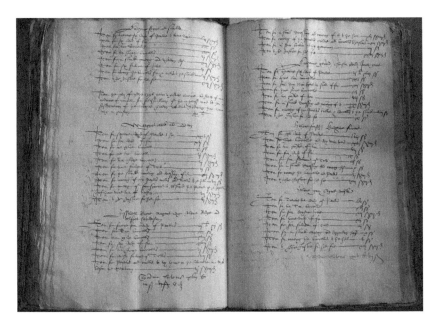

Figure 1.4
Pages from the Dean of Guild Accounts, Aberdeen, detailing the costs of burning witches in the year 1597. CA/7/2/1: Aberdeen City, Guildry Accounts vol.I (1452-1650). (Image by kind permission of Aberdeen City and Aberdeenshire Archives)

The Price of a Soul

What led to the spate of accusations in Orkney in the first half of the 17th century which brought Marable Couper and at least 14 other men and women to the fire on Gallowhill? To understand, we have to take a wider look at what was happening in Scotland. The Scottish Witchcraft Act was passed in 1563 but there were few prosecutions before 1589, when an anti-witch hysteria broke out which can be laid squarely at the door of King James VI. He visited Denmark that year for his wedding to Anne (the sister of King Christian IV) and encountered there a court seething with suspicion of sorcery. On their way home, gales drove the bridal party onto the shore of Norway where they were storm-stayed for several weeks. By the time he finally reached Scotland, the paranoid king had convinced himself that the storm had been caused by witchcraft. He unleashed a bloodhunt: more than 100 men and women were arrested in North Berwick and many of them confessed under brutal torture to having met with the Devil and conspired to poison the king or sink his ship. The high-profile trials stirred up anti-witch feeling and James kept fear and horror of witchcraft in the forefront of national consciousness with the publication in 1597 of his treatise on the subject, *Demonologie.*

The witch-hunts tended to be concentrated in central Scotland and the east coast: Aberdeenshire, Fife, the Lothians, the Borders. 1597 saw 23 women and one man burnt in Aberdeen. Every suspect arrested and interrogated named more individuals who were arrested and interrogated in turn. The last burning in Scotland occurred in Dornoch in 1722, when Janet Thorne was convicted of trying to turn her daughter into a pony with the help of the devil. (Her daughter had a congenital deformity of the hands and feet). In Orkney, most of the witch-hunting fell within the 50 years between 1595 and the mid 1640s, with peaks of persecution in this time but not the mass convictions and burnings seen in some areas. (In Finnmark, in the north of Norway, 91 people from a small rural population were burnt in the same period as the Orkney witch-hunts.)[25]

The Witchcraft Act was not repealed until 1735 and recent estimates suggest that over 1000, or even 2,000, people were executed in Scotland in the 170 years that it was on the statute books.[26] Many who did not receive the death penalty were branded or banished or died in prison from harsh treatment, starvation or suicide. The Burgh of Aberdeen financial accounts, for example, include a sum *for trailing of Manteith throw the streittis of the toun in ane cart, quha hangit hir self in prisoun.*[27] Roughly half as many executions happened south of the border, despite its much larger population. There was more scepticism towards witchcraft in England and the crime of witchcraft was treated quite differently: it was the severities of the injuries caused by witchcraft that mattered and there was a sliding scale of punishments for different levels of sorcery. In Scotland, the crime was being a witch; the extent of the harm – if any – that the witch had wrought to others was irrelevant.

The anti-witch fire that the king had ignited was regularly fanned by the Kirk. The General Assembly circulated every Presbytery in the country with copies of Condemnatory Acts ordering them to search out and prosecute witches, and we can see their effect in Orkney. The Act passed in May 1643, for example, was swiftly followed by the arrests of Katherine Craigie and Jonet Reid, who were burnt in Kirkwall that July, and a spate of accusations which targeted people in the North Isles. Four women in North Ronaldsay, three women and one man in Westray and one woman in Papa Westray were accused. Katherine had already been tried once in 1640 but reprieved, so it does look as if she was re-arrested directly as a result of the latest Act. Barbara Boundie, a 'wanderer' in both Orkney and Shetland, was *incarcerated for witchcraft* sometime in 1643 and examined, over several meetings, by the Orkney Presbytery.

When Barbara was arrested, Katherine and Jonet had gone to the stake only four months earlier so it is not surprising that she was so terrified that *she ran into the sea to her craig* [neck].[28] It is clear from the Presbytery minutes that she was subjected to prolonged interrogation by several ministers and put under considerable psychological or physical pressure to confess. Had she seen the Devil have sex with Marjorie Paplay? Barbara answered that *John Aitkin had promised her her life if she spake, and that she being feared for her life, spake more than enough of the said Marjorie at that time ...* Asked if she had said that Marjorie had murdered Thomas Lentrom, she answered that she had spoken what *was put in her mouth* by Master Patrick Wemyss, the Hoy minister. It was only after *long entreatie,* in other words coercion, that Wemyss broke Barbara down to declaring that Thomas had been bewitched by Marjorie. The upshot of this Presbytery meeting was that the Sheriff was instructed to keep Barbara in custody and, disturbingly, two ministers were to *forme a supplication to the Secret Counsell for purchasing a commission to put Barbara Boundie to tortures.* It is interesting that they did at least wait for this authorisation.

It is hard to know to what extent torture was used in Orkney in extracting 'confessions'. The case of Alison Balfour, who was accused of conspiring to murder Earl Patrick Stewart by witchcraft in 1594, is notorious both because it was well-known that this was an entirely politically-motivated accusation and because, even at the time, people were horrified at the brutality with which not only Alison but her elderly husband and young child were tortured. Torture was not legally sanctioned in the church courts but there are many references in Kirk Session minutes in Scotland to sleep deprivation being used to force a confession, with a rota of elders being appointed to 'watch and ward' a suspect to prevent them from falling asleep. This did not technically count as torture, but its effects in inducing hallucinations were well known and, combined with harsh prison conditions, it was highly effective in producing 'confessions.' There is no direct evidence that sleep deprivation was used in Orkney, but when the Presbytery determined that Barbara Boundie should be imprisoned until *all lawfull means of tryall that can be thought upon be used towards her,* it is obvious that their intentions towards the wretched beggar were grim.

Marjorie Paplay is an interesting suspect. She was first incriminated by a beggar called Elspeth Cursetter who had gone to the stake in 1633 naming her as *the greatest witch of them all,*[29] and accusations were still rumbling through Presbytery sessions a dozen years later. It becomes clear, as one slowly disentangles the Mafia-like web of Orkney family feuds, that Marjorie escaped being formally tried because of her social status. Boundie and Cursetter were vagabonds with no-one of influence to speak for them. If Presbytery felt that they had to fulfil some sort of witch-burning quota to appease the General Assembly, these women were ideal victims. Paplay, on the other hand, was the wife of a Kirkwall merchant and the mother of James Baikie of Tankerness, a prominent landowner and one of the wealthiest men of the county.

James Baikie protested his mother's innocence and wanted her accusers summoned for slander, but arrayed against him was the minister of Shapinsay, Henry Smythe, and his supporters who wanted Paplay brought to trial. (Smythe's mother-in-law had died suddenly after *some hard speeches uttered by the said Marjorie to her*. The ministers were quite as credulous as their flocks when it came to witchcraft). Unfortunately, the Presbytery minute books for the years 1647-96 were mislaid in the turmoil of the times so we do not know the end of the stories of Paplay or Boundie.

The literature on Scottish and European witch-hunts lays great emphasis on the significance of the Demonic Pact. It was believed that a witch had a real encounter with Satan, and in return for the material advantages which he promised her in this life, she renounced her Christian faith and promised her allegiance to him. This was normally sealed by having intercourse with the Devil and, as a visible sign of the Pact, the witch received the Devil's mark on her body which was supposed to be insensible to pain. Many wretched women were subjected to being 'pricked' all over their bodies by professional witch-prickers and burnt on the basis of the prickers' 'proof'. Interrogation and sleep-deprivation produced vivid confessions of 'Witches Sabbaths' with the Devil in attendance, generally very convivial and disorderly occasions with all the feasting and fiddling and dancing and uproar that the Kirk so sternly forbade and of which real life was so miserably deprived.

However, Demonic Pacts and prickers do not feature in Orkney witch-trials. The accused women rarely mention the Devil at all, let alone dancing and fornicating with him. It is entirely the interrogators – as we have seen in the sad case of Barbara

Boundie – who insist on dragging him in. In fact, assemblies of partying witches are rarely heard of and it seems that the Orkney witches had a dull time of it in comparison to their sisters further south. The nearest we get to a deal with the devil is in the case of the beggar Jonet Rendall who admitted at her trial that the misfortunes that she had been blamed for were caused by someone (or something?) she calls 'Walliman', but there are none of the lurid details of renouncing her baptism and having *carnall dealing* with the devil that occur in so many of the Scottish trials. According to her testimony, *Walliman came to her ... and she maintaining that she was poor and had nothing he said to her that she should live by almis.* It is worth noting how cheaply the devil is able to buy a soul, he does not need to offer riches or high living; the summit of Jonet's aspirations is the assurance that she will be given alms so that she can survive from day to day.

Sickness and disasters were frequently ascribed to the 'muttering' of a beggar who was refused food or lodging. At a time when everyone had so little, it is understandable that people were reluctant to part with any of the money or food that they possessed. It was easy to blame every mishap on the grumpy, grudge-nursing old woman whom everyone tried to avoid and perhaps this picture fits Annie Taylor from Sanday, who was tried and burnt in 1624. *Robert Miller refused you meal that he was grinding – you went away murmuring to yourself – Robert could not make the mill gang that day for all his skill ... Mareoun Paulsone took some meal from your girnel* [meal chest]. *You cursed her and she is dead ... You brought in peats to Annie Peace – she found fault with you and you said she would never burn the rest. The same night a great storm came and the sea washed away all the rest of the peats.*[30]

At a time when disease and sudden death were so common, it was inevitable that misfortunes frequently did follow curses, and the curser gained a fearsome reputation which she either exploited or started to believe in herself. It was an effective economic strategy. Patrick Gray saw Jonet shaking her blanket against the house and, fearing the worse, quickly went to the barn to give her a sheaf of corn. Unfortunately for the Grays, the curse had already taken effect: two horses died in the stable shortly afterwards and Patrick fell ill and dwined for nine months until he died.

Gypsies, of course, fell foul of the law as vagabonds as well as fortune-tellers and charmers. John Faw, who was tried in 1616, gave their vocation as *sorcerers, tellers of fortunes, and that they can help or hinder the profit of the milk of cattle.*[31] Magnus Linay and his wife were accused of learning their skills from *the Egyptians*, as gypsies were often called.[32] Their retribution for a slight could be terrible. Magnus' son neglected the cows he was herding and they wandered into Robert Gray's corn. The angry Robert *gave his son a cuff* and soon after his best horse died, and then all his cattle, sheep and horses died *and nothing thrives with him since.*[33] It seems that curses and maledictions were used to protect – or at least, avenge – employees from discipline or dismissal more effectively than any modern trade union.

Very occasionally, communities inflicted summary justice on a *notorious witch* instead of waiting for the legal process to take its slow course. According to Stronsay tradition, a woman known as Scota Bess made a habit of calling up fogs in order to wreck ships. Bess was beaten to death in the barn of Huip, with flails which had been dipped in the water in which communion vessels had been washed. Despite this counter-magic precaution, Bess was not to be got rid of so easily. Although her body was buried deep in the ground, the next morning it was found lying on the surface. The next night it was carried to the Muckle Water and sunk in the loch and load after load of turf tipped on it till an island was formed. If the details of the story sound apocryphal, it may contain a germ of truth. Similar mob executions happened in other parts of the country, such as that of Janet Cornfoot in Pittenweem who was accused by a child of being a witch and stoned, beaten and crushed to death by a mob in 1705.

If women were most likely to see witchcraft at work when their cow fell sick or its milk failed to be churned into butter, men were especially frightened when their sexual potency was threatened. When William Roy quarrelled with Marion Richart, she struck him on the back with her hand *and presently the power of his body was taken away in so much that he could not do the duty of a man towardis his wife, while two nights before he was all sap and able for his wife as ever he was before.*[34] On the other hand, Jonet Reid was able to restore Robert Sinclair's *wonted vigour and ability* by slipping something into his food. When someone had powers like that, it was better not to get on the wrong side of them.

It was the contemporary obsession of Kirk and State with sexual morality that linked feminine sexuality and supernatural power so fatally together, and the connection is explicit in several stories in which curses are accompanied by the action of women tearing off their courche, or cap, and literally letting their hair down. Helen Wallas so lost her temper with William Holland in an argument over *a piece of gras* that she *pulled the curtch off her head ... shook her hair about and ran to the Lady Chapel hard by, and went thrice about it upon her bare knees, praying curses and maledictions.* A *piece of grass* may sound to us like a trivial reason for such a tantrum, but if William had effectively stolen the only grazing for her cow or her precious hay crop by pasturing his own cattle on it, her situation would have been desperate. Helen was following long-established tradition in making a pilgrimage to a chapel and circumambulating it in order to obtain a favour, though perhaps unusual in praying for a curse![35]

The curtch or courche was not just the normal woman's head covering, it symbolized her chastity and modesty, it concealed her fatally attractive hair and no respectable woman would be seen out of doors without it.[36] By tearing off her curtch Helen was throwing away all social restraint and letting loose the power of unbridled sexuality. William Meslet knew that Isobell Young was at the bottom of his misfortunes when she was seen *taking off her courche and passing about widdershins*[37] (the spell made doubly strong by walking round against the sun) and it was enough to see Jonet Sinclair at the Noup in Westray *with her hair about her lugs* to know who had caused the man of the Noup to fall ill.[38]

When we read the charges against Katherine Craigie, at the time of every reported incident she was staying at a different house in her neighbourhood of Wasbister in Rousay. She was probably the local 'howdie wife', the woman you called on to be midwife at births and lay out the dead; someone you might also ask to stay in the house when a member of the family was sick and needed care when all the family were out working. Katherine had a tremendous store of folk-remedies and charms and considerable skill as a healer. When Magnus Harcus was tormented with an intolerable pain in his leg, *you came to him where he was lying, and desired to see the leg, and you stroked your hand tenderly on it, so it fell out that immediately after, the great pain slackened and ay became better.*[39]

Belief in the power of numbers, especially the number three and multiples of three, is almost universal, as is water as a magical or healing ingredient, and often they are combined in a charm. Katherine took a sick neighbour down to the shore at Saviskaill, before dawn, and poured three handfuls of water over his head, *and everie day thairafter, he convalescit and becam better.* Charms often used the language of prayers, sometimes muddled and misremembered but piously mixed with traditional incantations. Many were not local in origin or use but belonged to a huge pool of ancient folk-lore and are remarkably similar to those recorded all over Europe: spells to cast disease on animals or humans or to cure it, curses on the niggardly housewife who would not give alms to the beggar, charms to bring luck to a fisherman, milk to a cow or a husband to a girl.[40]

Figure 1.5
At least four medieval chapels were built on the margins of Wasbister Loch in Rousay. St Peter's on the crannog and Cross Kirk, where the walls of the graveyard now stand, can be seen in the photograph at the far side of the loch. This was a place of concentrated spiritual power, and it was believed that the sick could be cured by walking round the loch 'in silence before sunrise'.

The practice of visiting, or circumambulating sacred wells or lochs was also known all over Europe long before, and after, the arrival of Christianity.[41] Katherine had great confidence in the curative powers of the Wasbister Loch in Rousay, a place hallowed by the presence of at least four medieval chapels. By taking her 'patients' to walk around the loch, Katherine was undoubtedly following one of the old traditions that had been banned at the Reformation. When the patient was too sick to make the pilgrimage himself, she believed that it could be effectively made on his behalf. When William Flaws was ill, she told his wife: *Jonet, if you would have your husband receive some little health, you will go with me about the Cross Kirk of Wasbister, and the Loch of Wasbister, before sunrise, and desired her to keep silence and not speak a word.*[42]

This is the most poignant aspect of the trials: often the witch is not accused of causing harm but of healing, or trying to heal. In fact, hardly any of the charges against Katherine in her two trials blame her for malevolence. When her spells are not medicinal, they are usually designed to be helpful, as in bringing a new husband to widow Isabel Craigie, or favourable weather. *James Caithness having gone over to Westray on business and could not get home for ill weather, and his wife was thinking long for her husbands homecoming, you came to her and said; Give me a piece of cloth ... and your husband will get fair weather to come home shortly ... and upon the morn, the weather became fair, and James came home.*[43]

Katherine was denounced by the same people that she had helped, her neighbours. Clearly they had an ambivalent attitude to 'witches': they needed and employed them because they had no recourse to other medical help and because traditional lore regarding charms and spells was far older and more deeply entrenched than the teaching of the Kirk. At the same time, they were afraid of their powers and also frightened of being accused themselves of the crime of 'consulting'. For the Kirk, there was no ambivalence at all, the difference between black and white magic was non-existent. If a person had, or claimed to have, skills in healing, their powers came from the Devil. If the Devil seemed to be doing good things, that was just one of his subterfuges for deceiving people. So, when Jonet Reid charmed Henrie Sowie of his sciatica *and Henry, being unable to stir out of his bed for the space of fourteen days before, recovered his health, and was able for his work within two days after ...*[44] there was no question of seeing in Henry's good fortune either Jonet's skill or the mercy of Providence, but *witchcraft and devilrie.*

However, healers like Katherine and Jonet also came under attack from a secular direction. Medicine was increasingly becoming a professional, and therefore masculine, occupation from which women were officially excluded. An Act of Parliament of 1641 forbade anyone who had not been approved by the surgeons from practicing surgery, and threatened women who continued to practice unlawfully with prosecution under the Witchcraft Act.[45] Inevitably, until medicine became both affordable and reasonably effectual, people resorted to whatever remedies were offered, in the same way that we today try 'alternative' treatments when conventional western medicine has failed to provide a cure. Long after witchcraft had ceased to be a criminal offence, Presbyteries and Kirk Sessions fought a losing battle against what they called 'evil superstition' and their congregations would simply have regarded as clutching at straws.

What is puzzling is that women like Katherine persisted in offering their cures even when they were well aware of the retribution that would follow. After the terrifying experience of her trial in 1640, one would expect her to have been much more circumspect when she returned to Rousay and to have refused to exercise her talents. Instead, astonishingly, she continued to offer healing charms until she was arrested again in 1643.

There is no record of any witches being burnt at the stake in Orkney after the deaths of Katherine Craigie and Jonet Reid in 1643. It is possible that the spate of accusations in that year, especially against someone as well-connected as Marjorie Paplay, eventually led to a back-lash against the persecution. (The great witch-hunt of 1597 in Aberdeenshire was eventually brought to an end by James VI himself when he realized that the hysteria had got out of hand and high-status women were being accused.) In the 1650s, the occupation of Orkney by Cromwell's English troops, with their more sceptical attitude to 'witches', would also have discouraged witch-hunting. When Cromwell's Commissioners arrived in Edinburgh and found 60 men and women accused of witchcraft they *found so much Malice and so little proof against them that none were condemned.*[46]

From the mid 17th century, although men and women continued to be charged with sorcery, they were dealt with by the Kirk Session instead of being handed over to the civil court. In 1689 Thomas Swintone, for example, was *made to answer* [to the Session] *for his scandal in raising the wind that stormy Sunday* and so preventing God-fearing islanders from getting to the kirk. Slander – taking away someone's good name – was regarded as a very serious offence and, by this time, accusing someone of witchcraft was likely to be treated as slander and severely punished. Hugh Moare of Orphir, for example, was put in Marwick's Hole for maliciously declaring Barbara Hutchison a witch.[47]

Figure 1.6
This drawing of St Magnus from the Reverend James Wallace's 'A Description of the Isles of Orkney' (1693) shows the cathedral as it looked at the end of the 17th century. The wooden spire was much shorter than the original one which was destroyed by lightning in 1671. (OLA)

The Kirk also became far less likely to accept accusations uncritically. In 1666, a fishing tragedy occurred at Burwick. It widowed four women, one of whom lost two sons as well as her husband in the accident. The bereaved women were much troubled by rumours in the parish that the deaths had been caused by the curses of wicked people and they asked the minister to open the graves to see if they had been tampered with. This was duly done in the presence of the congregation and the baillie. The minister, finding no suspicion of witchcraft, *did publicly exhort all the people to lay aside all sinister or evil thoughts towards any persons then present. And if any should reproach any of these afterward, they should be condignly punished.*[48]

The very different attitude to superstition among the clergy by the end of the 17th century is evident in the Reverend John Brand's book of his travels in the Northern Isles. In 1700 he visited Papa Westray in his capacity as a Commissioner for the Kirk, with the brief of extirpating *heathenish and popish rites* from Orkney. St Tredwell's Loch was famous for miraculous cures, especially for eye diseases, and people came from far afield to walk around the loch, in silence, in hope of a cure. The rituals are the same as those Katherine Craigie had practised, and been condemned for, at Wasbister Loch in Rousay sixty years earlier. Although Brand strongly disapproved of *dregs of popery*, he was actually quite intrigued by the evidence of cures and there is no suggestion in his report that the pilgrims should be treated as criminals.[49]

It was not that the practice of sorcery had in the least diminished. Charms and spells continued to be common currency; cattle continued to be bewitched and sicken, or their milk suddenly cease to flow and as suddenly flow again, well into the 20th century. (Duncan Robertston wrote in 1924 of causing great anxiety to an islander when he set sail for another island after speaking sharply to an old woman; *she's drooned three men already.* A sudden squall in a calm June day nearly upset his boat.)[50] Nor was it that people became more tolerant and compassionate, but the obsession with creating a 'godly society', which had justified all the brutal persecutions of the late 16th and 17th centuries, was melting under the growing scepticism and rationalism of the age. As the state gradually redefined itself as a secular institution rather than the enforcing arm of the Kirk, Parliament was increasingly resistant to the lobbying from the General Assembly for renewing the acts against witchcraft and witch-hunting gradually came to an end.

From the 16th century the English had been amused, titillated and horrified by stories of witch-hunts, tortures and burnings north of the border. Woodcuts illustrating the grisly and ghoulish happenings amongst their more primitive neighbours were in hot demand in the more sophisticated south, and witches became part of the stereotypical image of Scotland. In 1780 Earl Ligonier wrote from Surrey to his sister Frances Balfour in the island of Shapinsay: he was ill *and what is worse, and absolutely incurable, I feel I grow old.* ***You*** *are fortunately situated in a part of the world where age is of no signification, for when Ladies advance in years in Scotland, they only mount a broomstick and become immortal witches. When you take it into your head to commence flying on the said conveyance, I shall hope to have the honour of seeing you.*[51]

Figure 1.7
In March 2019 the Orkney Heritage Society laid a memorial stone at the top of the Clay Loan, once Kirkwall's Gallowhill, to commemorate the victims of Orkney's witchcraft trials who were burnt on this spot. (OLA)

41

Confusion and Tumult

Above all else, Kirk Sessions were preoccupied with 'Discipline', the investigation and punishment of socially unacceptable behaviour and moral backsliding, and Discipline fell much more heavily on the poor who could not buy their way out of public humiliation by paying a quiet fine. The plus side of the system (for the historian, not the backslider) was the meticulous record-keeping of Presbyterian bureaucracy.

The common charges against women were slander (swearing at the neighbour who let their cow or sheep wander into their corn), Sabbath breach ('vaiging' or going for a walk, selling liquor or collecting shellfish to feed their starving children on a Sunday) and – by far the most common charge – sexual immorality. Men were also charged with fornication or adultery, but often they were conveniently absent at the fishing or in Hudson Bay, leaving their sweethearts to join the long procession of unmarried pregnant girls compelled to sit on the repentance stool or stand in sackcloth at the kirk door during service. Historian Julian Goodare commented that *the vigorous assault on sexual offences that characterized the Scottish Reformation was also, inevitably, a move towards the criminalization of women.*[52]

In 1627, the Kirk Session of St Magnus Cathedral, *considering the great growth and increasing of fornication*, ordained that every fornicator should fast on bread and water for 48 hours, and make a public penance, on several Sabbaths, standing upon the pillar of repentance.[53] Two years later, the Session admitted that, notwithstanding former acts, *this sin of fornication still abounds and increases daily more and more in this congregation.* Severer sentences were necessary: sinners were to be fined, chained in the joggs and *every woman falling in fornication heirafter to make their publicke repentance, without a pled or any other garment about them.*[54] While fasting, fines, pillar and joggs were to be the fate of both male and female fornicators, there is an unpleasant smell of prurience around this last punishment for women. One might think that these dire penalties would have had a salutary effect on loose morals, but as every single Session meeting, in every parish, deals with fornication/carnal copulation/naked bedding/prenuptial and antenuptial fornication and trelapses and quadrilapses (falling a third or fourth time into the same sin), they were evidently totally ineffectual.

Women had inferior status under Scots law. We know from late medieval rental records that some Orkney women owned and rented land in their own name but in criminal law they did not exist and, like children and felons, they were not admitted as witnesses in courts of law. Yet, within their own communities, women played a prominent (sometimes even dominant) role, and Kirk and society were only partially successful in keeping them in subjection. There is nothing tame about the feisty

Figure 1.8
The joggs, a very few still survive in parish kirkyards.

women summoned before the Circuit Court for 'ryoting', as when *with the tongis Christian Cromartie strack Margt Smyth upon the head*[55] and, even when they found themselves carpeted in front of the Kirk's grim all-male committees, they were quite often noisily defiant. The Orkney Presbytery summoned Elspeth Marwick *for her godless carriage upon the communion day in the matter of her publick repentance*, and Ursilla Cromartie *for her*

43

great and scandalous offences, in using of imprecations in the house of God. Katherine Heart *refused flatlie to give any kind of obedience* and Agnes Cursetter was to be excommunicated for slandering the Presbytery clerk.[56] It seems that, despite all the threats of fines, sackcloth, the repentance stool and even excommunication, women often refused to be browbeaten into submission by the men in power.

The Sessions referred to the Presbytery more serious cases of misdemeanour. Presbytery also dealt with Kirk issues of national importance and chose representatives to send to the General Assembly. The minutes of Presbytery meetings supply a remarkably unedifying picture of Orkney's leading citizens. If the peasantry were quarrelsome, unchaste and defiant of authority, the best educated and most privileged of the ruling elite hardly set examples of good behaviour. While the endless procession of fornicators and adulterers, penitent or otherwise, shuffled across the background of the social stage, in the forefront strutted a venal set of men who changed their principles as often as their clothes and vigorously *slandered and vilipended* one another at every opportunity. The particularly unpleasant Reverend Patrick Waterston, *an incendare and turmultuous person* storms through the pages of Presbytery minutes causing uproar at every meeting.[57] It was a vain hope of the Moderator that *the Brethren of the Presbytery would take some course anent the ordering of the house, for avoiding of confusion and tumult.*

The exchanges are sometimes unintentionally entertaining. In 1643 James Aitkin, the minister of Birsay, *complained upon John Sinclair of Hammer his parishioner 1) for not communicating ... 2) for the calumnies against himself in saying that he had mixed the wine in the Sacrament with water ... 3) for many contemptuous words used against himself, 4) for slandering of his wife, saying that she lied like a whore as she was.*[58]

In 1638 most of the Orkney ministers signed the National Covenant, pledging themselves to oppose the king's attempts to force English church practices upon Scotland. However, twelve years later the Marquis of Montrose was in Orkney trying to recruit an army to support the restoration of Charles II to the throne. Almost all the Orkney ministers hurried to sign the 'Loyal Address to Montrose', discarding the Covenant as rapidly as they had adopted it when it seemed expedient to do so. This time they had miscalculated the political wind and the result was disastrous. Montrose was defeated and executed; the General Assembly deposed all the ministers who had signed the Loyal Address and Cromwell sent troops to occupy Orkney. The islands were not only under military occupation but, until 1654, left with only two ministers to serve all the kirks (one of them the 'tumultuous' Waterston). St Magnus Cathedral was besieged and damaged, and then used by Cromwell's soldiers as a barracks and a stable.

The political power-swings of the 17th century, between King and Parliament, Bishops and Presbytery, left the whole country deeply divided and the angry confrontations between parties persisted well into the next century. The sheer vitriol in the clashes between Episcopalians and Presbyterians is hard for us to understand, but the issues at stake were not mere differences of church organization but deeply entrenched fears and insecurities. If the arguments are alien to us, the anger and aggression engendered when parties polarize is depressingly familiar.

For the 'gentry', with status and property to defend, the traditional hierarchy of society, with king and bishop in their proper places, meant the upholding of the landed interest. Presbytery, on the other hand, raised a frighteningly democratic spectre, with the kirks (and therefore society) ruled by committees that might even include *the trading and inferior sort*. One can imagine the lairds nodding agreement at Charles II's aphorism that *Presbytery is not a religion for gentlemen*.

It was only in 1688, (after the 'Glorious Revolution' which saw the forced abdication of the Catholic James II and VII and the accession of the Protestant monarchs William III and Mary) that Presbytery was finally recognised as the only government of the Scottish Kirk. Presbyterian ministers were placed in every parish and were generally cordially loathed by the lairds – and ladies. Thomas Traill of Holland in Papay repeatedly threatened, harassed, and assaulted the Reverend William Blaw – his brother-in-law. After a particularly violent scene in the Papay kirkyard in June 1718, Traill beat the boatmen who had brought Blaw over from

Westray and swore he would evict any tenant who transported the minister or gave him any shelter on the island.[59] Cristiana Crawford, Lady Melsetter, horsewhip in hand, strode into the kirk in Walls to attack the Reverend John Keith and his family *in the most base and upbraiding language ... and ... sent George Jameson to tell me that she had four charged pistols prepared for me and any messenger that came firth to crave my stipend from her.*[60]

Figure 1.9
St Boniface Kirk in Papay, the scene of the irascible laird's violent attacks on the minister. 'There hath been such swearing and cursing in the Kirkyard as might make the Kirk to sink with us all as the ground did to Sodom'.

Women were also often in the frontlines on the opposite side of the battlefield, defending their Presbyterian kirk with passionate nationalism. Their fury at anyone suspected of foreign 'popery' was well stirred by ministers like Thomas Baikie who vehemently denounced Episcopalians as Baal-worshippers from the cathedral pulpit. In scenes of mob violence such as we associate with Celtic versus Rangers encounters, the Reverend James Tyrie was attacked and *threatened to be tore in pieces* by the combined forces of the women of Stromness and Sandwick.[61]

The Jacobite rebellions ended any hope of toleration for Catholics or Episcopalians. Although there was some support for Prince Charles Stuart among the Orkney lairds, for most people the rebels were not only dragging the country into civil war but, by seeking the support of France to put a Catholic king on the throne, were inviting foreign invasion. The reprisals were savage. It was only after the Jacobites had been thoroughly crushed and a degree of stability brought to the country that animosities cooled, the Orkney gentry conformed, at least outwardly, and Orkney society grew less violent and embattled.

Chapter 1 Notes

1.   AM 135ff. All quotations from the trials of Marable Couper, Katherine Craigie, Marion Richart, Annie Taylor and Jonet Reid are taken from this volume, with the spelling modernized.
2.   ibid 142; Loanhead, at the top of Clay Loan, was also known as Gallowsha' or Gallowhill, a short distance above St Magnus Cathedral and, at that time, outside the city of Kirkwall.
3.   Marwick 1991, 376-81 lists references to over 70 people accused of witchcraft but the records are incomplete and there were almost certainly more.
4.   *Wiried*, strangled. The word survives in modern English only in the context of dogs worrying sheep. On the Continent witchcraft was regarded as heresy, and so witches were burnt; in England it was a civil crime, and so they were hanged. In Scotland they were usually both hanged and burnt.
5.   AM 137.
6.   Old form of barley, see glossary.
7.   The period of climatic cooling between c.1300 and 1850 known as the Little Ice Age reached its coldest in the 17th century. For its impact on Orkney, see Thomson 2001, 307-09.
8.   Barry, Appendix IX: *The Acts of Bailiary for executing of Justice through the County of Orkney; Act no. 34 anent Fugative Servants and Young Men going to Zetland*, 470-1.
9.   P. H. Brown, ed., 1904 *Supplication presented by the bishops of Orkney & Caithness to the Privy Council, Register of the Privy Council of Scotland* vol V 1633-35.
10.   OSA (Birsay and Harray) 153, n.
11.   AM 136-7.
12.   Exodus ch.22 v.18 (King James version).
13.   Maxwell-Stuart 212.
14.   The Ministry for State Security, the secret police agency of the German Democratic Republic.
15.   OP f.284.
16.   AM 157-8; Katherine Grieve is also referred to elsewhere as Katherine Miller, the use of both maiden and married surnames was common in Scotland.
17.   *Acts and Statutes of the Lawting Sheriff and Justice Courts within Orkney and Zetland MDCII – XLIV*, Maitland Club Miscellany vol.II part I (1840): *Act no. 16, 1615, anent the resoirt of uncouth Beggaris*, p.XLIX.
18.   Historicus, *Some references to witchcraft and charming*, Old Lore Miscellany vol. II, pt.II, 1909, 111.
19.   Marwick 1991, 346 quoting Sir George Mackenzie, *The Laws and Customs of Scotland in Matters Criminal* 1678.
20.   This is an intriguing statement. Why was Margaret taken the 20 mile journey to Kirkwall? To see a doctor or to make a clandestine visit to St Magnus? The cult of saints was denounced by the Kirk but the Court does not query Margaret's trip to Kirkwall, any more than her curious visit to the house of the woman she denounced as a witch. Margaret Corston can probably be identified with Margaret Mowat, see n.16.
21.   AM 137. An extract from Marable's first trial, which led to her banishment, is printed in C. Rogers, 1886, *Social Life in Scotland* vol 3, pp.300-01.
22.   ibid 144.
23.   According to contemporary belief.
24.   Stuart 65-69. The cost of one burning is significant. These sums would probably have paid a working man's wages for at least six months.
25.   The emotive Steilneset Memorial, opened in 2011, commemorates the extraordinary number of people executed in this remote rural area, both from the coastal fishing villages and Sami herding communities. See Liv Willumsen, *Steilneset* 2011.
26.   The School of Scottish Studies Survey of Scottish Witchcraft online database found 3,212 named individuals tried for witchcraft in Scotland and estimated some 67% of these were executed. Figures given in earlier sources are much higher.

27	Stuart 65.
28	OP ff.250-260.
29	ibid f.204.
30	AM 146.
31	Dalyell 235, the spelling of quotations in this volume modernised by Rendall.
32	Gypsies were thought to have originated in Egypt.
33	Dalyell 235.
34	AM 156.
35	Dalyell 449-50. A century earlier, Jo Ben described people making their painful way up the rocky path to the chapel on the Brough of Deerness on their knees (Ben, 10) and pilgrims were circling the chapel and leaving offerings of small coins there well into the 18th century.
36	Readers of Tracy Chevalier's novel *Girl with a Pearl Earring* will recognise the same strong cultural taboo concerning a woman's head-covering that prevailed in contemporary Protestant Holland.
37	Dalyell 458.
38	ibid 451.
39	AM 177.
40	The rite of *casting the heart cake* to find the cause of a disease, for example, was popular in Orkney but also recorded in Shetland and in different parts of Scotland and in Scandinavia.
41	Martin Martin saw people perform sun-wise circuits of sacred wells throughout the Western Isles at the end of the 17th century; Martin, M., 1703 *A Description of the Western Islands of Scotland* (London; facs. repr. Stirling 1934).
42	AM 167.
43	ibid 172.
44	ibid 183-4.
45	Larner 1984, 150.
46	ibid 75.
47	Marwick 1991, 374.
48	Craven 1911, 54 quoting minutes of Kirk Session of South Ronaldsay and Burray, 28-29/10/1666, the spelling modernised.
49	Brand 88.
50	Robertson 1924, 44-5.
51	Letter from Edward Ligonier, Cobham to Frances Balfour, Burray 12/8/1780, OLA D2/4/12.
52	Goodare 307.
53	Acts of the Kirkwall Kirk Session, Act XXXIX, Minutes 18/11/1627, OCR 14/74.
54	ibid Act XLI, Minutes 3/5/1629, OCR 14/74.
55	Circuit Court of the Stewartrie of Orkney, held in St Peter's kirk in South Ronaldsay, June 1685, OLA SC11/86/12/3/2.
56	OP ff.195,230,331,352.
57	OP 1643, ff 212-220. At this date the tumultuous Patrick Waterston the younger was minister of St Andrews and Deerness. As a fervent and vehement Covenanter, he antagonized all the other Orkney ministers. In 1660 he was sent to the Tolbooth for *treasonable speeches* denouncing Charles II and his ancestors and then *sent south from sheriff to sheriff till he reaches Edinburgh there to be incarcerat*. Fasti 273.
58	OP 1643, f.250.
59	NIPR 1718-19, OCR 3/1.
60	CPR 1730, OCR 2/1.
61	CPR 1747, OCR 2/1.

CHAPTER 2

The New World: Emigrants and Rebels

Prologue

The records of witchcraft trials and angry Presbytery meetings from 17th century Orkney reflect a society closed in on itself, tense with anxiety and riven with conflict. To move from these documents to letters written in the later 18th century is to open the curtains and let daylight into a darkened room. The rationality of the 'age of enlightenment' has banished much of the credulity and paranoia that fuelled the violence seen in the previous chapter, the Devil has been defeated more effectively by neglect than by the fires on Gallowhill. Life is still often hard; the threat of famine is a recurring theme, but people are looking outward, seaward, for new opportunities far from home. Their misfortunes are not caused by spells and demons but by events we can all understand: sickness, a storm at sea, financial failure, war.

From the 1730s onwards informal letters to family and friends become more common and handwriting much more similar to that of the present day. Some of the earliest letters to survive in the Orkney Archive were written by sea-captain William Manson. He was born in Kirkwall in 1744 and 'farstrayed' from there many times to ports all over the Mediterranean, the North Sea and Baltic and across the Atlantic. His family connections ramify through these stories. His mother was Marion Blaw, daughter of the Reverend William Blaw, the unfortunate minister whom we have met being attacked by Thomas Traill in scandalous scenes in the Papay kirkyard. One of his uncles was James Blaw 'of Jamaica' who made a fortune from his sugar plantations. A prolific letter-writer and letter-hoarder himself, his marriage to Elizabeth Balfour ensured that his letters would survive in the immense Balfour archive.

We can follow him at different stages of his career: skippering a cargo ship between ports north to Archangel (Arkhangelsk) and south to Madeira and to the southern colonies of America, leading a party of emigrants to found a new settlement in Georgia; transporting cargoes again between England and Jamaica for a rich plantation owner, and, finally, remarried and comfortably settled back in Orkney. He is rather an ambivalent character: a somewhat sanctimonious Quaker with a streak of violence that doesn't sit well with his Quaker protestations. However, his letters to his family in Kirkwall and the log-book of his voyages, written when he was a very young sea-captain, give a wonderful flavour of the horrors of long stormy voyages in small 18th-century cargo ships.

Far more terrifying were the experiences of the emigrants who fled desperate poverty in Orkney only to be caught up in the brutalities of civil war in America as the Revolution reached the southern states. A single letter from one emigrant, a young Kirkwall boy called Baikie Harvey, poignantly captures his confusion, disillusionment and fear.

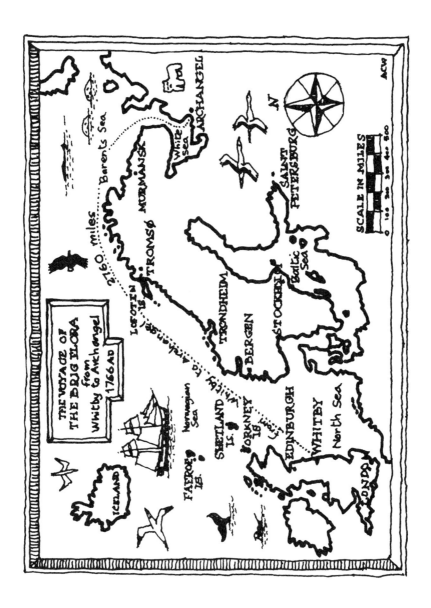

Figure 2.1

William Manson, Sea Captain

I've crost the Atlantic twice twenty times o'er
And far distant Countries I long did explore;[1]

Whitby, Halifax, Charlestown (Charleston), Dublin, Philadelphia ... these are just some of the places where the young William Manson mailed letters home to his parents. His father, William Manson senior, was a wright and furniture maker in Kirkwall, probably the owner of a large and successful workshop judging by the number of boys who were apprenticed to him. William junior, born in 1744, was the third child of a large and close family. His older brother James was sent to Jamaica, where his uncle James Blaw was prospering, and William was apprenticed to a merchant vessel in his teens. Clearly a capable and very hard-working young man, he was rapidly promoted. He was dutiful in writing to his family whenever landfall allowed and he also kept a beautiful ship's log for three years of his voyages.[2]

Letters from parents were infrequent, dependent on wind and weather and inevitably slow to catch up with peripatetic sons. In 1760 Manson wrote from Stromness, acknowledging the sad letter his parents had sent six months earlier. *I received your affectionate letter dated the 11th March wherein you acquaint me of the Death of my Dear Sisters which gives me some concern I am very sorry to hear of the indisposition of your family by reason of that Loathsome Distemper the Flux, but blest be God for your safe Recovery.*[3] The flux, or dysentery, had probably cut a swathe through many other families at this time; deaths of children were almost too common to be remarked on. Disease was also a far greater hazard at sea than shipwreck or enemy action. Manson's crew was evidently depleted for he added a message from the master, asking his family *to enquire if you can get*

4 or 5 or 6 Lads of Creditable Parents from 14 to 16 or 20 years of Age to be Indentured when we arrive at Orkney. Shortly afterwards his ship was based in Halifax for 18 months but letters from home failed to reach him; *you have not sent me no letters for this 2 years past* he reproached his parents. [4]

Much later, in a letter to his own son, we learn about William's career as a merchant seaman, *in the employ where I made a long Apprenticeship and when I got my Indenture from my Master, having faithfully served him 5 years, before I was 21 years of Age he gave me the Command of a Ship and the Consignment of the Cargo to myself.* [5] His employer was the wealthy Whitby ship-owner and trader Jonas Brown, for whom William captained the brig *Flora* on merchant journeys that took him between Whitby and Archangel and back and forth across the Atlantic to Madeira and Charlestown in South Carolina. From 1766 to 1769 he kept a log-book of the *Flora's* journeys and the bold flourish with which he heads the first page suggests his justifiable pride. *A Journall of a Voyage by God's Permission from Whitby towards Archangel in the Flora of Whitby – Wm Manson Commr.*

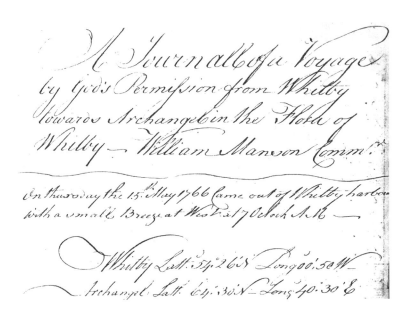

Figure 2.2
The log-book of the Flora 1766-1769. Captain William Manson begins the log of his first command with a proud flourish. (OLA)

57

The ship left Whitby in mid May and, battling storms and ice round the North Cape, through the Barents Sea and finally into the White Sea, reached Archangel seven weeks later. Just to look at the map is to be impressed at the journeys that these little ships made, though the log gives little detail other than the wind and weather, with only occasional observations on the landscape. Lying off the coast of Lapland on 20th June, Manson wrote: *There is no Inhabitants at this place only 2 familys that Live in Small hutts about 6 or 7 miles up the River Tokina – on the Island is a Great many Eggs and Numbers of Seafowl of all kind. here is a Good Watering place likewise some Driftwood for fireing that Drives about with ye Tide But no Woods to be Seen ashore or Nothing but high Mountains and Rocks covered with moss. There is Thousands of Seals.* The *Flora* was probably an old ship, there are certainly plenty of references to her leaking, and labouring in heavy seas. *Ship Labours very hard, ships a deal of Water over all and makes Deal of Water in her Hold more than Usual.*

Before leaving Whitby, Manson had news of the shortage of food in Orkney and had planned to bring some supplies for his family but was thwarted by the weather. *I am very sorry that we could not have an opportunity to call at Orkney either in Going out nor Coming home we had nothing but Gales of Wind as we passed it both times ... am very sorry to hear of the Great Scarcity that has been in Orkney this last year not Doubting but that you have been very hardly put to it for which Reason I had bought some Flour, Bread and Pease for you which I brought in our own ship in Expectation of Calling at Orkney in Going out but was Disappointed ...*

Frustratingly, Manson does not record what he was carrying to or from Archangel. The town's position at the mouth of the river Dvina gave it good communications with the interior but it was a long and dangerous journey from western Europe, and the White Sea was only free of ice for a few months between May and August. Russia produced iron, hemp (for rope), flax, tallow and timber; all these were in demand in Britain and exported from Archangel when prices were high enough to justify the transport costs of bulky goods. Pitch, tar and train-oil (from whales) were all produced in the vicinity of the port, and small volumes of luxuries such as wax, caviar and furs were also exported. One of Britain's main exports to Russia was broadcloth, so bales of Yorkshire cloth may well have been stowed in *Flora's* hold for the outward journey, and potash (needed for dyeing cloth) brought back to Yorkshire mills.

The only mention of the *Flora's* cargo is in the log of a voyage to Charlestown, via Madeira, with a hold full of unfortunate horses. They had not long left Whitby when it records: *28 Sept 1767 A Great Swell from ye East Ship Labours Hard, the Horses are hard matcht to keep upon their Legs*. One poor animal was only kept on his legs by being *hung by the slings*. It is astonishing that, after the vicissitudes of a three-month journey, only one horse sustained an injury and they arrived in Charlestown *all very well and have good stomachs for their victuals*!

More often than not, the *Flora* seems to be battling through gales and *Monstrous Seas* but, occasionally, there was a break of fine weather and the crew could be set to repairing the rigging or other jobs on deck. On their way home from America in May 1767 there was an opportunity to air their fetid bedding. *Little Wind & fine Clear Water all sails set ... our Deer Skins upon Deck and Air in the Sun and Beat the Worms out.* It was probably quite a brief reprieve. A month later the weather was more normal. *Blows Excessive hard Ship makes very Bad Weather of it ... Sea monstrous high to the End.*

It was probably in 1765 that William married a Whitby girl, Margaret Jackson, from one of the prominent Whitby ship-owning and merchant families, and the following year a daughter was born, Betsy. Margaret must have been an adventurous spirit for in 1769 she left Betsy with her grandmother and accompanied William on the five-month round trip to Carolina. It was an exciting crossing of the Atlantic. *30th March. our Tiller broke ... the Sea runs monstrous high ... Washed away a Top mast off the deck & our ship Broached Too several times fit to wash us all overboard ... the Ship steers to badly and the Sea running over and over us fore and aft obliged us to Clap to ... Blows Excessive hard.* The experience did not deter Margaret from crossing the Atlantic with William again, a few years later, when heavily pregnant.

William did not spare his parents descriptions of his most harrowing adventures. A winter voyage from Hamburg to Leith took a month of gales. *Never since I came to sea have I endured such hardships as we suffered in that time – but we have Reason to be thankfull to God for his Mercys in saving our Lives – I am credibly Informed that there is upwards of a Hundred Sails of ShipWrecks on the Coast of Holland betwixt the Texell and the Schaw Riff – in the Gales of wind we was out, thank God we are Alive and well to tell of it.*[6]

By 1771 the *Flora* was sold and Manson was in Philadelphia taking charge of a larger ship that had been built for new employers, John Horne and Thomas Kemp, merchants of London, *Worthy Goodmen and of that sect of Christian called Vulgarly Quakers.*[7] He was excited about his new ship, the *Arundel, above 400 tons Burthen as fine a Ship as ever was put in the water*[8] and soon he was sailing her to Leghorn [Livorno, Italy] and from there to the Baltic with a cargo of salt. Manson's family were also Quakers, which probably explains his employment in Whitby where there was a considerable Quaker community. It is at this stage that Manson's letters home take on a sternly pious and sanctimonious tone. *Dear Parents I hope that you in your old age are Pressing forward with your Faces Zionwards ...*

He continues with a damning indictment of the state of religion in Orkney, especially the character of its ministers. *The Christian Religion has dwindled away into a mere name and empty show owing in a great measure to the shallowness of many of their teachers who mind nothing but getting their stipends payed them and make a kind of a Show of Preaching and Singing . . .when them that are called Ministers will get Drunk and Quarrel among themselves, brother going to law with brother and always disputing and envious about Stipends how can Love of God be said to dwell amongst such ...*[9] It would sound like calumny, unless one had read the minutes of 18th-century Presbytery meetings in Orkney which are evidence that Manson's diatribe was, in fact, sadly accurate.

It was when Manson skippered the *Arundel* to Savannah in Georgia that he heard of vast, fertile, empty lands being offered to settlers and he hatched his plan to leave the sea and found his own Quaker settlement, with his family and a boatload of emigrants as the foundation stock.

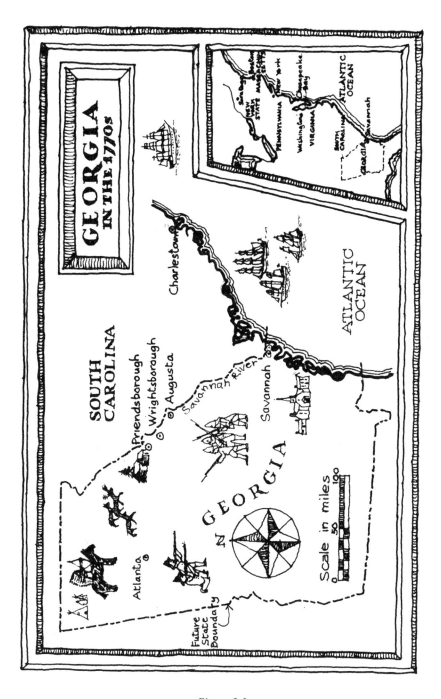

Figure 2.3

Voyage into War

In 1774 and 1775 a number of emigrants set sail from Orkney for Georgia. They had been promised an escape from poverty to a brave new country where land was fertile and plentiful. They had no idea that the 'empty ' lands that they were promised were the home of native peoples, or that the American Rebellion, which had broken out in the northern colonies, would soon spread to engulf the south as well in a brutal civil war.

Georgia was a relatively recent colony, founded in 1732 by James Oglethorpe, English soldier, philanthropist, MP and member of a parliamentary committee which investigated debtors' prisons. Oglethorpe obtained a charter to found a new colony where urban poor and ex-prisoners could get a fresh start. He sailed with the first settlers and established a town at the mouth of the Savannah River, laying it out on a neat geometrical plan. Scots from both the Highlands and Lowlands soon joined the colony which was intended as a settlement of yeoman farmers and artisans, overseen by a group of trustees and directed by Oglethorpe. Wanting to avoid the class divisions of England, he prohibited slavery and large landholdings, but his idealistic scheme was soon defeated by the settlers. In 1752 the trustees surrendered all power in the colony to the British government and, by the time that the Orkney emigrants arrived, it was fast becoming a country of large sugar, rice and indigo plantations, relying heavily on slave labour.

The early settlements were on the swampy and malarial coast but Jonas Brown and his ambitious son Thomas had heard reports of exciting opportunities to obtain grants of territory inland. The 'backcountry' was described as both richer and healthier land and – best of all – a thousand miles from rebellious Boston which was starting to foment discontent at British colonial rule. In 1773 the government of Georgia bought a huge tract of territory and offered plots for sale on enticing terms to new immigrants to the country. Brown, a prosperous Whitby merchant and ship-owner and former employer of William Manson, was enticed; his son Thomas was also eager to exchange the life of merchant and skipper for that of 'gentleman planter'. Jonas purchased a large block of land and advertised around Whitby for would-be migrants, promising every head of family transported a large block of virgin land.

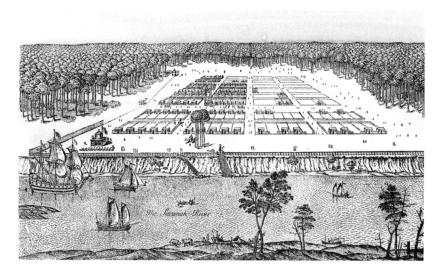

Figure 2.4
The town of Savannah as laid out in 1741 by James Oglethorpe, who planned a colony of 'yeoman farmers'. (North Wind Picture Archives)

On August 12th 1774 Brown's ship the *Marlborough,* a 300 ton Whitby-built 'cat',[10] sailed for the port of Savannah 'north-about', calling at Kirkwall and collecting Orkney emigrants on the way. The ship had a safe passage, the twenty-four-year-old Thomas was well received in Savannah and was so enthusiastic about his prospects of becoming a New World-style Lord of the Manor that he sent the *Marlborough* back to England in January 1775 and advertised a second transport. There was little response in Whitby, as it was a busy port with high employment, but the north of Scotland and Orkney provided plenty more applicants eager to escape agricultural depression and poverty.

In September 1775 a sixteen-year-old lad from Kirkwall called Baikie Harvey embarked on the *Marlborough* and sailed for the New World to better his fortune. It is not hard to imagine the excitement that Baikie and other servant lads must have felt, seeing the sailing ship in Kirkwall harbour and the recruiting posters, appealing to all who were able-bodied and had a spirit of adventure to leave their life of toil and hunger and cold for the life of free, landed, men under the warm and sunny skies of America's southern states. Brown's description of his property must have seemed a fantasy of paradise to the poor in Orkney (or anywhere in Britain) living a hand-to-mouth existence in a time of harsh climate and frequent hunger. Could they even imagine a land of thick forests with an endless supply of timber for the taking, deer and turkey for the shooting; rivers full of fish and land so fertile that it grew corn and fruit and vegetables in abundance: melons, cucumbers, peaches, pears, apples and plums ...?

Nor was there need to worry about finding money for the fare. Anyone who could not afford to travel as a paying passenger could be indentured as a 'covenant servant' to Brown for the space of three years in return for a free passage. It was a system which had supplied servants and plantation workers to the colonies in America and the West Indies since the 17th century. Not only had numbers of the very poor indentured themselves voluntarily (the term was normally five or seven years), but cities such as Edinburgh and Glasgow had sold batches of prisoners, vagabonds and other undesirables to the plantations. In the 18th century the good citizens of Aberdeen were profiting by kidnapping street children and selling them to the colonies: slave labour at £16 a head.[11]

At the start, however, the three year term of servitude would have seemed to the Orkney emigrants a small price to pay for the amazing dream that they were sold. Every single man would be allotted 15 acres of arable land and a house; corn, cattle and tools would be supplied until the first crop was raised. Every married man would have an additional ten acres for his wife and five for each child over ten years old. When their contract ended they would pay Brown a small rent but they would be free men and women settled in their own homes, ploughing their land with their own horses and oxen. There would be no factor riding over the hill to demand payment for the hovel in which they lived or for the few miserable patches of exhausted ground which had so repeatedly failed to feed their families.

We know a little more of Baikie Harvey than of all the others who went to Georgia because of one letter that has survived in the Orkney Archives. On 30 December 1775 he wrote from America to his godfather, Thomas Baikie of Burness in Firth. We do not know if young Harvey was a relative of Baikie, perhaps an orphan but fortunate in being sponsored by a man of some property and social status. We can guess that it was through his influence that Baikie had been given a position as servant in one of the houses in Kirkwall – an easier life than that of a farm servant but hard enough. It is little wonder that he, and some of the other servants, weighed up the certainty of a future of poverty against the uncertainties of a long sea voyage and a new life in a strange land, and signed the document that would take them to Georgia.

At 16 years old Baikie was by no means the youngest emigrant. With him in the ship were Peter Petrie, a farm servant in St Andrews parish and John Loullet,[12] beggar in Stromness; both were only ten when they sailed and unaccompanied by any family. The majority of those who went out as indentured servants were boys in their teens but there were also single women, most of them giving their occupation as farm or house servants, and whole families. Among nearly 90 emigrants on Brown's ships there were 13 couples and 31 children. They came from Mainland parishes and a few from the nearby islands: Shapinsay, Rousay and Egilsay. All gave very similar answers to the question: why did they want to emigrate? Peter Petrie went *in expectation of doing better*.[13] It is unlikely that they could imagine that their situation could be worse in America than it was at home.

Families encouraged friends and relations to leave with them and the parish of Evie in particular seems to have been emptied by the flight from destitution. Adam Corrigel, age 32, farmer in Evie, left with his wife Janet and three children aged one to six because of *bad crops and loss of cattle*. His neighbour George Brough had also *sustained loss by his cattle dying and cannot support his family* and sailed with his wife and four children. Nicol Johnston, 28, emigrated with his wife and infant daughter and two unmarried sisters. John Linay, another neighbour, *cannot support his family owing to bad crops and high prices* and took wife and two children on board; Ann Turnbull, 23, an unmarried servant on an Evie farm, went *to seek better encouragement than she gets in this country*.[14] One wonders how those who were left behind viewed this mass exodus of 32 individuals whom no-one expected to see again; it must have left a painful gash in the parish.

Orcadians were accustomed to young people, especially the men, leaving home for years at a time to find work: in the Royal or Merchant Navy, at the whaling or in Hudson Bay, and long absences were the norm. Orkney merchant-lairds travelled extensively and, in the course of the 18th century, increasing numbers of them settled in ports like Boston and Charlestown and then were joined by young relatives to be trained in the business. (A significant number of Traills from Rousay, for example, ended their days in Boston). The departure of whole families of impoverished farmers, however, was unusual at this date.

The *lack of encouragement* which so many of the emigrants cited is corroborated by the Reverend George Barry. Thirty years later he wrote in his *History of the Orkney Islands* of the *low state of agriculture, the smallness of the farms, and the little respect in which those connected with the cultivation of the soil are held* which impelled so many to *leave this place, in the hopes of better in another country*. He estimated an annual exodus of some 400 Orcadians, *the whole of these, as it may well be supposed, are our most vigorous, spirited and industrious young people, of both sexes*.[15]

At much the same time as the *Marlborough* sailed out of Kirkwall in September 1775, another emigrant ship anchored in the bay. The *Georgia Packet* was captained by William Manson who had made several voyages to Georgia, transporting cargoes from England to the merchants of Savannah. In 1774 he found the colony in *a very settled and flourishing condition* and immediately set out on horseback to see the new 'Ceded Lands' for himself.[16] He was impressed by their potential for farms and plantations and determined to found his own settlement. He reserved 2000 acres in the Lands and bought further tracts in the adjoining township, Wrightsborough, which had been founded a few years earlier by a Quaker community and named after the Governor of the colony, Sir

James Wright. Brown's emigrants had founded their own colony, Brownsborough, in the same area.

The naturalist William Bartram had visited Wrightsborough with a survey party in 1773 and described an idyllic landscape. *The Soil is very fruiteful, hill and Vales watered and beautified by numbers of salubrious waters ... the flowery hills and verdant lawns ... Mills are erected on the swift flowing streams ... The inhabitants ... Plant Wheat, Barley, Flax, Hemp, Oates, corn, Cotton, Indigo, Breed Cattle, Sheep and Make Very good Butter and Cheese.*[17] Manson hired a family to cultivate his farm and returned to England to find his settlers. At home his plans grew very much more ambitious. He entered a partnership with two extremely wealthy Newcastle merchants, the Chapman brothers, who had decided to invest heavily in American plantations. They obtained huge estates in Florida and Georgia and agreed to provide four-fifths of the financial backing to establish new settlements; Manson would supply the remainder and retire from the sea and manage Company affairs in Georgia for an annual salary.[18]

Manson had probably originally planned to fill his ship with his fellow-countrymen but found few to go with him as Brown had only just recruited in Orkney. However, there were plenty of poor tradesmen in Newcastle and unemployed from Scotland who were willing to sign on as indentured servants. He also brought a friend, Dr Taylor, and his 16-year-old brother Tom who came out as his 'under-clerk'. In August 1775 Tom wrote confidently to his mother: *According to the description my brother gives of the country, the Inland parts are healthy and the soil exceeding rich and I hope there will be no fear of my doing well.*[19]

At the same time Manson was writing from Newcastle to two of his sisters, Betty and Barbara ('Babie'), to leave their employment and housekeep for him in the new settlement. *I am now fitting out a ship at this place for Savanna in the province of Georgia and taking on board Servants and Passengers to settle on our Plantations in that country ... I intend please Providence when I arrive there to leave of the Sea and settle in that country with my brother Tom and our servants ... Therefore my request is that as soon as you receive this letter that one or both of you will immediately set out for this place with all speed as you will both be very useful and serviceable to me to manage the affairs of my house in that country – and without one of you I shall be much at a loss for a Person to confide in as a housekeeper. Besides we shall be company for one another ... I think it will be for both your Goods and better than being in Service and I shall take Care that you want for nothing.*[20]

His wife, Margaret Jackson from Whitby (possibly a relative of Brown's),[21] was an experienced sailor, having (rather surprisingly) travelled with her husband on several of his trading voyages, but she was pregnant and William considered *it will be a Risque for her to run to come out in that condition.*[22] Nonetheless, when the ship left Newcastle, Margaret had evidently decided to run the 'Risque' and was on board with their nine-year-old daughter Betsy. Betty and Babie had evidently not been deterred by the very short notice from leaving their employment and taking up their brother's offer, so he was well supplied with housekeepers.

The *Georgia Packet* called at Orkney for provisions before setting out on fourteen weeks of stormy and miserable voyage. Smallpox broke out on board, half the passengers were sick with fever at any one time, four of the children died and three were born, including the Mansons' son Billy.[23] The ship and its exhausted passengers finally reached Savannah in December 1775, not long after the arrival of the *Marlborough* with its second contingent of emigrants. The ships had left Orkney just in time; in 1776 the British government closed any further emigration from Scotland. The almost perpetual state of war with France and the rebellion in America had caused anxiety that Britain was losing potential cannon-fodder to the colonies just as it was demanding (and pressganging) more recruits into her army and navy.

Brown and Manson had obviously painted a glowing picture of the country but the new colonists must soon have been alarmed to discover two major factors that their leaders had disregarded. One was that the 'empty' Ceded Lands which the Georgian government were selling to settlers were in fact the territory of Cherokee and Creek tribes who had been put under huge pressure to give up some two million acres of good land in return for the cancellation of the money debts they had run up with sharp and unscrupulous white traders. The dispossessed people had not taken kindly to the theft of their lands and there had been brutal raids on settlers.[24] Shortly after Governor Wright's proclamation in 1773, advertising the sale of the new lands, an angry war party of Creeks had massacred a white family on Christmas Day. Strained relationships were made worse by the contradictory British policy which tried to open the country to settlers while at the same time remaining on good terms with the native peoples because they wanted to maintain the profitable deerskin trade. There were further ambushes and hostilities stirred up by aggressive settlers. When chief Mad Turkey came to Augusta (the main inland town) to negotiate peace terms, he was murdered. When Brown returned to Georgia to settle, he had to accept that the boundary Ceded Lands were altogether too dangerous and restrict his settlements to the Lower River area near Augusta.

The other factor – even more alarming and long-lasting in its effects – was that the immigrants had arrived just as the simmering discontent in the American colonies erupted into open war with Britain. In Georgia, mixed reaction to the rebellion led to a vicious conflict between loyalists and rebels. Jonas Brown had printed circulars in England which assured applicants that Georgia had *no connection or concern with the trouble now subsiding with Great Britain.* However, when they landed in Savannah it was to find his son Thomas, a fervent loyalist, badly scarred and crippled from the brutal torture he had suffered at the hands of the rebels a few months earlier.

The earlier stages of the American Revolution had erupted in the northern colonies. From 1765 onwards, resentment against taxes imposed by the British Parliament without any representation from the colonies grew from grumbles to armed opposition. The 'Townsend Acts' which levied duties on a number of essential goods were rejected as unconstitutional. In 1770 feelings were inflamed by the 'Boston Massacre', a scrap with the militia in which five civilians died. In 1772 rebels/patriots (named according to one's point of view), including one John Brown, burnt a British warship that had been enforcing the unpopular trade regulations. In 1773 the Tea Act led to the most famous incident of the war: the Boston Tea Party. Incensed by the imposition of taxes from London to pay for their own control, angry colonists boarded three East India Company vessels that were attempting to offload a huge surplus of tea that had been lying unsold in their London warehouses. £9,000 worth of tea was thrown into the harbour.

On 17th December the revolutionary leader John Adams wrote: *Last night 3 Cargoes of Bohea Tea were emptied into the Sea. This morning a Man of War sails ... There is a Dignity, a Majesty, a Sublimity in this last effort of the Patriots that I greatly admire. The People should never rise, without doing something to be remembered – something notable and striking.*[25]

George IIIs' Britain was in no mood to lose its grip on Empire, but its retaliation only hardened resistance. The Coercive Acts, designed to punish Boston and thoroughly reassert British authority, were known in America as the Intolerable Acts and united the colonies in rebellion. Late in 1774 patriots formed their own alternative government to coordinate resistance and the First Continental Congress declared a boycott on British goods. The Americans began drilling their own militia and fighting between patriots and British regular soldiers broke out at Lexington and Concord in Massachusetts in 1775. Later that year the first major battle of the war was fought at Bunker Hill. It was a military victory for Britain but on all sides she was losing political control. Soon, in all 13 colonies, the patriots would overthrow existing governments and draw up new constitutions for territories that would now be known as States rather than colonies. The raw militia that had been defeated at Bunker Hill was being drilled into an effective Continental army under its Commander-in-Chief, General George Washington.

The country that the *Georgia Packet* returned to in 1775 was thus a very different place from the one that Manson had left the previous year. Unrest had escalated in Savannah and the governor, Wright, was now *a mere cypher* with the real power in the hands of a rebel Council of Safety. The atmosphere of disorder and violence encouraged some of both Brown's and Manson's servants, (probably disgusted with the conditions of the voyage,) to claim harsh treatment by their masters and take the first opportunity to escape from their servitude. Half a dozen of Manson's men rapidly enlisted with the rebels and attacked the house where he was staying. Trade was totally disrupted by the boycott – the cargo of coals that the last of Brown's servants had brought for sale was thrown overboard. (Manson was more fortunate; because a friend of his was president of the Council, he was allowed to unload his British goods). Brown himself had been attacked at his house near Augusta by rebels who demanded that he sided with them. When he refused, they tied him to a tree, burnt his feet with blazing torches and tarred and feathered him. He survived, to lead an avenging troop of King's Rangers, but was crippled and suffered from headaches due to his horrific head injuries for the rest of his life.[26]

Presumably hoping that things would be more peaceful inland, Manson sent Dr Taylor to lead half of his people to the lands he had purchased near Wrightsborough and, despite an appalling journey through snow storms, Taylor sent back positive reports that they had come to a rich country with a mostly loyalist population. However, a country that was a battleground between Native Americans and settlers and between loyalists (or Torys as they were called) and rebels can hardly have seemed the Promised Land flowing with milk and honey that the new immigrants had been promised. Some, especially those who had come with young families, must have thought that poverty and hunger at home would have been easier to endure than scalping parties and shoot-outs between rival militias.

In neighbouring South Carolina the rebels were joined by some of Brown's disillusioned servants. *Dear Godfather*, Baikie Harvey wrote on 30th December 1775, *I am very sorry that I did not take your advise and stay at home with you.* Probably without the slightest idea of who was fighting who or why, Baikie had joined the large force of Colonel Richard Richardson that was hunting down loyalists. For the Orkney lad, who had probably never handled a firearm in his life, it was a shock to see the skill with which his American contemporaries handled a gun. Despite the trauma of tumbling into a war zone, Baikie had quickly appreciated that this was a country where, for the free man with a trade and a capacity for hard work, there far more opportunity to make a good living than there had been in Orkney. The first impediment had been his status as an indentured servant, and therefore little better than a slave to his master, and it seems that many of his fellow-servants had determined to rid themselves of this shackle as soon as they got to America. This was only one problem, however. Baikie saw that his newly-arrived countrymen, in their naivety and inexperience, were as helpless among the hardened American colonists as the wretched negroes newly landed from slave ships.[27]

In a stroke of good fortune, Baikie met Le Roy Hammond, a merchant with a large plantation in New Richmond in South Carolina, who bought out the rest of his indenture from Brown. Baikie was well treated by Hammond and his wife but he realised that in order to 'better himself' in America he needed a trade and he asked his godfather to send out any money that was owed to him so that he could apprentice himself to a tradesman. The revolution, however, growing in violence and viciousness on both sides, brought an abrupt end to Baikie's ambition to learn a peaceful trade and Manson's to be Founding Father of a prosperous settlement. Manson and the rest of his 100 immigrants reached his lands in safety in February 1776, but the news from Savannah was hardly reassuring. British warships had arrived in the port to obtain provisions for the army in Boston, and when they were refused they seized ten merchant vessels – including the *Georgia Packet*, still being loaded with rice. Manson lost his cargo and also had to bear part of the cost, £400, of the ship *being obliged to sail in Ballast, not being permitted to take her Cargo aboard.*[28] Governor Wright and his council fled to the warships and with them the last symbol of royal authority in Georgia.

Always an optimist, Manson proceeded with his land purchases and settlements. Plans dated March 1776 show that he obtained from Governor Wright a parcel of 600 acres of *good oak and Hickory land ... out of the lands ceded to his Majesty by the Creek and Cherokee Indians*, next to Thomas Brown's land, and then a separate block of 3,500 acres.[29] He carefully glossed over the war in his letters to his mother in Kirkwall. In April 1776 he wrote to her reassuringly: *We are now settled upon our Plantation which we have named Friendsburgh, my wife and Betsy with Brother Tom and my sisters are well in health – and all the People are settled much to their satisfaction. I would not have thee to be uneasy about us as these troubles are a little alarming but does not affect us much being a long way up the Country about 180 miles from the Sea Coast.*[30] William would have been sure that his choice of name would please Widow Manson, a devout Quaker, as were many of his friends and in-laws in Whitby. William's own beliefs are less clear; although his letters to his parents are stuffed with pious injunctions, Quaker principles did not prevent him from owning slaves in Georgia or from later taking revenge on his enemies with violent military action.

Three months after William wrote his optimistic letter home, in July 1776, the Continental Congress issued the Declaration of Independence, throwing down the gauntlet to 'the tyrant' George III. There was no turning back from this point but Britain and her German allies reacted by sending more troops to crush the rebellion. Places far from the main battlefields were torn apart by civil war because many Americans did not support the rebellion. In Georgia, the merchants wanted independence because they wanted to avoid paying taxes to Britain, but the backcountry settlers were more anxious about hostile natives and felt that their safety depended on being supported by government forces. How many of the young emigrants who left Orkney on Brown's ships to find a better life, got caught up in the turmoil? There were certainly Orcadians fighting on both sides.

Manson, a wily survivor, seems to have managed for a while to remain on terms with both rebels and loyalists and run a prosperous trading business, but in 1777 raids by the dispossessed native people forced him and his family to flee Friendsborough for Augusta. The next few years were action-packed as the tide of war turned and turned again over the country. In 1778 a British invasion force captured Savannah and marched into the Georgia backcountry. Manson took an oath of loyalty so that he could remain on his plantation and led the troops into Augusta, but when they retreated before the rebels he found himself arrested as a collaborator and his considerable property confiscated. Later he claimed that he had been imprisoned for several months.

Manson's friend Dr Taylor took the chance to escape to British-occupied Philadelphia. He was an ardent loyalist and almost certainly the source of damning reports to the Chapmans of their partner Manson's equivocal activities. They passed on the news to poor Widow Manson in Kirkwall, as a justification for cutting off her annuity. *The last accounts we had of him were about a year since by some Gentlemen from Georgia – They do not speak so well of his Conduct and Principles as we could wish . . .You have no doubt heard that your two Daughters left him very early and went to places in some Genteel Families in the Neiborhood who took compassion on their situation ... Mrs Manson to whom we must in a great measure attribute the otherwise unaccountable behaviour of her Husband. Your daughters have not only left him but likewise your Son Thomas who we have the satisfaction to acquaint you is well settled with a Housekeeper in St Augustine E Florida. Besides your own children almost all those who went out as Indentured Servants have left Mr and Mrs Manson on Acct of their usage of them. Mr Manson for sometime separated himself from his Wife but unfortunately took to her again ... It gives us pain to communicate to you some of the Circumstances in this letter and still more so as in consequence of them we are necessitated to desist paying your Annuity.*[31]

It is understandable that Manson's backers were uneasy about their large investments and ceased to pay his bills when they had heard nothing from him in 18 months – they did go bankrupt as a result of the war and the confiscation of their properties. However, it seems unlikely that William's family seriously fell out with him in Georgia. His sisters returned to Britain with him in 1781, his brother a little later and they all carried on an affectionate correspondence. One would give a great deal to know how Betty and Babie viewed their whole adventure. The war made correspondence with Britain difficult and, after France entered it, virtually impossible. Mail from England could only be sent to neutral Holland and from there to a French port in the hope of finding a ship bound for Savannah or Charlestown, which might well be intercepted by British warships or privateers on the way. Amongst all the chaos, Manson had a personal problem: his wife disappeared.

What happened to Margaret remains a mystery. Was she the reason for Betty and Babie leaving their brother's household? Did she run away with a rebel lover? The Chapmans seemed to blame her for siding with the rebels. By 1779 the Mansons had separated for good, William taking the two children with him; he never saw his wife again. Two years later, in England, he was still trying to find out what had happened to Margaret. *One request more I have to make you is this,* he wrote to a friend in Georgia, *that you will please to make inquiry of any Savannah Gentlemen or people from Georgia, to be informed whether the poor unfortunate woman Mrs M is alive or not, or what has become of her and I beg you will inform me by the earliest opportunity of it.*[32]

He was also concerned at the fate of the negro slaves of his household: *Let me Beg of thee to take under thy particular care that Negro Woman Tyra [?] and Boy Tom Belonging to me,* he wrote in the same letter, *I left them at James Manson's but I am afraid they may be lost ... I had rather thou would take care that they do not want for any thing needfull and I will pay thee when please Providence we meet.*[33] Another slave is mentioned in his list of confiscated property. *A very valuable Negro Man, carried over the Mountains by Rebels and thereby lost.*[34]

Augusta was not in the hands of the rebels for long. In 1780 Georgia and South Carolina were overrun by British troops, including a detachment led by the indomitable loyalist Thomas 'Burntfoot' Brown who had been campaigning ever since he escaped from his torturers. Brown testified that Manson *having had resolution and virtue enough to preserve his loyalty unshaken in the worst of times, has been under sentence of banishment for refusing to take an oath of abjuration ... in consideration of so extraordinary an instance of his firmness and loyalty I am happy to bear testimony to his merits and particular services since the arrival of the Kings Troops under my command.*[35] Manson was hired to travel to the Ceded Lands under a flag of truce and offer surrender terms to the last of the Georgia militia. Most of them accepted and Georgia became the only American state to be reduced to a colony again; Governor Wright returned to office; *Captain William Manson again became an Augusta merchant ... with a royal garrison for protection and as a customer.* [36]

Something of the nature of the garrison's custom is evident in Manson's invoice of 1780 addressed to Brown, now Commandant of the King's Rangers and his Majesty's Superintendent of Indian Affairs. It included his personal expenses while on the King's service, *'with Flag'* [of truce] and an eclectic range of other items: *7 Cows and Steers Killed and Used by the Indians when Encamped in my field; Sundry tools for the fortifications; a New Cart with Cover and Harness Compleat ... to bring ammunition down to the troops when you was in the swamps after Mckay (lost); 3 Wiggs spared you for the Indian Warriors they cost me £4: 10.*[37]

In an interval of relative peace, Manson did well. *I speculated in Divers Branches of Commerce in which I was generally successful which in the course of a few years accumulated greatly, with which I purchased Lands, (which I thought the surest property a man could possess, in a Country the Seat of War) to a considerable amount.*[38] It was only a lull, however. French and American pirates raided shipping off the coast, gangs looted, rustled livestock and murdered inland. A company of irregulars besieged Brown and his garrison in Augusta and the loyalists retaliated savagely, devastating the Ceded Lands with the help of Native Americans. *One hundred farms, all of the forts and the courthouse were reported destroyed. Hundreds of men, women and children – black and white – were driven or fled into a wintery, wilderness exile with little more than the clothes on their backs.*[39]

By over-reacting to the uprising, the loyalists had re-started a general war and as Manson supplied their garrisons, he was a target of rebel revenge. Later, claiming compensation from the British government, he wrote: *That your memorialist to the utmost of his power opposed the measures of the Usurpers/the rebels, which often brought him much loss and damage by their plundering and taking away his property by force and many attempts were made to take away his life which Compelled him repeatedly to leave his House and Family and sleep in the Woods by which means his Sufferings were very great.*[40] William finally decided to return to Britain in the hope of sorting out the dispute with the Chapmans, and took his sisters and his children to Charlestown for safety until they could take ship. He planned to return to Augusta to sell the last of his property but, before he could do so, irregular rebel soldiers had once more occupied the town.

In January 1781 I formed a Resolution of coming home to England to settle affairs ... the Kings Troops at that time being in possession of Georgia and Carolina, and all pretty quiet in that Quarter; But a Reverse of Fortune took place! The Kings Fort in Augusta which was within 200 yards of my Dwelling House was Besieged and taken by the Rebels! who plundered and Destroyed all my Personal property and Everything in my House which they razed to the ground (had I been there I would certainly have been taken as was the case with many of my neighbours who were murdered after they had surrendered as prisoners of war).[41]

This was the point at which any Quaker ideals of pacifism that Manson may have held definitely snapped. He returned to the sea and took command of a schooner, the *Peggy* of Charlestown, with which he took revenge and hoped to get recompense for his losses by capturing American merchant ships. When the patriot general Thomas Sumter[42] looted the houses of loyalists in Georgetown, South Carolina, Manson retaliated by setting fire to the wharf and bombarding the townspeople who tried to put out the fire. Wind fanned the flames and most of the town was burned. It was a sad end to the hopes with which he had set out from Kirkwall for the New World six years before. [Manson] *had gone to America hoping to create a new settlement and had ended by destroying an existing town.*[43]

This was the dramatic finale to William Manson's American career. He and his family made it safely back to Britain. His sisters found work – Babie as a teacher in a London boarding school, while Betty returned to Kirkwall – and presumably thrilled friends and relatives for the rest of their lives with hair-raising tales of narrow escapes from scalping parties and other adventures. For a time his brother Thomas fought with the loyalists, an experience of *Losses, Perils and Disappointments ... which made me quite sick of the army*[44] and he too returned to England. After an anxious time seeking employment he ran a successful business as an insurance broker and raised a family of ten children in London. William was employed for three years skippering trading ships to Jamaica. Friendsborough did not outlast the revolution, but presumably many of the settlers did and they became a small part of the European diaspora that peopled America. Some, like Baikie Harvey from Kirkwall, perished in the fighting between loyalist and rebel gangs.

Other Orkney men died fighting in the King's regular army. Earl Ligonier, an outstanding soldier and Colonel of the 9th Foot, had made his Orcadian brother-in-law, Thomas Balfour, an ensign in his regiment. The post was a sinecure, designed to give Balfour an income without the inconveniences of active service, but the British army was badly needing replacements and Ligonier asked him to recruit in Orkney. In February 1777 he wrote to Balfour: *You will be pleased to send your recruits in the most expeditious manner ... as one of the additional companies is ordered for immediate embarkation for America ... the ships will sail as soon as they are victualled.*[45]

The journey across the Atlantic was hazardous as British vessels were constantly harassed by American shipping; Ligonier had just lost the entire consignment of uniforms he had sent for his men. *The whole clothing of my Regt has been taken by a Rebel Privateer ...*[46] Balfour found enough men sufficiently desperate for the King's shilling to enlist and Ligonier was impressed by the Orkneymen. *I have pleasure to acquaint you with the safe arrival of your Recruits which are as good men as it is possible to wish for ... On their arrival at Norwich, some of the Rabble of that Town, unaccustomed to some part of their dress, thought proper to insult them, and an Affray ensued, in which your Countrymen acquitted themselves so well, tho 10 to 1 against them, that I believe they may walk the streets of Norwich in peace for the rest of their lives, under whatever habit they think proper. In short, they proved themselves a hardy, spirited Race.*[47]

The alarming news from America evidently had no impact on the gaiety of Georgian England. Thomas Balfour's sister Peggy was visiting her in-laws at Cobham in Surrey and, in the same letter, Ligonier assured Tom that his sister's launch into high society was uncurtailed by the war. *In spite of the general convulsion of the State, Dissipation reigns triumphant in this part of the Realm, Masquerades, Concerts, balls etc occupy the Gay world, without the least interruption.*[48]

Tragically for the Orkney recruits, and all the regiments sent to subdue the rebellion, the war went increasingly badly for Britain. The king's troops held New York City and some ports but could not decisively defeat *General Washington, so called from being the Rebel Chief.*[49] The autumn of 1777 brought humiliating disaster. General John Burgoyne invaded from Canada with a large army, including Ligonier's regiment. He had hoped to meet up with two other British forces but they failed to arrive and he was surrounded in upstate New York by General Horatio Gates. Defeated in two battles and forced back to Saratoga, the British lost 440 men dead to the Americans 90 and Burgoyne surrendered the remnants of his entire army, 6222 men.

For the wretched prisoners of war, it was only the beginning of their suffering. The officers were left to languish in prison camps and, as Ligonier wrote to Balfour: *the remnants of my poor regiment are ordered into the remotest part of Virginia, a march of some hundreds of miles and I much fear, without Shoes, or Cloaths. It is too horrid a subject to dwell upon any longer.*[50] If any of the *hardy and spirited* recruits ever made it back to Orkney, it would only have been after (perhaps long after) the war was finally concluded by the Treaty of Paris in 1783 which acknowledged the United States as independent sovereign states. The articles stipulated the repatriation of prisoners and the return of property confiscated from loyalists. As William Manson was to discover, the last article was frequently ignored.

Saratoga was a turning-point. France, eager for revenge after being defeated by Britain in Europe and India, joined the war on the American side and the following year Spain did the same, escalating the rebellion into a global conflict. Britain was forced to withdraw troops to defend her valuable colonies in the Caribbean and to face the enemy at sea as well as on land. Peggy Balfour wrote to her mother in Westray about the gossip in Surrey: *We have great talk of a French war our ambassador has come home and theirs is gone away some time ago a war is looked upon as unavoidable ... it is every day expected that the Spanish ambassador will also be recalled, how we are to combat all those foes join'd together I am not polititian enough to find out when we could not subdue America alone.*[51]

New regiments such as the 76th Foot, Macdonalds Highlanders, were raised to serve in the American war and they joined Lord Cornwallis' campaign in the south. Despite successes in Georgia and South Carolina (where Cornwallis defeated General Gates), as they fought their way north the country behind them just dissolved into a chaotic guerilla war between rival militias. In 1781 Cornwallis was besieged by a combined American and French force under George Washington at Yorktown on the Virginia coast. A large French fleet prevented the rescue from the sea that he had expected and he was trapped in Chesapeake Bay. On 18th October he surrendered a second British army. Like the wretched prisoners of Saratoga, the troops were marched in detachments to different parts of Virginia to wait out the rest of the war.

It was inevitable that the British soldiers who served with Burgoyne and Cornwallis fought against some of their own countrymen and the lists of officers include several Traills from Orkney on either side. Robert Traill (originally from Rousay) went to Philadelphia in 1763 and became a major in Washington's army. Captain Jack Traill was in Cornwallis' army that surrendered at Saratoga. Colonel Patrick Traill also fought for the British and appears in the records of 'Distressed Loyalist Refugees' who claimed for goods and livestock looted from their home in Charlestown when it was occupied by the rebels in 1782.[52] Another Robert Traill married Mary Whipple whose brother, General William Whipple, signed the Declaration of Independence and led the New Hampshire militia at Saratoga. The family was solidly patriot apart from Mary, who *was a Loyalist to her death, and whenever Independence Day came round, instead of joining in the general rejoicing, she would dress in deep black, fast all day and loudly lament our unhappy differences with his Most Gracious Majesty.*[53]

After his spell on the Jamaica run, Manson remarried in 1787, to Elizabeth Balfour. Leaving his children in schools in England, he retired to Kirkwall where he and Elizabeth lived very comfortably in the house called Hell he bought from his uncle James Blaw, *late of the island of Jamaica.*[54] They had one child, Mary, who enjoyed a much more settled and privileged childhood than her half-siblings. Backed by his influential Balfour relations, William eventually secured compensation from the British government for his substantial losses of land and property in Georgia (valued at £9,255: 17: 6) and was given an undemanding position as Comptroller of Customs. *In consequence of domestic tranquillity, hospitable social intercourse, splendidly substantial meals, light official duties and a sedentary way of life he grew uncommonly fat.*[55]

Thomas 'Burntfoot' Brown had a lively career. Undaunted by his terrible experience in Augusta, he continued to champion the loyalist cause, in politics and war, in South Carolina. He spent time living with the Creek Indians and later settled in Florida (then British) where he received a huge grant of land and acquired 170 slaves. When Britain surrendered Florida to Spain he moved to the Bahamas, where he established a prosperous plantation on Grand Caicos and raised a family. 27 years after leaving Whitby he was back in his home town, negotiating to exchange his estate for one in St Vincent. In 1807 he was in England again but was jailed in Newgate for two years on a charge of forgery. The irrepressible

Thomas survived, paid off a vast debt and lived till 1825, a 'gentleman planter' on St Vincent.[56]

What happened to the Orkney emigrants who sailed to Georgia with Brown and Manson? Most of them just disappeared without trace. From one letter and a fragment of information we know that teenage Baikie Harvey, who left Kirkwall *to seek a better way of living*, spent four years of the war soldiering with the rebels and was killed in a skirmish. I wish I knew what happened to Peter Petrie, aged ten when he left his life as a farm-servant in St Andrews parish to sail on the *Marlborough, in expectation of doing better.*[57]

Rebels and Torys

Baikie Harvey was 16 years old when he joined the Orkney emigrants on the *Marlborough*. After a few months caught up in the confusing turmoil of rebellion and civil war he wrote to his godfather Thomas Baikie of Burness from LeRoy Hammond's house at Snowshill. His letter combines regrets, fear and an intelligent perception of the difference between the *smart industrious* crack-shot Americans and the naive and totally unprepared new arrivals from the old world. In 1777 Baikie was in a rebel troop again, a private in William Caldwell's Company, and he was killed during an assault on a British redoubt at Spring Hill on 11th October 1779, aged 20.

To Thos Baikie, Burnass in the Parish of Firth, The Orkneys, North Britain

Dear Godfather,

I am very sorry that I did not take your advise and stay at home with you as I have found to my sad Experience that I ought not to have slightig your advise. Mr Gordon[58] was vere good to me but Mr Brown us'd me vere ill and I Runaway from them and went to the Army that was marching up to the Back parts of south Carolina against a set of people they call Torrys in this Country and when I came back I went to one Mr Leroy Hammond merchant in S Carolina and he bought my time which I am very glad of, for he and his Lady uses me vere well and gives me Cloaths and I Ride with my Master and Loves them Both You Please to send me all the money you can colect that is my Due by the first safe opportunity that I may be enabled to Buy my time and Put myself to some Tradesman to Learn his calling for a Tradesman has good wages in this Country I beg that none of my Relations may come to this Country Except they are able to pay their passage themselves and then they may come as soon as they like this is a good poormans Country when a man once getts into a way of Living but our Country people knows Nothing when they come hear the Americans are smart Industrious hard people and fears Nothing our people is only

82

Like the New Negroes that comes out of the ships at first when they come amongst them I am just returned from the Back parts where I seed Eight Thousand men in arms all with Riffels and Barrill guns which they can hit the Bigness of a Dollar betwixt Two and three hundred yards Distance the Little Boys no Bigger than myself has all their Guns and marches with their Fathers and all their Cry is Liberty or Death Dear Godfather tell all my Country people not to come hear for the Americans will kill them like Deer in the Woods and they will never see them they can lie on their Backs and Load and fire and every time they Draws sight at anything they are sure to kill or Criple and they run in the Woods like Horses I seed the Liberty Boys [rebels] *taking Between Two and three hundred Torrys and one Liberty man would take and drive four or five before him just as the shepards do the sheip in our Country and they have taken all their arms from them and put the men in Gaile* [gaol] *so that they will niver be able to make head against them any more – Pray remember me etc.*

I am dear Godfather your most Obedient and Humble Godson Baikia [sic] *Harvey*[59]

Chapter 2 Notes

1   From a poem by William Manson, *A Lammas Fairing for a Friend's Private Use* 1798, in Frances Balfour, *Some Trifling Originals and Some Selections Written for the Amusement of a Solitary Hour*, OLA D2/119.

2   The original log-book of the brig *Flora* is owned by the Whitby Literary and Philosophical Society. A copy is in OLA D1/260.

3   Letter from William Manson, on board ship, Stromness to his parents, Kirkwall 5/9/1760, OLA D2/9/14.

4   Letter from William Manson, Whitby to his parents, Kirkwall 5/9/1763, OLA D2/9/14.

5   Letter from William Manson, Kirkwall to his son Billy, London 4/9/1793, OLA D2/34/16.

6   Letter from William Manson, Leith to his parents, Kirkwall 16/12/1769, OLA D2/9/15.

7   Letter from William Manson, on board the *Arundel*, Dover Road to his parents, Kirkwall 5/7/1773?, OLA D2/8/12.

8   Letter from William Manson, Philadelphia to his parents, Kirkwall 6/12/1772, OLA D2/9/15.

9   Letter from William Manson on board the *Arundel*, Dover Road to his parents, Kirkwall 5/7/1773?, OLA D2/8/12.

10 'Cat' is an acronym of 'coal and timber'; these were wide-beamed, shallow draught vessels built in Whitby, primarily for the coastal trade but Captain Cook's ship *Endeavour* was a converted Whitby 'cat'.

11 Janice Hopper, *Chilling Trade*, History Scotland vol.16 no.6, 201.

12 Perhaps a misspelling of the Orkney name Loutit.

13 List of indentured servants brought to Ceded Lands 1774-75, compiled from records in the British Public Record Office, Davis 1982, 3-15.

14 ibid.

15 Barry, 330-31.

16 Narrative of William Manson n.d. OLA D2/9/10.

17 The Wrightsborough Quaker Historical Site, http//freepages.religion. rootsweb.ancestry.com.

18 Davis 1983, 4.

19 Letter from Thomas Manson, Newcastle to his mother Marion Manson, Kirkwall 19/8/1775, OLA D2/8/16.

20 Letter from William Manson, Newcastle to his sisters, addressed to his mother Marion Manson, Kirkwall 6/8/1775, OLA D2/8/16.

21 The Jacksons were another prominent Whitby family, Quakers and merchants.

22 Letter from William Manson, Newcastle to his sisters 6/8/1775, OLA D2/8/16.

23 Davis 1983, 5.

24 When Oglethorpe arrived in Georgia, he was hospitably received by the local people. The chief of the Yamacraw (a Lower Creek tribe), Tomochichi, became Oglethorpe's ally and travelled to London in 1734 with him and several of his tribe for the ratification of the treaty between their peoples. What the Creek had not anticipated, of course, was the numbers and aggressiveness of the later settlers who effectively drove them out of their own lands.

25 Diary of John Adams 17/12/1773, http//www.masshist.org/publications. Adams was one of the foremost leaders of the movement for American Independence. He negotiated the peace treaty which ended the war in 1783 and was appointed ambassador to Britain in 1785. He was the first vice-president of the United States, under George Washington, 1789-97, and its second president 1797-97.

26 Davis 1983, 7.

27 Letter from Baikie Harvey, Snowshill, Georgia to Thomas Baikie, Burness Orkney, 30/12/1775, OLA D3/385.

28 Valuation of Real and Personal estate of William Manson, confiscated in consequence of his Loyalty to His Majesty and Attachment to the British Government, n.d. OLA D8/1/4.

29   ibid.
30   Letter from William Manson, Savannah to his mother Marion Manson, Kirkwall 8/4/1776, OLA D2/8/12.
31   Letter from the Chapman brothers, Newcastle to Marion Manson, Kirkwall 26/10/1778, OLA D2/9/15.
32   Letter from William Manson, London to William Digby, Georgia 23/2/1782, W Manson Letter-book, OLA D2/60.
33   ibid.
34   Valuation of Real and Personal estate of William Manson, confiscated in consequence of his Loyalty to His Majesty and Attachment to the British Government, n.d. OLA D8/1/4.
35   Handwritten reference by Thomas Brown, 23/7/1780, OLA D2/44/18.
36   Davis 1983, 17.
37   Invoice from William Manson to Lt. Col. Brown at Augusta 1780/81, OLA D2/44/18.
38   Narrative of William Manson n.d. OLA D2/9/10.
39   Davis 1983, 18.
40   ibid 19.
41   Narrative of William Manson n.d. OLA D2/9/10.
42   Thomas Sumter 1734-1832, general in S. Carolina militia during War of Independence.
43   Fereday 1990, 121-2.
44   Letter from Thomas Manson, London to William Manson, Jamaica 27/2/1784, OLA D2/15/16.
45   Letter from Edward Ligonier, Cobham to Thomas Balfour, Orkney 6/2/1777, OLA D2/4/12.
46   ibid.
47   Letter from Edward Ligonier, London to Thomas Balfour, Orkney 30/4/1777, OLA D2/4/12.
48   ibid.
49   ibid.
50   Letter from Edward Ligonier, Cobham to Thomas Balfour, Orkney 30/1/1779, OLA D2/4/12.
51   Letter from Peggy Balfour, Cobham to Elizabeth Balfour, Westray 20/4/1778, OLA D2/9/1.
52   Ritchie 272.
53   ibid 329-30.
54   Hossack 198.
55   Fereday 1990, 124. William died in Kirkwall in 1808.
56   Cashlin; gregg784.com/2017/04/29/Thomas-browne-of-grand-sable-st-vincent.
57   Davis 1982, 12.
58   James Gordon was a partner of Thomas Brown, Davis 1983, 4.
59   Letter from Baikie Harvey, Snowshill, Georgia to Thomas Baikie, Burness Orkney 30/12/1775, OLA D3/385.

CHAPTER 3

Seafarers, Slaves and Pressed Men

Prologue

Letters that were written from sons abroad to their parents in Orkney tell stories of other 'farstraers' scattered across the world in search of a living. Like William Manson, many young men went to sea but there were other, even more perilous, options for those with a good education and a head for business. The demand for sugar was soaring and this provided opportunities for men to work as clerks and overseers on the slave-worked sugar plantations in the West Indies. There was always the hope that they would be among the lucky few who did not die of yellow fever, become 'planters' themselves and come home wealthy men.

The appalling treatment of the African slaves, on the ships which transported them across the Atlantic and on the plantations, was well documented by campaigners for the abolition of the slave trade. What is perhaps less well known is the murky part played by both the British government and Scots landlords who disposed of criminals and prisoners of war (especially Jacobites and Covenanters) and surplus tenants by sending them to the plantations. The last 20 years have seen many attempts to 'open up' the story of the involvement of Scots in slavery which had been almost blanked-out in a collective amnesia.[1]

At the same time as William Manson was trying to establish his settlement in war-torn Georgia, two teenage boys from Kirkwall were struggling to find a foothold on the 'planter' ladder in the West Indies. Their letters are more revealing for what is omitted than for what is written: they describe their hardships from hurricanes, fever and the French, but never mention slaves. At home, prominent Orcadians owned slaves and a few made fortunes from slave-worked plantations. At the same time, the Orkney kirks were active in sending petitions to Parliament for the abolition of the slave-trade.

The journey to the Caribbean was itself often dangerous. If the horrors of a long voyage on an 18th-century sailing ship are too ghastly to imagine, first-hand accounts come to the rescue. Lieutenant Sandy

Watt, shipwrecked once and then suffering three months of storms and near-disasters before his ship even reached Gibraltar, spared his parents nothing when he wrote home about his voyage in the ill-fated fleet carrying General Abercromby's army to the West Indies to fight the French.

The shadow of war hangs over many of the chapters in this book. There were few years in the entire 18th century when British troops were not engaged in at least one theatre of war, if not in several at once, and the demand of His Majesty's army and navy for men to serve in Britain's far-flung battlefields was insatiable. Letters and official papers document the activities of the pressgangs in Orkney after the outbreak of the Seven Years War in 1756 and bring home the hardship that they caused, both to the men dragged away to the brutality of military life and to the families left at home without a breadwinner.

Throughout the Napoleonic wars, the pressgangs were active again and men who worked at sea on fishing or cargo boats – as so many Orkney men did – were especially vulnerable to being seized by naval vessels. No fewer than five brothers in one Orkney family were pressed into the Royal Navy, at least two of them surviving major sea-battles. Some particularly unlucky individuals were pressed and then captured by French or Spanish ships and held as prisoners of war.

Whaling fleets from Dundee or Hull made their annual hazardous expeditions to the Davis Straits west of Greenland and collected stores and crew from Stromness on the way. Of all the hair-raising descriptions of shipwrecks and terrifying sea voyages that I have read, the most harrowing is a diary kept by a crewman on the Dee, one of the whalers that sailed in the spring of 1836 and was trapped in the ice, only returning to Stromness with the starved remnant of its crew a year later.

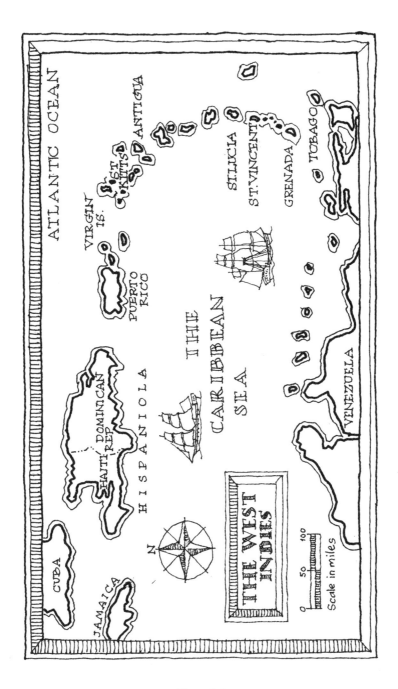

Figure 3.1

Of Sugar and Slaves

I pity them greatly, but I must be mum;
For how could we do without Sugar and Rum?
Especially Sugar so needful we see;
What, give up our Desserts, our Coffee, and Tea?[2]

In 1794 the Reverend William Clouston of Stromness and Sandwick in Orkney's West Mainland penned a splendidly informative description of his parishes for the first *Statistical Account*. The minister was proud of the advances that had been made in the course of the 18th century and he listed some yardsticks of the economic and cultural progress he had noted. *In 1700, for example, there were only 5 houses with slated roofs, and a few scattered huts in the village of Stromness ... In 1794, there are 130 houses with slated roofs, and in all 222 inhabited houses ... In 1700, the use of tea was unknown, even in the families of gentlemen of the first landed property. In 1792, 860 pounds of tea were imported, and tea is drunk by tradesmen and mechanics.[3]*

It may not at first be obvious that there is a direct connection between the tea-drinking habits of the mechanics of Stromness and Orkney's link with the islands of the Caribbean and the slave trade. In the 18th century tea-drinking became a national addiction in Britain. It was China tea rather than Indian that was drunk, without milk as milk was often not available, but invariably with sugar. The British appear to have early acquired a very sweet tooth: in the course of the 1700s our annual consumption rose from four pounds to 20 pounds a head, ten times more than that of our enemies the French.[4] In the same period we were usually at war, with the French and often with several other countries as well, so we needed more warships and more crew to man them. The size of the Royal Navy trebled, to some 129,000 men by 1800,[5] and all those men required to be fuelled with a daily tot of rum, made from sugar. (At that time a tot was half a pint of rum, added to water, which means that the Navy was consuming nearly 3 million gallons of rum in a year).

In the early 17th century it was tobacco that was the main cash crop in the British colonies in America and the Caribbean and the planters relied on European labour, either men who had signed on to serve a period of years as indentured servants, or convicts serving a penal sentence. As soaring demand made sugar the most profitable crop, France and Britain fought for possession of the valuable West Indian colonies and, one after another, the islands were stripped of their native people and vegetation and planted from coast to coast with sugar canes. The climate was lethal for Europeans and, as sugar production expanded, it became impossible to procure enough white labourers to work in the fields or the mills which processed the canes. By the middle of the 17th century most planters were turning to African slaves as the most profitable form of labour. In 1672 the Royal African Company was formed which gave England a virtual monopoly of the slave trade and from that time Jamaica became one of the largest slave marts in the world. In 1494 Columbus had described it as *the fairest isle that eyes have ever beheld*. Two centuries later, for the many thousands who ended very short lives there, it was a hell.

It is the ghastly trade in Negro slaves that is notorious but many of the slaves who were shipped to the Caribbean were not from Africa. Over half of the people named in an index of early Scots colonists to America and the West Indies were not voluntary emigrants but convicts and political prisoners who were transported and sold as labourers, most of them to Virginia or the Caribbean colonies.[6] Britain's prisons were overcrowded with men and women waiting for capital punishment for offences down to petty theft. Selling thieves, forgers and sheep-stealers to the plantations was regarded as a practical solution and a merciful alternative to hanging. The normal period of transportation was fourteen years, and convicts were treated just the same as the African slaves, as this poem by James Revel (who served his sentence in Virginia) makes clear.

No shoes nor stocking had I for to wear,
No hat, nor cap, both head and feet were bare.
Thus dress'd into the Field I next must go,
Amongst tobacco plants all day to hoe,
At day break in the morn our work began
And so held to the setting of the Sun ...
We and the Negroes both alike did fare,
Of work and food we had an equal share ...[7]

Then there were the 'politicals'. Oliver Cromwell addressed his 'Irish problem' by deporting many thousands of Irish as slaves to the plantations in Barbados, Antigua, and Montserrat. In 1655 he sold some 1200 Royalist prisoners of war,[8] and Charles II's government dealt with rebellious Covenanters in the same way. After their final defeat at the battle of Bothwell Brig in 1679, more than 1100 Covenanter prisoners were imprisoned for months in the open air in Greyfriars kirkyard in Edinburgh where many of them died from wounds and exposure. Only 257 survived to be despatched to America to be sold as slaves to plantation-owners. *The Crown of London* sailed northward from Leith that December but was wrecked off Orkney in a storm. Captain Patterson and his crew reached the shore but most of the captives, locked below the decks, were drowned in Deerness Sound.[9] Some may have escaped but were almost certainly recaptured and successfully shipped to the colonies; they were hardly more fortunate.

'Ordinary' convicts were free at the end of their sentence, if they lived, but there was little hope of a return home for political prisoners. A dozen or more ships were chartered to transport Covenanters in the late 17th century,[10] and at least ten shiploads of Jacobites were transported after the failed rebellion of 1715. An estimated 3,500 prisoners followed in 1747 after the disaster of Culloden, most of them shipped (in appalling conditions) from Leith or Liverpool to Jamaica or other islands of the West Indies, or to states such as Virginia, Maryland and South Carolina which relied heavily on slave labour.[11] They were not expected to survive the climate or the harshness of their treatment.

Figure 3.2
The Covenanters Memorial on Deerness Sound was built in 1888 to commemorate the prisoners who were drowned when the ship taking them to America was wrecked near here in 1679.

Exceptionally, one convict from Orkney apparently not only survived Jamaica but prospered there. The minister of Firth and Stenness parishes, the Reverend William Nisbet, was tried in Inverness in 1765 on a charge of adultery. The case was all the more scandalous as the minister had only recently married and his lover was related by marriage. Nisbet was sentenced to two months in Inverness Tolbooth *to be fed upon Bread and water only ... till an opportunity shall offer for Transporting him to one or other of His Majestys Plantations in America ... and they hereby Banish him during all the days of his Life. They grant warrant to and ordain the Magistrates of Inverness and Keepers of their Tolbooth to deliver over the person of the said Mr William Nisbet to any Merchant, Shipmaster, or other person ... and Report a Certificate to the Court of Justiciary of his being so Transported and landed.* If Nisbet returned to Scotland he was to be returned to the Inverness Tolbooth and *taken out and whipped at the usual times and places, and again transported.* Nisbet sailed for Jamaica in July 1766, leaving a destitute wife behind.

The minister himself, however, thrived in his new surroundings; he subsequently acquired land in Jamaica and some of his family followed him from Orkney.[12]

It was the sugar colonies of the West Indies that brought wealth to Scotland as a whole and transformed her economy. Glasgow and Liverpool became major hubs of the trade. British ships carried manufactured goods (firearms, liquor, trinkets) to the American seaboard, reloaded with rice to feed the slaves on the plantations, sailed to the Caribbean and finally homeward with cargoes of sugar and molasses to distil into rum. Scottish estates were bought and new mansions built on the profits of sugar. In the second half of the 18th century some 17,000 young Scots made their way to the Caribbean, especially to Jamaica, Trinidad and the Windward Islands of Grenada and St Vincent, in the hope of sharing this wealth.

For a few, the rewards were enormous. Charles Stewart, born in Kirkwall in 1725, became rich in North America as a government contractor in the French and Indian wars, ended up with the lucrative post of Receiver General of Customs and was able to establish his nephews on his plantations in Tobago and Jamaica.[13] Kirkwall sea-captain William Manson sailed cargo ships to and from Jamaica for the fabulously wealthy plantation-owner Simon Taylor, who left £1 million sterling on his death.[14] Orkney-born Malcolm Laing and his nephew James also made fortunes from the plantations. These were some of the celebrities of the plantocracy, but their careers were built on a colossal gamble: that they would live long enough to enjoy their wealth. Three of James' brothers died of fever in Jamaica as very young men, two of them in the same year. Their stories were far more typical.

The successful ones found opportunities for their young relatives; there was always a plentiful supply of nephews with genteel but impoverished parents anxious to find them a 'situation'. Present-day sentiments of pride in and affection for Orkney had no place in the 18th century, when even the better-off were so desperate to find a livelihood for their children that sending them to a place where the chances were stacked so high against them ever returning was preferable to the disastrous option of staying at home. Trying to help his younger brother Tom to a career, William

Manson wrote: *the Orkneys in my opinion will never do anything for him.*[15] Orkney was a dead-end; to escape from it an urgent necessity.

Sometimes a parent's reasons for despatching their children to the distant colonies were even more pressing than the purely economic. Thomas Traill of Tirlet in Westray enlisted the help of all his relations to ship his son William as far away and as quickly as possible. *He has been so unfortunate as to form a connection with a worthless woman who has influenced him to do what has given his family much uneasiness, and they apprehend no less than a disgraceful marriage if the partners are not kept long asunder. With this view his father desires most earnestly that he may be put apprentice to a merchant vessel in some foreign trade or if that cannot be easily accomplished that he may be entered on board a man of War.*[16] Only six weeks later the Orkney network had succeeded and Thomas Manson in London was able to write to his brother: *Please to acquaint Uncle Tirlet that I have agreed with one of our Captains in the Antigua Trade to take William an apprentice for 3 years.*[17] Death in battle or from fever was clearly much to be preferred for one's son and heir than a *disgraceful marriage*.

William was duly shipped to Antigua but too late: a few months after this correspondence his son was born in Westray and baptised in January 1788. William came home to marry his love, Ann Reid – probably *a worthless woman* only in the literal sense of having no tocher (dowry) to bring to the marriage – and they had many more children.

A 'connection' was the vital key which opened the door out of Orkney and to employment in the colonies, and parents had eager but unrealistic hopes that this would soon lead to remittances sent by prosperous sons to cushion the real hardships of life at home. In fact it often led only to a very low rung on the ladder, as a clerk or junior overseer on a plantation, and promotion was not easy. In the 1770s the Mowat brothers from Kirkwall were sent to the West Indies as soon as they were 16. Their uncles Thomas Baikie and John Mowat had successfully enriched themselves in Jamaica and clearly the family had loaded Hugh and Robert with their expectations. However, the boys found that the war with America had made all provisions expensive and they were struggling to live on their meagre salaries. *You may be sure it is terrible hard living in this country at present,* wrote Robert from St Vincent in 1780. *Will you believe that a firkin of butter cannot be bought here for less than £5, a barrel of indifferent salt beef much about the same, in short every article of provisions, Cloathing etc are at least about three times as dear as ever they used to be.*[18] Letters from home reminded them of the hopes pinned on them that they were unable to fulfill. In 1783, when crops had failed right across Britain, Hugh wrote to his mother from Grenada: *all I lament is that it is not in my power to give you and your family the assistance I would wish to do was it otherwise with me.*[19]

For the junior white employees like the Mowat boys, life must have been lonely at best. There were only a small number of white people on the estates and hardly any white women. Letters were a very rare event, often lost on the way *through the precariousness of the times*. Robert wrote that he had not heard from his father in Orkney for some 20 months, or even from Hugh in Grenada – the nearest island – in 16. They were also at the mercy of the unpredictable weather in the Caribbean, being lucky to survive the 'Great Hurricane' of October 1780 which killed 22,000 people in the Windward and Leeward Islands. Hugh wrote home in the spring: *Crops have been so very short this year by reason of the Hurricane that people cannot expect augmentations to their salarys, they may even be thankfull that they are kept in imploy in such hard times. We finished Crop this day and have only made 86 Hogsheads Sugar and wont make over 6000 gallons Rum. We last year made 220 Hh Sugar and upwards of 13,000 Gl Rum ...*[20]

Even more potentially serious for the Mowats was the volatile political situation. They had gone out to British colonies but in 1779 first St Vincent and then Grenada were captured by the French and the small British population was in fear of being shipped to France as prisoners of war. One can sympathise with Mrs Mowat, trying to bring up the rest of her *numerous family* in an Orkney that was suffering repeated years of food shortage; waiting for a year, or two years or more, for news of her teenage sons; hearing, long after the event, that their islands have fallen to the enemy. *I am exceeding sorry to see that you have been so very anxious regarding our welfare,* Hugh wrote to his mother[21]and, reading the boys' letters over her shoulder, she must have been exasperated as well as anxious. She didn't really care how many hogsheads of sugar they had made that year, but she must have worried about the military occupation, about their safety, and wished they would supply some information about the island and their daily life. We can guess the kind of questions any mother would have been asking, but it is hard to know just how much of the realities of a slave-worked plantation was understood or discussed at home.

Figure 3.3
Slaves working on a sugar plantation in the West Indies. (Mary Evans Picture Library)

Early settlers in the West Indies, like the dynasty of Campbells from Argyll who acquired vast tracts of Jamaica, put down permanent roots in the islands but the climate was so unhealthy that, from the mid 18th century, most of them aimed to return to Britain as soon as they had made enough money. They did not establish families, or build schools and churches as in other colonies, but left their estates in the hands of managers who themselves wanted to maximise profits so that they could get rich quickly and leave. The result was that conditions for the slaves were generally even worse than for those in America. Men and women worked long days in the fields at the heavy labour of clearing ground and planting new canes, malnourished and brutally treated. High mortality and a very low birth rate meant that new slaves were constantly needed. Only when replacement slaves became more scarce and expensive, after Britain banned the slave trade in her territories in 1807, were conditions slightly improved. Young overseers like Hugh and Robert Mowat were expected to keep the field slaves working as hard as possible, but their letters reveal only their own hardships and slaves are never mentioned. Did they or their families ever reflect on the ethical issues, or did they just not see them as issues?

If Mrs Mowat and her Orkney friends had seen the human cost of the sugar that they stirred into their tea, would they have been unduly distressed? Janet Schaw, from the Borders, travelled to Antigua with her brother in 1770 and, though at first a little discomfited by the sights she saw, was soon consoled with her 'knowledge' that black people were not human. *When one becomes better acquainted with the nature of the negroes, the horrour of it must wear off. It is the suffering of the human mind that constitutes the greatest misery of punishment, but with them it is merely corporal. As to the brutes it inflicts no wounds on their mind, whose Natures seem made to bear it and whose sufferings are not attended with shame or pain beyond the present.*[22] Did many of her contemporaries salve their consciences the same way?

There were writers on both sides of the Atlantic who did not take such a sanguine view of the way in which slaves were treated. The American Philip Freneau, for example, detailed some of the atrocities he observed on plantations in Jamaica at much the same time as the Mowats were working in Grenada and St Vincent.

If there exists a hell – the case is clear –
Sir Toby's slaves enjoy that portion here;. . .
One with a gibbet wakes his negro's fears,
One to the windmill nails him by the ears;
One keeps his slave in darkened dens, unfed,
One puts the wretch in pickle ere he's dead:
This from a tree suspends him by the thumbs,
That, from his table grudges even the crumbs ...[23]

For the white employees, their deadliest enemy by far was not hurricanes or French but yellow fever. In September 1780 Robert Mowat wrote that he had been seriously ill for ten months, *during all which time you wou'd hardly have given a shilling for me.* He was desperate to go home, but getting a passage to Scotland was far from easy. *I actually sailed two different times on board a sloop for St Lucie in order to take a passage from thence for Britain, but somehow or other we were always put back and detain'd till a few days ago and now I think it is too late of the year to venture into a cold climate after having been these three years and a half toasted in this frying pan.*[24] Early the next year he tried again, taking a ship to Grenada, back to St Vincent, then to St Lucia and finally to Antigua before finding a vessel bound for Britain. It took him only as far as Liverpool, where he waited three weeks for a ship that battled contrary winds for five days before delivering him to Port Glasgow in July.

Before heading for Leith to find a ship for Orkney he wrote to prepare his father for his arrival. *There is one thing I have to tell you, that is, you must not expect to meet one come home with a fortune but, one that has had the fever and ague 21 months, Tanned as brown as a piece of leather, Drove away by ye Indians of St Vincent and plundered to very Clothes on his Back.*[25] I wish I knew just what had happened to him. Robert was dead a few months later, aged 21. The letter that finally brought the news to Hugh told him that his 18-year-old brother Tom who had gone to sea had also died in the same year.

In 1795 the French stirred up the slave populations on Grenada and St Lucia to rebel and 'the Brigands' succeeded in driving the British out of most of Grenada and St Vincent. It was an intolerable loss of trade and prestige to Britain, and the government despatched

General Abercromby with a fleet of 155 ships to recapture the islands. It was late November. Lieutenant Sandy Watt from Skaill was in one of the ill-fated ships that was storm-battered for days in the English Channel before the tattered remnant was washed ashore in a chaos of wreckage. *Dear Father, I now inform you that I have escaped the danger of the Sea which makes me think I am not born to be drowned as I shall never be in greater danger than what I have been in,* wrote Sandy from Spithead.[26] He was quite wrong about the danger. Sixty ships had been lost and mass graves hastily dug on Chesil Beach, but the demand to secure the sugar islands was so urgent that in only a fortnight an even larger fleet had been assembled and Sandy embarked again, on an ill-starred voyage that would take three terrifying months to get as far as Gibraltar.

In fact Sandy was extraordinarily lucky. He was not drowned at sea and he was not one of the many British soldiers killed recapturing the islands. The hapless fleet finally made it to the Caribbean in the spring of 1796 and, after a month-long campaign, Abercromby's troops drove the French from St Lucia. Sandy was with them for the final assault at the end of May and then at the retaking of St Vincent and Grenada. Luckiest of all, he was not one of the soldiers left to garrison the islands. The 4000 men left with Sir John Moore to garrison St Lucia were swiftly reduced to 1000 fit to stand, with 1500 dead and 1500 sick.[27] Sandy Watt was only too glad to be posted away from a place where *there has been more lives lost by the Climate than by the enemy.*[28]

At the time of Abercromby's expedition, there were more than 300,000 slaves in Jamaica alone. The statistics of the slave trade are hard to digest. In the 1760s, the peak years of the trade, Britain's shipments averaged 42,000 slaves a year: men, women and children. Warring tribes in central Africa sold their captives to slave traders who took them to the coast to sell to European slavers. In the four years between 1781 and 1785 there were 53 recorded slaving voyages from the Gold Coast (now Ghana) to Jamaica, which landed an estimated 22,800 slaves. That figure of course is well below the number of slaves who were taken on board. Two ships *Nelly* and *Anne* which sailed from Liverpool in 1782 lost one-quarter of their slaves, 278 souls, on the way from West Africa, dying on the ghastly 'Middle Passage' across the Atlantic or thrown overboard alive as sick and unmarketable. It has been estimated that well over 15 million enslaved people had reached the Americas by the mid 19th century, plus over two million who died on the voyage.

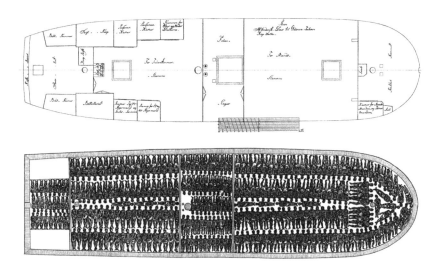

Figure 3.4
Deck plan of a slave ship, showing slaves transported like cargo. Images like these were used in the campaign against the slave trade to stir the conscience of the public. (North Wind Picture Archives)

Voices were raised in protest in Britain from the late 17th century, mostly from the Quakers, but it was another hundred years before there was any significant debate about the trade. From the mid 18th century, a few anti-imperialist voices spoke out against the cruelty perpetrated on the peoples of Africa, America and Asia when they were 'discovered' by Europeans. Samuel Johnson wrote in 1759: *The Europeans have scarcely visited any coast, but to gratify avarice, and extend corruption; to arrogate dominion without right, and practise cruelty without incentive.*[29] Johnson's friends John Hawkesworth and John Maclaurin wrote poems criticising slavery but most people were too preoccupied with enjoying the considerable economic benefits of the slave trade to question its ethics. The first petition to ban the slave trade, from a Quaker committee, was only submitted to the government in 1783.

The conscience of the British public was at last being stirred, however, and several widely-publicised legal cases focused attention on the barbarities of slavery and gave significant impetus to the anti-slave trade campaign. Charles Stewart, originally from Orkney, brought a slave called James Somerset to England from Boston in 1769. It was not unusual for house-slaves to accompany their masters back to Britain and there were some 15,000 black slaves in England at this time. Their status as the property of their masters was not normally questioned, as testified in some 800 'Runaway Slave' and 80 'For Sale' advertisements placed in British newspapers (including *The Scotsman*) between 1700 and 1780.[30] Somerset escaped but was recaptured and Stewart ordered that he should be put on a ship bound for the West Indies to be sold to a plantation. However, Somerset had supporters among prominent campaigners who applied for a writ of habeas corpus, removed him from the ship and brought a test case before the High Court, arguing that slavery was not legal in England and therefore Somerset was a free man. After a lengthy case, Lord Chief Justice Mansfield made his famous pronouncement in 1772 that slavery was *so odious, that nothing can be suffered to support it ... and therefore the black must be discharged.*[31]

Five years later, a similar case centred on Joseph Knight, a slave who was brought to Scotland from Jamaica by John Wedderburn. When Knight left his service and claimed his freedom, Wedderburn took his case to the Perth Court which found in his favour. Knight appealed to the Court of Session and was supported, among others, by Samuel Johnson and James Boswell. Eventually the judges declared that *the state of slavery is not recognised by the laws of this kingdom* and Knight was recognised as a free man.[32]

In 1783 Lord Mansfield again found against the slave-owners in another famous case, that of the slave-ship the *Zong* which was bound for Jamaica with more than twice the number of slaves on board that a ship that size could safely carry. The ship was navigated past the island by error and the crew threw 132 slaves overboard, arriving in Jamaica with only 208 of the original 442 to sell. The owners claimed insurance for the drowned slaves on the grounds that they were short of water and it was legal for them to jettison part of the cargo to safeguard the rest. The case was brought to the court of the King's Bench where Mansfield pronounced that the insurers were not liable to pay for the crew's error. It was a cautious judgment, a very long way from condemning slavery, but the case drew attention to the inhuman treatment of slaves on their journey to the plantations and was greeted by the abolitionists as a significant encouragement for their cause.

Figure 3.5
Slaves thrown overboard from a slave ship in a storm. Hand-coloured woodcut. (North Wind Picture Archives)

In 1787 the Society for Effecting the Abolition of the Slave Trade was founded. Prominent campaigner Thomas Clarkson rode all over the country delivering speeches and pamphlets in support of abolition. The churches, both in England and Scotland, were active in drawing up petitions to the House of Commons pleading for a ban on the trade.[33] The Kirkwall Presbytery sent in its own petition in 1788.[34] Inevitably, there was considerable opposition. The alarmed gentry of Liverpool, by far the biggest slave-trading port, immediately retaliated with their own petition against abolition, which would be so prejudicial *to the town of Liverpool in particular ... the landed interest of the Kingdom in general ... ruin the property of the English merchants in the West Indies, diminish the public revenue ...*[35]

The Orcadians who grew rich on plantation profits became designated not by the name of their Orkney lands but by their Caribbean properties, and their families were inextricably intertwined. Thomas Ruddach of Tobago inherited a plantation in that island from his uncle Charles Stewart. Malcolm Laing of Kingston, his nephew James, John Mowat of Orkney Hall, Dr James Blaw and Thomas Baikie were all known as 'of Jamaica'. Everyone knew the source of their wealth, but there was a deafening silence about its implications.

In 1791 Wilberforce's Bill to ban the slave trade was debated in Parliament. Despite the chilling evidence that the Abolition Society laid before the House of Commons, the Bill was easily defeated by 163 votes to 88. With Parliament composed exclusively of men of property, many of whom were benefiting from the revenues from slaves, sugar and shipping, it is not surprising that all the subsequent Bills which Wilberforce proposed over the next 20 years were thrown out by either the Commons or the Lords or both. Although he had supported Joseph Knight, James Boswell defended slavery in his 'Life of Johnson' and other writings and attacked the anti-slavery movement as an aspect of the lamentable democratic tendency of the age. He was expressing the views of many when he condemned the 'Noodles' who would ruin Britain's economy

> *Noodles, who rave for abolition*
> *Of th'Africans improv'd condition*
> *At your own cost fine projects try;*
> *Don't rob – from pure humanity ...*
> *What frenzies will a rabble seize*
> *In lax luxurious days, like these;*[36]

The evidence that the Abolition Society gathered was circulated among the Presbyteries. As a result of the failure of the first Bill, in 1792 another nation-wide campaign deluged the House of Commons with 519 petitions, the largest number that had ever been submitted on a single issue. In Orkney the North Isles Presbytery, meeting in Sanday, *took to their consideration the unhappy circumstances of the african natives unjustly reduced to the state of Slavery by the subjects of Great Britain carrying on a cruel and unjustifiable trade to that coast as stated in a pamphlet transmitted to each of the members. They unanimously agree to express in the strongest terms their abhorrence of such practices* [and to draw up a petition to be sent to Mr Wilberforce] *for the abolition of that traffick; and for the instituting such Regulations and acts, as might render the situation of the slaves in the British west india islands more comfortable, and effectually to prevent a Tyrannical and cruel treatment, or death with impunity to be perpetrated on them, as appears hitherto hath been done, and too frequently the case.*[37]

The wording is interesting. The good members of Presbytery are asking for the 'traffick' to be abolished, and cruel treatment of the slaves, but one senses a nervousness that too much righteous indignation against slavery itself might affect their own interests. There is a cautious distancing of the members from knowledge of the situation, *as **appears** hitherto hath been done,* as if they knew nothing about the slave trade before they read the pamphlet. The members' coyness sounds disingenuous. They could hardly have all been unaware that young men had been going out to the plantations from Orkney for decades, or of who or what young overseers like the Mowat boys were sent to oversee. It is also impossible that they knew nothing of the widely-publicised cases of James Somerset and Joseph Knight. Both cases were highly controversial and it is inconceivable that they were not known and discussed in Orkney where Charles Stewart, Somerset's master, must have had plenty of kin.

There is plenty of contemporary evidence for the way that slaves were treated in the West Indian newspaper advertisements for runaways. 4,150 missing slaves appear in the pages of the Jamaica press during the 18th century, and a further 3,278 in merely eight years at the beginning of the 19th. In the *Weekly Jamaica*

Courant for 30 July 1718, for example: *Run away, from Mrs Drakes a yellow Negro wench named Rose, marked LC upon her right shoulder. Whoever brings the said Negro to her mistress shall be well rewarded, and whoever entertain her be it at their peril.* In a 1730 issue: *Taken up, the 10th inst at Mr Montgomerys pen in Liguanea, an Ebo Negro woman. Whoever can prove their just right, and describe her marks, may have her, paying charges. Likewise for a young bay horse without mark.*[38] Slaves had their owner's mark burnt into their skin – usually branded on the breast – but they were also often described by their ethnic group, as Eboe, Congo, Coromante, Mundingo and so on, and it is interesting that white Jamaicans were well aware of the ethnicity of the slaves and could identify them. Many Africans were also distinguished by their own tribal scarification on their faces. There is an almost unbearable poignancy in reading that that a slave has the 'bruchee' cut, the mark of a man of very high rank and dignity.

Runaway slaves could also often be recognised from their sores and disfigurements, from smallpox, from diseases caused by malnutrition or parasites, or from accidents (an extraordinary number are described as having fingers or toes missing) or from mutilations inflicted as punishment. *Escaped out of the prison of this parish ... a mulatto man slave named Dan, He is a stout made man, about 28 years of age and had a wooden leg ... He had his leg cut off for robbing the late Mr John McDonald ...* Another conspicuous renegade was Cuffee, *a desperate villain and the leader of the gang; he had his nose cropt for being formerly a runaway.*[39] Recaptured and recalcitrant slaves were jailed in the workhouse, but these often refused to accept slaves who were carrying infectious diseases or seriously injured, as *Jasper ...* [who] *is not in a condition to be sent to the workhouse having been severely flogged.* Many of the advertisements refer to children, small boys like Monday [who] *had on when he went away a check shirt, without any breeches, as he could not wear them on account of a whipping he had a few days before.*[40] Even when no physical ill-treatment is recorded, the names the slaves were given reflects the way in which they were dehumanised. *Run away from Bellfield estate, two Congo Negro men, named Edinburgh and Glasgow, marked IC;* or *Run away, two new negroes named Somebody and Robinhood.*[41]

The sugar plantations absorbed the greatest number of slaves in their fields but also in their factories, which required skilled workers. *Titus is ... a good boiler and sawyer and can turn his hand to almost anything on a sugar estate, being a piece of a jobbing carpenter.*

The other fellow Peter is 6 ft high, stout and well made, an extraordinary good boiler and compleat sawyer, and has filed teeth.[42] However, the advertisements demonstrate that slaves were employed in a great variety of other ways. They were stockmen on the farms, housemaids and valets and cooks and grooms in private houses and joiners and coopers, butchers and barbers and entertainers. Some were just hired out to whoever required them, like Dublin who had been hired as a pioneer to the 16th Regiment and ran away from Lucea Barracks.

Those with special skills changed hands for many times the average price, and sometimes a hint of individual personality comes through in the long columns of classified ads. It is hard to imagine how runaway George Sterling remained hidden. *He is a likely negro, speaks English, French and Spanish, shaves and dresses hair well, plays on the violin, with a variety of other accomplishments, but is very much given to excessive drinking, and well known all over the North-Side of the island.*[43] Another character that stands out is *a young Negro man named Sharper ... he is a complete waiting-man and barber, and had on when he went away a pompadour* [pink] *coat, with frogs of the same colour. It is probable that he may attempt to pass as free, having already under an imposition of that kind taken a cruize in one of his Majestys ships of war, by the name of Tom Jones.*[44]

The perseverance of the abolitionists finally achieved, in 1807, the Act of Parliament which prohibited the trading of slaves to British colonies but it would be another 26 years before Emancipation made it to the Statute Books, let alone to reality. Meanwhile there were still profits to be made from the plantations, at home as well as abroad. In Orkney Samuel Laing, the youngest of the Laing brothers, was in financial straits. He had lost much of the Jamaican property he had inherited *by the neglect and mismanagement of the Executors;* his post managing his brother's leadmines had devalued when the price of lead fell at the end of the Napoleonic war; his speculations were disastrous, and he had children and an extravagant mother-in-law to support. His autobiography takes up the story.

I went to London to consult my brother James what I should do. He was then living in splendour like all West indians. He suggested the supplying of his estates in Jamaica with herrings. This was the origin of the Herring Fishery in Orkney ... I proceeded to Orkney, collected coopers and materials, and prepared for curing herrings on an extensive scale.[45]

James Laing's suggestion was not a new idea. The Scottish fishing industry had boomed from the sale of cheap salted herrings to the plantations. By the end of the 18th century almost 85,000 barrels were being exported to the West Indies from British ports annually, an estimated 61% of them from Scotland. The herring fishing created considerable employment in the coastal towns and villages and petitions against the emancipation of slaves were sent to Parliament from the merchants and fish curers in Wick and Cromarty and Tain.[46]

Samuel's project was made easier by the fact that two of his brothers owned land at Papa Sound where there was an excellent harbour and good access to the fishing grounds: Malcolm owned what would become the busy curing station at Whitehall in Stronsay, and Gilbert the small island of Papa Stronsay opposite. Before this there had been no herring fishing in the North Isles but 1816 saw a good season and the following year 400 boats were fitted out in Orkney. *For some years the House of Spenser & Co took all the fish, repacked them and shipped them off direct to the West Indies.* The contract with Spenser was lost after a few years but the fishery continued for more than a century, supplying markets in Britain and Europe. It never succeeded in bailing Samuel out of his financial difficulties but he proudly claimed that it *has diffused comfort, intelligence, independence and enterprise among the lower classes.* [47]

While Samuel's fishermen were enjoying the benefits of supplying herrings to feed slaves on Jamaican plantations, the campaign for emancipation was gaining momentum, but also acrimony. Right up until 1833, when legislation was being finalized in Parliament, the campaigners were pushing a massive boulder uphill to challenge public attitudes as well as the vested interests in slavery. Deacon Flett in Kirkwall received a smirking letter from his nephew in Edinburgh. *We are amused here with a most Eloquent lecturer in favour of the immediate Emancipation of the Slaves, and his opponent a Mr Borthwick who is inferior by advocating their gradual Emancipation.*[48]

Despite all the opposition, the tide was turning. In December 1831 a peaceful protest in Jamaica turned into a slave revolt – one of many that had occurred in the West Indies – and the loss of life and property jolted planters and politicians towards thinking that only emancipation could prevent further rebellions. The following year, the Reform Act of 1832 significantly widened the franchise in Britain and brought more pro-emancipation MPs into Parliament. Finally, in August 1833, (a month after the death of William Wilberforce), the Slave Emancipation Act was passed. To gain the assent of slave-owners, substantial concessions were made to them. Slavery would be theoretically abolished from 1st August 1834, but only children under the age of six would be immediately free; all other slaves would serve a period of 'apprenticeship', or compulsory labour, for their former masters: four years for domestic servants and six for field hands. Additionally, the British Government granted £20,000,000 to compensate planters for the loss of their property, a sum equivalent to 40% of the government's total annual expenditure. So many people had some kind of interest in a plantation that in the end over 45,000 awards were made to owners, mortgagees, legatees, annuitants and their agents for 800,000 freed slaves.[49]

Emancipation Day, the first of August 1834, was celebrated with jubilation in the West Indies, but the clause which bound slaves to work for their former masters for six years effectively extended their slavery, even though they were now theoretically paid labour. Before emancipation, the children of slave mothers were automatically the property of their owner and, when new slaves could no longer be easily imported, there was an incentive for masters to offer easier conditions to pregnant women and new mothers to ensure a new generation of slaves. After emancipation, the children of 'apprentices' were free and so there was no such incentive. Women made up the majority of field workers in Jamaica and were expected to do the hardest of labour for ten hours a day even when pregnant or nursing. Recalcitrant workers were sent to workhouses where both men and women were punished with flogging or the treadmill. Former slaves were not allowed to leave their plantation, or to own more than a small garden plot of land. The terrible abuses of the system were publicised by the Anti-Slavery Society, who made an inspection tour of the West Indian colonies in 1836, published first-hand accounts by apprentices[50] and barraged Parliament with pamphlets and petitions. Their evidence forced the government to bring full emancipation two years ahead, to 1838.

The records of compensation paid to former slave-owners are meticulous and they allow us to see who they were and the scale of their properties. On average, they received £20–£25 for each slave, rather less than their market value. Some owned just one or two slaves, these would be domestic servants, and then there were the small plantation owners, like Edward Clouston of Kingshouse in Harray, who was paid £448. 3 s. 5d for his 21 slaves in the parish of St Thomas in the Vale in Jamaica. A few years earlier he had bought freedom for his slave mistress Eliza Fox and their child, the property of Henry Lascelles, the earl of Harewood, who owned a plantation in the same parish. Lascelles owned five other plantations in Jamaica and Barbados and was awarded £26,309 for nearly 1300 slaves. Eliza must have been a highly regarded servant, for Edward paid £120 to manumit her and their son.[51]

Given the almost total lack of white women in the Caribbean, it was inevitable, and quite socially acceptable, for white planters to employ black or mulatto 'housekeepers'. The women often regarded themselves as married, they referred to 'my husband' and were loyal partners, but for the men it was a temporary arrangement until they could return home with enough money to establish themselves in society and make a suitable marriage. While it would have been socially unthinkable for them to bring a black wife home, many brought their mixed race children back to Britain and they seem to have suffered no stigma. Edward Clouston was typical in abandoning Eliza in Jamaica when he returned to Scotland in 1833. He took their two children, Henry and six-year-old Isabella, with him and Isabella apparently lived happily with her Scottish stepmother. Her skin colour was no bar to a 'good' marriage with Robert Thin of Edinburgh.

Nineteenth-century Stromness seems to have been happily free of colour prejudice. It was a cosmopolitan town, often loud with the tongues of foreign sailors and home to a few Indian wives of Hudson's Bay men. There were also the children of men who had made 'country marriages' in the Bay with native women. Henrietta Maria Stewart, the daughter of Orcadian planter Walter Stewart and a negro slave in St Kitts, must have been a little more conspicuous but clearly neither colour nor illegitimacy nor her slave mother affected her status as 'gentlewoman'. In the 1821 census Henrietta and her aunts were the only women in the town designated as 'Miss', and she finally inherited her father's Masseter estate in South Ronaldsay.

Figure 3.7
The Whitehouse in the 19th century, Stromness, home of the Stewart family.

Shipwreck

Captain William Manson's letters and log-book conjure up a vivid picture of a small brig *labouring hard* through Atlantic storms, but at least his merchant vessels were usually carrying only cargo and a crew of experienced seamen. Far more harrowing is Lieutenant Sandy Watt's description of his voyage in a troop ship. Unlike merchant vessels, troop ships had a naval crew but were crammed with soldiers, many of whom had never been to sea before and were surely sea-sick, terrified and totally without the skills to assist the ship in a crisis. After the first fleet carrying General Abercromby's army to the Caribbean had been wrecked in the English Channel with huge loss of life, a second fleet was hastily assembled and it set out with 19,000 men on 218 ships. After three storm-tossed weeks at sea it had got no further than three days sail from England and it was three months before Sandy's stricken ship limped into Gibraltar. He described the journey in a letter to his parents in Orkney, the dramatic effect heightened by the shortage of punctuation.

We sailed the 9th of December and parted with the fleet the 21 in a severe gail by which we received verry much damage, some days after we foul in with a Fregat and 3 Transports whome we spoke, but could give us no Accounts of the Admiral. We were again separated by another Storm our Ship now being in a dangerous situation having carried away our Main topmast and the forehead of the Vessel being so much shattered that we were under the necessity of having it fixed with Ropes. Some times after we fail in with 25 Sail of the fleet and not one of the Convoy [naval escort] with them. They bore down for us seeing our distressed situation and were to have given us some assistance the next day had we not received another Storm, much worse than any of the rest. Our situation became distressing having started two of her Planks which drew so much water that both Pumps could not keep her up. We then hoisted a Signal of distress to the Fleet but they could render us no assistance as the Sea running so high, upon which we bore away for this place. At that time was over 900 Miles from it. Upon this tack she drew much less water which cheered us all up. We at last mead this place [Gibraltar] *but were unfortunately drove past in the night time, the Current being so strong and then we beat for 3 Weeks but could not get up.*

Eventually the ship reached Carthagena, now Tunis; Sandy described the countryside as *much worse than the hill above Stromness.* They had been at sea for ten weeks of acute danger and misery; *the troops being so long on salt Provisions and worn out with fatigue in Pumping the Ship and their berths being constantly wet, sickness began to increase* ...[52] What Sandy's poor mother, home in Orkney, felt on receiving that letter one can only guess. When they finally made it to Gibraltar and could haul the ship out for repairs, they loosened the ropes with which they had tried to hold the leaking hull together and the planks fell apart. Presumably another ship was found to carry the troops across the Atlantic to do battle with the French in the West Indies.

His Majesty's Service

There were few years in the 18th century when Britain was not at war somewhere, often fighting on several fronts at once. From 1739 onwards, hostilities with Spain merged into the War of the Austrian Succession, swiftly followed by the global conflict known as the Seven Years War which was fought across not only Europe but in India, North America, the West Indies, West Africa and the Philippines. Britain emerged as a super-power with a clutch of foreign colonies but it was not long before she was challenged in the American War of Independence, with France and Spain taking revenge by siding with the rebellious colonists. Barely ten years of uneasy peace elapsed before the French Revolutionary Wars set Britain on a war footing again, with the rise of Napoleon drawing out the conflict until his eventual defeat in 1815.

Every fresh outbreak of hostilities brought new Acts of Parliament for enforced recruitment and a flurry of War Office circulars to the Justices of the Peace in every county to demand supplies of men. Orkney and Shetland men working at sea were easy targets for the Navy 'Press' but landsmen were not safe from troops of soldiers who arrived to 'enlist' deeply reluctant recruits. When Britain became embroiled in the Seven Years War of 1756-63, the activities of the pressgangs intensified.

In 1757 the Orkney JPs wrote to all the parish constables ordering them *to search for and apprehend all such able-bodied men within our district who are Idlers and out of service and between the years of seventeen and fourty five years and not under the height of five feet four inches in bare soles and to bring them before the said justices in order to their being inlisted to serve his Majesty.*[53] For the unfortunate constables, the orders to pluck their friends and neighbours from their homes and work placed them in an impossible position, threatened with heavy fines if they did not produce the men and vilified by the community if they did.

In March 1758 the constables of Rousay wrote a heartfelt letter to the JPs, pleading that there was no one that could be spared from the island ... *after we had taken the said order to consideration there was no Idler to be found within our Bownds fit for to be inlisted in HMs service ... the JPs sent us another Precept (more severe than the first) ... that we Constables should Impress Two Men and bring them into Kirkwall on or before the 22nd of this month of March ... But did the Honourable Justices know the Present State of our Isle through the want of Servants to Manure and Labour the Land we are of the Oppinion that they would have a Simpathie with the Labouring Man, And not lay the Constables under such a weighty fine as is threatened ... For our Isle through the want of servants is almost like to ly lay* [ley, uncultivated] *... We also crave and Intreat that the Hon Justices would Chuse others in our place ... and not Inflict more on us than we are able to bear. Subscribed by David Marwick for Wm and Rowland Marwick's and himself Constables in Rousay – March the 14th 1758 years.*[54]

The unfortunate Marwicks had good reason to want to retire. In the same year the constables of Hoy were ordered to appear before the JPs for neglect of duty in failing to impress any men but their laird explained their reluctance. *For the whole people both men and Women have all along threatened to Deforce the Constables or any other party that would presume to take a man out of the place ... Mr Sands the minister of Hoy and his wife have been the Chief formenters of this lawless and disorderly spirit among the populace and sent out this morning two of his Women Servants, at least they were with about 30 or 40 more most active in Deforcing Ben Barnotson and William Swanson this morning when they had seized upon a young fellow ... the two constables were beat and abused with stones and otherways, particularly William Swanson who was cut in the face by old Wm Stout ...* [If those] *who were most Active in this Riot ... go unpunished you may assure yourself the like Riotous Spirit will Diffuse itself over the rest of the Country* [and] *farewell to all order and Government in this part of the world.*[55]

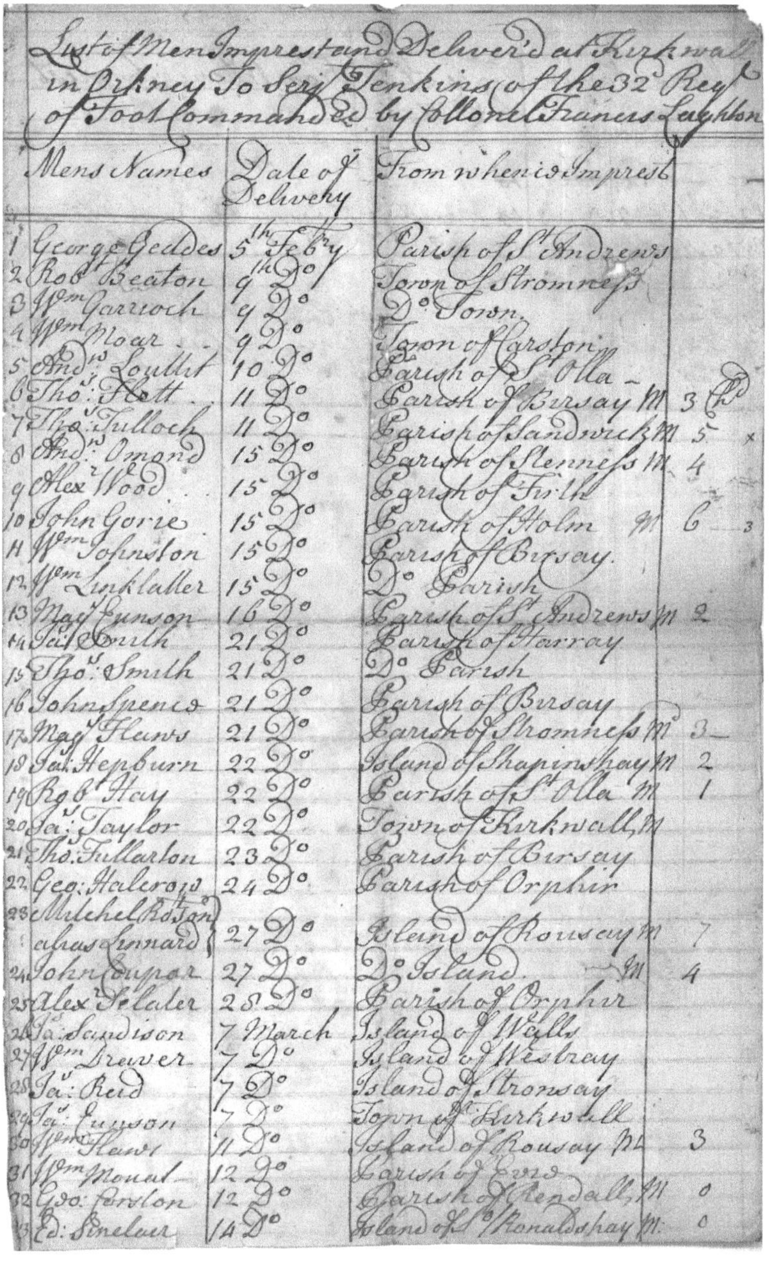

List of Men Imprest and Deliver'd at Kirkwall in Orkney To Serjt Jenkins of the 32d Regt of Foot Commanded by Collonel Francis Leighton

	Mens Names	Date of Delivery	From whence Imprest		
1	George Geddes	5th Feby	Parish of St Andrews		
2	Robt Beaton	9th Do	Town of Stromness		
3	Wm Garrioch	9 Do	Do Town		
4	Wm Moar	9 Do	Town of Harston		
5	Andw Louttit	10 Do	Parish of St Olla		
6	Thos: Flett	11 Do	Parish of Birsay	M	3
7	Thos: Tulloch	11 Do	Parish of Sandwick	M	5
8	Andw: Omond	15 Do	Parish of Stenness	M	4
9	Alexr Wood	15 Do	Parish of Firth		
10	John Gorie	15 Do	Parish of Holm	M	6
11	Wm Johnston	15 Do	Parish of Birsay		
12	Wm Linklatter	15 Do	Do Parish		
13	Magt Eunson	16 Do	Parish of St Andrews	M	2
14	Jas Smith	21 Do	Parish of Harray		
15	Thos: Smith	21 Do	Do Parish		
16	John Spence	21 Do	Parish of Birsay		
17	Magt Flaws	21 Do	Parish of Stromness	M	3
18	Jas: Hepburn	22 Do	Island of Shapinshay	M	2
19	Robt Hay	22 Do	Parish of St Olla	M	1
20	Jas: Taylor	22 Do	Town of Kirkwall	M	
21	Thos: Fullarton	23 Do	Parish of Birsay		
22	Geo: Halcrow	24 Do	Parish of Orphir		
23	Mitchel Robertson alias Linnard	27 Do	Island of Rousay	M	7
24	John Couper	27 Do	Do Island	M	4
25	Alexr Sclater	28 Do	Parish of Orphir		
26	Ja: Sandison	7 March	Island of Walls		
27	Wm Drever	7 Do	Island of Westray		
28	Jas: Reid	7 Do	Island of Stronsay		
29	Jas: Eunson	7 Do	Town of Kirkwall		
30	Wm Flaws	11 Do	Island of Rousay	M	3
31	Wm Monat	12 Do	Parish of Evie		
32	Geo: Forslon	12 Do	Parish of Rendall	M	0
33	Ed: Sinclair	14 Do	Island of S Ronaldshay	M	0

Figure 3.8
'List of Men Imprest and Delivered at Kirkwall Orkney to Sgt Jenkins of the 32nd Foot' 1758. (OLA)

The names of the men who were successfully pressed and their parishes were documented by the JPs. One *List of Men Impressed ... for the Speedy and Effectual Recruiting His Majesties Land Forces* names 30 men from all over Orkney. Another list from the same year, 1758, names a further 39 men delivered to Sergeant Jenkins of the 32nd Regiment of Foot. Married men received 15 shillings as incentive, £2 if they had a family; the constables received twenty shillings for every man they apprehended. David Hercus left a wife and five children in Westray; one wonders if he or any of the men he marched away with ever returned to their homes.[56]

Officially, it was only *able-bodied, idle and disorderly Persons,* who were to be pressed and heritors were not to use the Recruitment Acts to clear their parish of undesirable residents. *I must earnestly recommend that no Person unfit for HMs service be pressed on the Officers, however obnoxious he may be,* warned the War Office.[57] Men with a full-time occupation, especially if they had families, were theoretically exempt from the draft, but frequently the pressgang did not scruple to arrest citizens who were fully and usefully employed. John Traill of Elsness petitioned the Justices on behalf of Edward Sinclair who had come to Kirkwall with him as one of his boatmen and *was seized by three men said to be Recruits and Dragged in a most Inhumane Manner to the Tolbooth of Kirkwall without any crime committed by him or alledged against him ... with intent to get him made over by your Honours as a Soldier,* even though he was a farm servant on land that *must lye waste for want of a Plowman now in the labouring season.* Magnus Work had similarly been dragged into prison even though he was a respectable shoemaker, *remarkable in the Town of Kirkwall for sobriety and application in his business, never known to be guilty of any vice or addicted to the too much prevailing Custom in this place of spending his time in Idleness and his money in tippling or ale houses among debauched company.* One is glad to read that poor Magnus was eventually released.[58]

There were very occasional dissenting voices to the claim that there were no 'Idlers' to be found. Scribbled on a circular regarding recruitment, a disgruntled Stromness man wrote: *We have idlers in plenty in this place tho not a man of them fit for the service nor anything else thats good, and I wish the Justice of Peace would order the place to be cleared of them.*[59]

Like John Traill, all the heritors were as reluctant to lose their workforce as the men were unwilling to be drafted; they resorted to every possible delaying tactic to avoid answering the Justice's demands. A letter from William Balfour of Trenaby and other Westray heritors assured the Justices that they had *considered what you recommend with all possible Inclination to advance the public service ... have made very strict inquiry into the Circumstances of the Inhabitants but do not find a single Man in the Island fit for military service that can with any Propriety come under the Definition of the Act.* They claimed that the islands had already provided a considerable number of men to the sea service and it was the excessive demands of the Justices that was resulting in *the failure of our Crops for three years past, in this Island, so much more than that of any other part of the country.*[60]

Trenaby received a sarcastic reply. *The Gentlemen Justices in this place are Extremely well satisfied to hear of the Gentlemen in the North Isles their Inclination to promote the Success of the Recruiting Act. And it would give us still greater pleasure to Receive your quotas of Men ...*[61]

As the scale of Britain's wars escalated, so did the size of her armed forces. The government passed Quota Acts which specified the number of men that each county and port had to provide but the navy had such an appalling reputation for its brutality that it was almost impossible to recruit volunteers; crews were assembled by kidnapping. Five brothers from Nether Onston in Stenness sailed in the whaling fleets hunting the Davis Straits and on transports taking coal to London and timber from the Baltic and Archangel. All of them were press-ganged into the Royal Navy in the early 1800s.

The oldest, William Leith, born in 1760, joined the Merchant Navy and, in a rather bizarre interlude in the war with France, spent the winter of 1800/1801 a prisoner in Russia.[62] In 1804 he was pressed and sent to HMS *Illustrious* as a gunner. In 1810 the ship was embarking troops in India for an expedition to attack Mauritius and William died in an epidemic of cholera. The news reached Stenness not long after the family had heard that the youngest brother, Charles, born in 1782, had died on the way to the Baltic. He was also a merchant seaman but was pressed onto HMS *Rose* in 1805. James is first heard of plying the coal trade between London and Northumberland but he was serving in HMS *Polyphemus* at the battle of Trafalgar in 1805. Sadly we hear nothing of his part in Nelson's great victory but a few months later his ship *put into Madeira for water and captured two fine Spanish ships laden with cochineal, sugar, Indigo, cocoa and Drugs from Vera Cruz bound to Cadiz.*[63] James was in Quebec in 1820 and his last letter was written from Cork that year; he was bound for Jamaica but was never heard of again.[64]

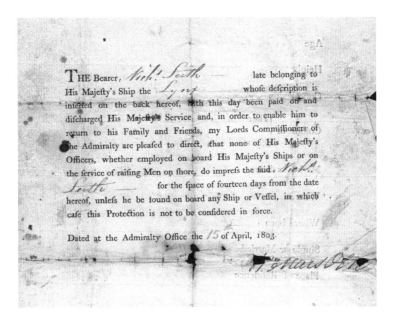

Figure 3.9
Certificate exempting Nicol Leith from impressment for 14 days 'to enable him to return to his Family and Friends'. (Leith family)

The surviving brothers were more fortunate. Peter, a ship's carpenter, was pressed in 1804 but soon released because of his essential trade. The following year, finding *the Press so hot* he joined a ship sailing to Malta to avoid recapture, but he returned home to Nether Onston after William's death and farmed there until his own death in 1861. Nicol was sailing to Hudson Bay and to the Davis Straits but in January 1801 he was pressed at Longhope from a fishing boat onto HMS *Lynx*. Lieutenant William Balfour of Trenaby joined this ship the following year and Nicol may have had to take part in press raids himself under Balfour, who was deputed to *Impress Seamen ... and receive no bribes for Sparing, Exchanging or Discharging any Person or Persons Impressed ... as you will answer it at your Peril.*[65]

By 1804 Nicol was serving alongside his brother William on the *Illustrious* and seeing plenty of action. In 1809 their fleet won *a great victory* over the French in the battle of the Basque Roads, *we burned 5 line of battle ships and 2 frigates and drove 2 line of battle ships on shore, 9 ships were destroyed. We lost very few men but there was great loss among the French and a great many perished in the flames.*[66] In 1811 Nicol was invalided out of the navy in Cape Town, but he came back to Stenness, and the very next year was fit enough to head back to the Davis Straits on the whaling ship *Truelove*.

Life on whalers was probably just as dangerous as on a battleship in wartime. Accidents on whaling vessels were frequent and Nicol had his share. On one voyage he sustained fractured ribs and a compound fracture of the leg in a fall, but he was also incredibly lucky in dodging death. One of his first whaling ships, the *Latona*, was lost in the Straits fifteen years later. In 1816 and 1817 he sailed on the *Thomas*, one of the ships crushed in the ice in the disastrous expedition of 1836, when most of the crew died of starvation, cold and scurvy. In fact, and presumably to the irritation of the naval paymasters,

Figure 3.10
Naval General Service Medal with Basque Roads clasp awarded to Nicol Leith. (Leith family)

he survived to claim his pension until he was 94. Seamen over a certain age were not made to go aloft but could serve as gunners and Nicol had evidently added 14 years to his age when he was pressed. An official pension certificate of 1865, when he was 90, gives his age as 104!

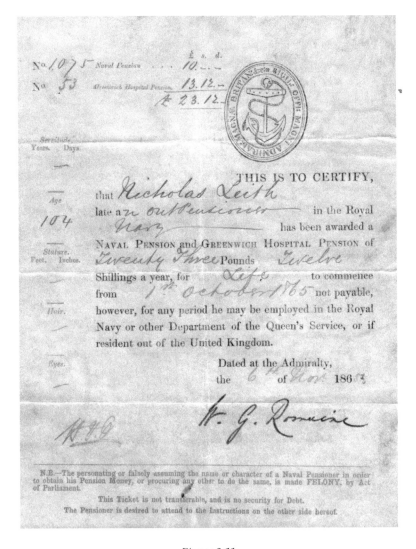

Figure 3.11
Nicol Leith's Naval Pension certificate, 1865, gives his age as 104. Nicol was 90 but had lied about his age when he was first pressed into the navy. (Leith family)

In 1770 Samuel Johnson commented: *Being in a ship is being in a jail, with the chance of being drowned. A man in a jail has more room, better food and commonly better company.*[67] Sailors' wages had not been raised for 140 years; the compensation paid to injured men was pitiful and their share of prize money delayed for years while fortunes poured into the pockets of admirals and navy board officials: Nicol Leith was still trying to obtain his small share of the *Lynx's* prize money 40 years later.[68] The food was terrible and scurvy, typhus and accidents caused far more deaths than the enemy. Unsurprisingly, crews deserted as soon as they could, so they were often allowed no shore leave when the fleet was in port. James Leith was unable to see his brother even when their ships were in the same harbour as his crew *was confined to the ship on account of deserters.*[69] However, it seems that some relaxation on board was occasionally allowed. From the *Polyphemus* in Spithead James wrote to his brothers: *Some days ago the ship got sailing orders and all the women were sent ashore, foretopsail loosed and salt petre hoisted, but then contrary orders came and all the women came back on board.*[70]

If compulsory service on a naval vessel was generally grim, the situation was even worse if the ship was captured by the enemy and a number of Orcadians spent years languishing in foreign prisons. A story was told of an Orkney man captured by one of Napoleon's ships on its way to Egypt and held prisoner of war in Alexandria for three years until the city was retaken. *John waas taaken bae da French and keepid i' prison i' Alexandria twar-tree year, fill 'e teuk scurvey an' waas a puir ting tae da end o' 'is days.*[71]

Charles Garrick, a POW in Arras, wrote home: *Dear Mother, I take the oppertunity of informing you that I am verry well in health at present, thank God, hopping this few Lines will find you in the same condition; dear Mother, I was captured in a Prise belonging to the Le Bonne Citoyenne in the British Channel the 21st Feby 1809 and has wrote you two letters since and has never had any answers from you, which makes me doubt of your wellbeing; I have sent you home a Certificat of Life; in purpose that you may receive my half Pay. . .*[72]

If prisoners could not make contact with friends or family at home and receive some funds, they had little to survive on. In 1805 James Riddoch, Collector at the Kirkwall Customs House, received a desperate letter from some Orkney men held in the Citadel of Valenciennes. Evidently an earlier letter had received no reply. *We implore your goodness should this come safe to hand to take our disagreeable situation into Consideration and Contribute but a little to our relief ...* [signed] *John Tilloch Kirkwall, William Tilloch Kirkwall, John Linak Stromness, William Hercus Papa Westrey, William Mitchell Shapanshay, George Guthrie* Feiriy [Pharay? letter damaged] *John Grieve Aggleshay.*[73] Inevitably, even when relief was sent from home, it could take many months or even years to reach its destination. In 1808 the parish of Holm raised a subscription of £4 12s 10d for John Laughton in Valenciennes and sent it to a Captain Foubister in London, but because he was in Jamaica at the time the money did not reach John until ten months later.[74]

There must have been considerable war-weariness in the country, and it is not surprising that there was reluctance to enlist voluntarily. I leave the last words to James Watson, commanding the Orkney Volunteers (a Home Guard regiment), exhorting his captains to fill up their companies and keep them in readiness to defend their country. *Now when we have every reason to believe that a powerful and unplacable enemy will ere long endeavour to invade our happy country, it becomes the duty of every good citizen to prepare for the event. However remote and obscure our situation in Orkney may be, this would not secure us from participating in the Consequences of any misfortunes that might happen to our common country and I trust that we are all as interested in the comfort and happiness of our homes and families, and feel equally animated as any others of our fellow subjects, with the glow of Patriotism, and ambitious of sharing with them in the honor of defending our "dear native land."*[75]

The Sufferings of the Dee

Harsh as conditions were in the Navy in war-time, the most harrowing stories come from the crews of whaling ships. The press-gangs competed with whalers for crew and, from the mid 18th century, whalers from Hull, Dundee and Aberdeen would call at Kirkwall or Lerwick on their way to the Greenland fishing. Orkney was an ideal place for picking up supplies (sides of beef hanging from the yardarm were soon frozen), and crewmen who were accustomed to privations and poor enough to sign on for lower wages than men from further south. As the waters between Spitzbergen and eastern Greenland became over-exploited, the whalers moved to the Davis Straits west of Greenland, and Stromness, with its excellent natural anchorage in the bay of Hamnavoe, became a convenient harbour for ships to gather on their way to the whaling grounds. In the boom years of the industry, from about 1813 to the early 1820s, there might be as many as 20 to 25 men recruited per ship. In 1820 Stromness agent Christian Robertson engaged 186 Orkney crewmen for 13 whalers but, as whales grew more and more scarce, so the ships took greater risks in sailing further north and staying till later in the season in the hopes of getting a profitable catch.

At the same time, the seasons were deteriorating. A grim warning came in the summer of 1830 when 19 British whalers and one French vessel were crushed by enormous ice floes in Melville Bay. It seemed that some ships would be ice-bound all winter but, though badly damaged, they eventually escaped and there was astonishingly little loss of life. The particularly harsh winter of 1835/36 brought far worse disaster: the ice closed in early and the ships were frozen in. Completely unprepared to survive an Arctic winter, the sufferings of the crew were appalling. In February 1836 the *Lady Jane* and *Viewforth* limped into Stromness, only eight of the crew of 64 on the *Lady Jane* able to crawl. Thirteen of the 25 Orcadians who had sailed on her had died and the survivors, *in a dreadful state of suffering*, were taken ashore to Humphrey's hospital.[76] *From the intense cold, amputations were found necessary in some cases.*[77]

Figure 3.12
The dangers of whaling. Illustration from 'The Arctic Whaleman ... being a narrative of the wreck of the whale ship Citizen *of New Bedford in the Arctic Ocean' by the Rev Lewis Holmes, Boston 1857.* (Smithsonian Libraries, Wikimedia Commons)

Despite these events, the ship-owners sent their fleet of whalers out that spring without extra provisions. Ships left Stromness in early April, but it was mid August before the first whale was killed. Again, the ice closed in on the ships early and by mid September it was realised that there was little chance of breaking out. The diary kept by some of the crew gives a faint idea of the desperate conditions on board as food and fuel and hope ran out. It was a whole year after they departed before some of the stricken ships were towed back into Stromness; by then 47 men had died of starvation, cold and scurvy.

A Narrative of the sufferings of the crew of the Dee while beset in the ice at Davis straits during the winter of 1836[78]

After 10th October real suffering of crew commenced. Fires were extinguished from 8pm to 5.30 am, beds damp and uncomfortable . . . a fatal squeeze from the ice was feared . . . boat dragged 3 miles to nearest berg for ice for fresh water . . . The night of 29th was terrible, ship rolling to and fro, crew on ice alongside, no shelter or fire . . . On 26th a bear was seen, but escaped so no fresh food . . .weather changed for worse. On 2nd Nov the dock gave way in several places and ice threatened to crush the vessel . . . supply of coal nearly exhausted; one of boats broken up for fire and soon another . . .

On 12th November sun almost gone and excessively cold . . . On 15th sun never appeared . . .

December opened with gloomy prospects. Men had coughs, swelled limbs and general debility with depression of spirits. On 3rd Dec 2 foxes shot. On 12 Thomas of Dundee listed over by pressure of ice. On 13th had become a total wreck . . . an equitable distribution of Thomas' crew and provision was made between the other ships . . . Scurvy now began to harass the greater part of the men. Gums became swollen and excruciatingly painful. On 18th 21 men ill with scurvy, some suffering severely. Ice again gave way and threatend to squeeze everyone of the vessels.

Jan – On 11th first man died William Curryall [Corrigall] *of Stromness (age 56). Sun appeared again on 16th January, and this gave the men some hope . . . During the last week of the month several whales were seen, some of them very near, unicorns* [presumably narwhal] *were also observed in the lanes of water, but there was no one now caring about anything but his life.*

Captain Gamblin died on 3rd February . . . Vessel was drifting slowly south, but the frost increased. Water in casks was soled [soiled], *the pillows were frozen and the blankets covered with soled ice. Vermin began to swarm in the beds and caused additional suffering. Men were also seized with violent diarrhoea . . . the lack of fires was felt most painfully.*

From this day onward more deaths were recorded every day. At last, on the 24th April, islands were seen to the south of them, by this time only three hands were fit to go aloft. A Dundee ship took them in tow and by the night of 26th April they were anchored in Stromness, more than a year after their departure.

The total number of deaths on board the Dee was forty-six; of these nine belonging to the Thomas of Dundee. Since the arrival of the Dee at Stromness, one of the invalids has died, thus making the loss no fewer than forty-seven souls.

Figure 3.13
Sperm whale tooth carved with whaling ship and polar bear, photograph by Rebecca Marr, © Stromness Museum

Chapter 3 Notes

1   Since writing this, the move in 2020 to remove statues and street names commemorating people and places associated with slavery suggests that this history will be buried rather than acknowledged.

2   William Cowper 1731-1800, *Pity for the Poor Africans* 1788, Basker p.297. Cowper was one of the most prolific and influential anti-slavery poets of the 18th century.

3   OSA (Sandwick and Stromness) 139-140.

4   Devine 6.

5   Robertson 2011, 2 n2.

6   Dobson 1989 passim.

7   James Revel, *The Unhappy Transported Felon's Sorrowful Account of His 14 Years Transportation, at Virginia in America* c.1680, Basker 22-23.

8   After defeat at the battle of Dunbar in 1650, an estimated 6,000 Scots were captured and all who could walk marched to Durham and imprisoned in the abandoned cathedral and castle. Around 1000 died on the march and another 1700 in prison. It is surprising that there was a remnant left to be marched to England for shipment to the colonies in 1655, along with Royalist prisoners captured at the battle of Worcester in 1651.

9   The crew hacked down the mast and used it as a bridge to the shore. It is said that one of the crew passed a key to the trapped prisoners and about 50 reached the shore but were either pushed back into the sea on the captain's orders or recaptured.

10   eg, the *St Michael of Scarborough* left Leith for the West Indies in 1678 and the *John and Nicholas* for Barbados in 1685 with cargoes of Covenanters, other shiploads sailed for Virginia. Dobson 1989 passim.

11   Dobson 1989 passim.

12   Hossack 292, Dobson 1989 no.5359. Nisbet's lover was Margaret Agnew, his brother's sister-in-law. A further twist to the tale comes in a letter from William Balfour in Inverness to his wife Elizabeth in Westray, 30/5/1766, OLA D2/12/15. He has heard that *Nisbet is in jail and is now supported on Charity, and if he cannot pay for his passage to America, he must be sold by a 7 years Indenture.* If his friends did gather the funds to pay his fare, presumably he would have arrived in Jamaica a free man, though banished from Scotland for life. This would make his subsequent success much more plausible.

13   Charles Stewart's nephews were the sons of his sister Cecilia, the widow of the Revd Alexander Ruddach, minister of Kirkwall Cathedral. He established Thomas in Tobago, Charles in Jamaica and Alexander in the Royal Navy. Thomas Ruddach of Tobago's will, 1796, is in OLA, D1/96.

14   Of Scots descent but Jamaica born, Taylor was 'by much the richest proprietor on the island'; on his death in 1813 he left a million pounds to his nephew. Devine 89.

15   Letter from William Manson, on board the *Arundel* in Dover Road, to his parents in Kirkwall 5/7/1773, OLA D2/8/12.

16   Letter from Thomas Balfour, Shapinsay, to William Manson, London 9/8/1787, OLA D2/22/18.

17   Letter from Thomas Manson, London, to his brother William Manson, Kirkwall 21/9/1787, OLA D2/22/18.

18   Letter from Robert Mowat, St Vincent, to his father Hugh Mowat snr , Kirkwall 6/9/1780, OLA D3/345.

19   Letter from Hugh Mowat jnr, Beaulieu estate, Grenada to his mother Barbara Mowat, Kirkwall 3/2/1783, OLA D3/345.

20   Letter from Hugh Mowat jnr, Beaulieu estate, Grenada to his mother Barbara Mowat, Kirkwall 26/5/1781, OLA D3/345. The Great Hurricane of 2/10/80 caused widespread devastation in the Caribbean.

21   ibid.

22   Devine 10, quoting *The Journal of a Lady of Quality being the Narrative of a Journey from Scotland to the West Indies, North Carolina and Portugal in the years 1774 to*

	1778, ed. E.W Andrews and C. McL. Andrews (Yale University Press 1939).
23	Philip Freneau 1752-1832, *The Island Field Hand* 1784, Basker 245-6.
24	Letter from Robert Mowat, St Vincent, to his father Hugh Mowat snr, Kirkwall 6/9/1780, OLA D3/345.
25	Letter from Robert Mowat, Glasgow, to his father Hugh Mowat snr, Kirkwall 29/7/81, OLA D3/345.
26	Letter from Lt. Alexander Watt, Spithead, to his father William Watt of Breckness, Kirkwall 27/11/1795, OLA D3/267.
27	Hewison 120.
28	Letter from Lt. Alexander Watt, Gibraltar, to his father William Watt of Breckness, Kirkwall 3/4/1796, OLA D3/267.
29	Samuel Johnson, introduction to *The World Displayed* 1759, Basker 126.
30	The 'Runaway Slaves in 18th century Britain' project has created an online database of over 800 newspaper advertisements referring to slaves, www. runaways.gla.ac.uk.
31	For a detailed account of the Somerset case, see S.M. Wise, *Though the heavens may fall, the landmark trial that led to the end of human slavery* (London 2006).
32	Knight married Ann Thomson, a servant of the Wedderburns, but nothing is known of their later life.
33	In England, the Quakers, Methodists and the evangelical Clapham Sect were strong supporters of Abolition, in Scotland both the Church of Scotland and the dissenting churches supported the petitions.
34	Minutes of the Kirkwall Presbytery 1788, OCR 4/9, 62.
35	Petition of Liverpool to the House of Commons 14/2/1788. 64 anti-abolition petitions were presented from Liverpool and Clarkson received death threats when he visited the city.
36	James Boswell 1740-95, *No Abolition of Slavery* 1791, Basker 238. The slave trade was made illegal in British possessions with the passing of the Slave Trade Act in 1807.
37	Minutes of the North Isles Presbytery 7/5/1792; OCR 3/3, 83.
38	Chambers, *Weekly Jamaica Courant* 30/7/1718, 24/6/1730.
39	Chambers, *Cornwall Chronicle* 12/7/1783, 26/3/1786.
40	Chambers, *Cornwall Chronicle* 4/2/1777.
41	Chambers, *Cornwall Chronicle* 18/12/1776, 16/8/1772.
42	Chambers, *Cornwall Chronicle* 11/12/1781.
43	Chambers, *Cornwall Chronicle* 10/8/1786.
44	Chambers, *Jamaica Mercury* 30/4/1779.
45	Fereday 2000, 140.
46	Dr David Alston, citing Parliamentary committee 1798, *The Scotsman* 9/8/2020.
47	Fereday 2000, 143.
48	Letter from James Watt to Deacon Flett, Kirkwall, 26/3/1833, OLA D35/1/4.
49	See the UCL Legacies of British Slave-ownership database, ucl.ac.uk/lbs/ project.
50	Campaigner Joseph Sturge published *A Narrative of Events, since 1st August 1834, by James Williams, an Apprenticed Labourer in Jamaica*. The book was a powerful tool in bringing the apprenticeship system to an end.
51	List of Persons Manumitted 1828, PRO, copy in OLA D1/825/5/1. Edward Clouston owned properties and was attorney (factor) for others in St George, the Blue Mountain region of Jamaica where a number of Orcadians managed or owned estates.
52	Letter from Lt. Alexander Watt, Gibraltar, to William Watt of Breckness, Kirkwall 1/3/1796, OLA D3/267.
53	Copy letter from JPs to Parish Constables 1757, OLA D10/11.
54	Letter from Rousay Parish Constables to Orkney JPs 14/3/1758, OLA D10/11.
55	Letter from Malcolm Groat, Hoy to 'Dear Cousin' (a JP) 24/3/1758, OLA D10/11.
56	List of Men Impressed by the commissioners for the District of Orkney ... Delivered over to the Lieut. Edward Eyre of the 56th Regiment of Foot, 23/5/1758; 2nd List ... men delivered to Sgt Jenkins of the 32nd Regt of Foot, OLA D10/11.

57   Printed circular from the War Office to the county sheriffs 16/6/1778, OLA D10/11.
58   Petition from Magnus Work to the JPs 19/5/1758, OLA D10/11.
59   Unsigned letter regarding recruitment in Stromness 11/3/1758, OLA D10/11.
60   Letter from the Westray heritors Jerome Dinnison, Thomas Traill and William Balfour to the Justices of the Peace in Kirkwall 10/2/1758, OLA D10/11.
61   Letter from the Justices of the Peace in Kirkwall to the Westray heritors 20/3/1758, OLA D10/11.
62   When Napoleon attacked Malta in 1798 some of the Knights fled to Russia and nominated their supporter, Tsar Paul I, Grand Master of the Order. Paul tried to reclaim Malta for the Knights but the British had taken control of the island. In retaliation the Tsar ordered that British vessels in Russian ports should be seized and their crews imprisoned. Tsar Paul was assassinated in 1801 and his successor, Tsar Alexander I, released the prisoners.
63   Letter from James Leith, Spithead to his brother Peter Leith 24/5/1806, Leith family.
64   Letter from James Leith, on ship *Grace* in Cork to his brother Peter Leith, Stromness 8/2/1820, Leith family.
65   Commission to Capt Willoughby Marshall of the *Lynx* to impress, which he deputed to Lieutenant William Balfour 25/5/180,3 D2/19/16.
66   Letter from William and Nicol Leith on HMS *Illustrious* to their father William Leith, Stenness 8/5/1809, Leith family. In April 1809, the French Atlantic fleet was attacked in the Basque Roads off Rochefort by a British squadron with bomb vessels and fireships. The Naval General Service Medal was a campaign medal issued in 1849 and awarded retrospectively to both officers and men for various naval actions between 1793 and 1840; each action being represented by a clasp on the ribbon.
67   Quoted in Robertson 2011, 4.
68   Letter from the Naval Prize Office, Admiralty, Somerset House to Nicol Leith, Stenness 15/2/1843, Leith family.
69   Letter from James Leith on HMS *Polyphemus* to his brother William Leith 15/2/1806, Leith family.
70   Letter from James Leith on HMS *Polyphemus*, Spithead to his brothers William and Nicol Leith 26/6/1808, Leith family. Saltpetre is an ingredient of gunpowder.
71   Leask 129.
72   Letter from Charles Garrick, Arras to his mother Christiana Garrick, Banks near Kirkwall 29/3/1810, OLA D5/3/1/6.
73   Letter from Orkney prisoners in Valenciennes to John Riddoch, Kirkwall 1/8/1805, OLA D10/9.
74   Graemeshall papers, OLA D5/3/1.
75   Circular letter from James Watson, Crantit to the Captains of Volunteer Companies 16/1/1806, OLA D10/11.
76   Letter from John Baikie to Thomas Balfour, MP., 24//2/1836, OLA D2/28/10.
77   Troup 30, quoting *John o' Groat's Journal* and *Caithness Monthly Miscellany*, 1836.
78   Marwick Papers, OLA D31/35/3a.

CHAPTER 4

Merchant Wives, Mothers and a Touch of Gossip

Prologue

It is time to shift the spotlight from Orkney men, travelling far afield to make a living, to the many remarkable, strong-minded and capable women who were holding everything together at home. Reading 18th- and 19th-century letters, I am often reminded of the women who feature in the Norse sagas, drawn in axe-sharp pen-portraits as wise, highly competent, and sometimes ruthless. Women did not 'farstray' geographically as their men did, but with so many men working far from home – sometimes for years at a time – it was inevitable that a disproportionate number of women were left in the islands, and that they were often forced to stray well out of the usual female roles and take on the work of men. The wives, sisters and widows of the men at sea or labouring in Hudson Bay were left to do all the heavy work on the land to feed their families and pay the rent. The womenfolk of the merchants and landowners had to take over all the responsibility of managing their estates or businesses as well as the running of their households, with the shadows of war and famine rarely far away.

The letters of the Balfour family of Trenaby in Westray are a historian's goldmine. In them we can discover not only their personal affairs but also the 'Affairs without doors' that fell on the shoulders of merchant-lairds' wives in the second half of the 18th century. Elizabeth and Frances Balfour ran their family's island estates during their husbands' long absences. It was not an easy time, politically or economically. After the crushing of the Jacobite rebellion in 1746, Elizabeth, a young wife with her first baby, was managing Trenaby while her husband William was skulking in caves, in fear of execution if discovered by government troops. Frances, catapulted from fashionable society in the south of England to a small agricultural estate in Orkney's North Isles, was the ultimate ferry-louper (a word in use to describe incomers to the islands since at least the 17th century). In physical distance and in culture she could hardly have strayed further within Britain.

The letters of the Balfour wives tell us a great deal about Orkney's economy, but they also tend to be more personal than those written by men and reveal much of their family life. A thread of anxiety runs through Frances' letters: for husbands and sons away at war, for crews and cargoes lost to storms or piracy or enemy shipping, for the threat of French invasion. If she sounds high-wired at times, she had much to be emotional about: her sense of always being an outsider, the callous neglect of the husband she adored and the death of everyone she loved.

In town as well as on the island estates, women often had to be at the helm. Stromness was a town of 'numerous widows' of all social classes who had to find ways of providing for their families. Women like Christian Robertson and Margaret Login, left on their own with large debts to pay and children to raise, ran successful businesses and contributed significantly to the development of the town. Margaret Humphreys, whose sons had dispersed to all corners of the world, was working hard into her old age to support her grandchildren, yet never lost her faith that God would provide 'unforeseen mercees'.

Women's letters also provide more light-hearted moments. Peggy Balfour provides a brilliantly funny vignette of the court of George III, Marion Balfour purveys the latest scandals from Edinburgh, and Anne Waters 'sports' her new veil and parasol in Kirkwall. Their own words bring them so close you can almost hear them giggling.

The Balfours of Trenaby

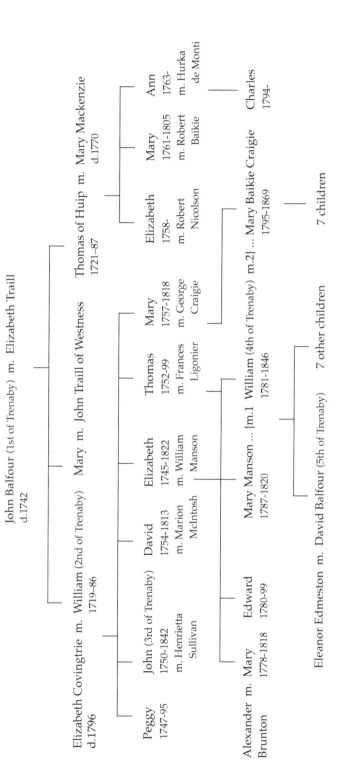

Figure 4.1: The Balfour Family

Merchant Ladies

The names of gentlemen such as William Watt, Thomas Traill, Patrick Fea, James Stewart, William Balfour and their contemporaries are written large in every account of 18th-century Orkney. As lairds of estates, they were all heirs to unproductive acreages of badly-farmed land, a competitive need to make more of a swagger in society than their contemporaries, and considerable debts. They were truculent Jacobites, adventurous merchants, sometimes agricultural 'improvers', wily businessmen and politicians and they appeared to control every aspect of Orkney life. Fortunately, the survival of many letters written by and to the female members of the Balfour family allows us to see a much more balanced picture of the time. Reading the correspondence of Elizabeth Covingtrie, the wife of William Balfour of Trenaby, and of her daughter-in-law Frances, it becomes obvious that the 'merchant-laird' phenomenon was only possible because of the stalwart ranks of 'merchant-ladies' who actually ran the estates while their men were absent.

William Balfour was one of the Orkney lairds who were incriminated as Jacobite sympathizers. They had signed a letter offering support to Prince Charles Stuart which was intercepted and, after the failure of the 1745 Rebellion, they were sentenced to execution and hunted by government troops.[1] While they hid in caves in Westray, William's young wife Elizabeth was left literally holding the baby. She saw her house burned down and most of her property confiscated and, when an amnesty finally allowed William out of hiding, she then had to take over the day to day management of their ruined estate while he was away in Edinburgh or Shetland trying to restore their fortunes. Overseeing all the seasonal work of ploughing, sowing, harvesting, carting seaweed, cutting peat and burning kelp; hiring servants, finding a new tenant, repairing the mill, arranging shipment of cargoes of produce for William to sell in Edinburgh: these were just a few of the tasks that fell to her on top of running her own household. A sensible and extremely competent woman emerges from the pages of her letters, faced with the difficult task of running a *profitless farm* and raising a large family through times of famine and political insecurity.

Not a man to accept defeat, William seized all the money-making opportunities that came his way in order to restore Trenaby and provide for and educate his children. He had wide-ranging trading interests, he salvaged shipwrecks, and for years he was the factor of Sir Lawrence Dundas' estate in Shetland. By the time he died, his hard work had successfully set his family on an upward economic slope. While he was away from home, letters of instructions arrived regularly in Westray. From Edinburgh he wrote to Elizabeth: *If therefore I should stay away longer than I wish or expect, you must take courage and set a stiff heart to a steep Brae and exert yourself so much the more not only in the case of your family and children but also of Affairs without doors, as to which I shall help you with my Directions from time to time and must leave you to execute them as best you can.*[2]

No doubt Elizabeth was already exerting herself looking after her family; she had six living children by this time and she would have been thought lucky to have lost only two. She came from a well-established Orkney family and had grown up learning all the skills of running a large household: the baking and brewing and salting of fish and meat so there was enough food stored to last the long hard winter; the huge amount of cooking at times like sheep-shearing and harvest when there would have been extra labourers to feed. *Three or four weeks of very great throng* as she describes it.[3] All this would have been normal women's work, but she also had to take on the *Affairs Without doors* which would normally have been her husband's province.

The theme hammered home in letter after letter is disastrous weather and crop failure. With hopelessly inefficient farming methods and equipment, Orkney somehow managed to produce enough oats and barley to feed a population of approximately 23,000 people[4], with enough surplus to pay the rent and the feu duties and even to trade, in a good year. But how often were there good years in the latter 18th century? In 1765 a violent summer storm destroyed virtually all the crops in the islands. In 1770 Elizabeth had to ask her neighbour Thomas Traill in Papay for meal; he could only spare her a little as his tenants were being forced to feed their seed corn to the cattle.[5] In the 1780s William Watt wrote to his brother: *You cannot conceive the situation of this country at present: there is not an article it produces but has failed as well as the crops. The death of cattle has been a sore strock to the poorer sort of people. The butter debt which they pay to the Supr and Masters has ruined them. Of rabits which this Country abounded with, there is none in the warrans, the badness of the season has killed them all, so that the bread is not left.*[6]

Figure 4.2
William Balfour 1719-85, 2nd of Trenaby. Photograph by D. Shearer of painting formerly in Balfour Castle. (OLA)

William, always one to snatch advantage from disaster, sent a boat from Kirkwall to Westray in the hungry spring after the 1765 hurricane with meal and 156 stones of potatoes – still a novelty in the North Isles. *Cause cry them at the Kirk on Sunday to be sold on Monday* he told Elizabeth. It was not a charity run. The unfamiliar food was to be sold at 11 pence a stone at a time when labourers earned less than a shilling a day.[7]

When William was in Edinburgh on business, his letters of instructions were leavened with a good dose of city gossip. In 1767 he asked Elizabeth to send him Orkney produce to trade. *Be sure to speak to some of your Dealers in the Neighbourhood to buy me a thousand Goose Quills immediately I mean about Martinmas, and I entreat you remember the Geese and all the Tongues you can procure. You will have heard of the death of his Royal Highness the Duke of York, it is said here, he was stabd through the body, and his Paramour with him, in the Embraces of a Lady, whose Husband took this Method of repairing his honour upon both offenders, and both are dead as they deserve.*[8]

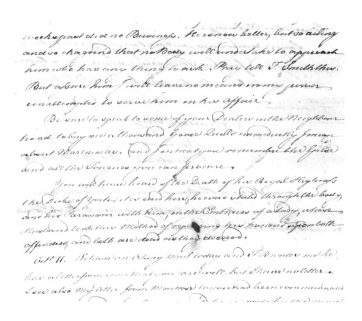

Figure 4.3
Letter from William Balfour to his wife Elizabeth, asking her to send him pens (quills) and goose tongues from Westray to sell in Edinburgh, and passing on some scandal from the capital concerning the Duke of York. (OLA)

Elizabeth comes across as eminently capable; in another age she would have been Chairwoman of the WRI and most of the other committees on Westray. In William's absences and after his death she carried on managing the Trenaby estate, very much the matriarch and the linchpin of her family. She can hardly have been optimistic of the outcome when her second son Thomas brought home as a bride a diminutive aristocrat from the south of England, whose knowledge of farming amounted to the view out of the carriage window.

In the close network of Orkney gentry, Frances Ligonier was a conspicuous outsider. Absolutely nothing in her first 34 years of life prepared her for living on an Orkney estate, let alone managing its farming and trading concerns through years of war and frequent food shortage, her negligent husband's long absences and after his death. She was not from the saga mould like Elizabeth. Her letters reveal someone lacking in confidence and self-esteem who often felt overwhelmed by her responsibilities. The Ligonier family, however, who had come to England as Huguenot refugees escaping persecution in France, had not inherited but earned their high rank through distinguished service to their adopted country and bravery on the battlefield. Duty and loyalty were the mottoes that Frances grew up with and it was these which sustained her through her often lonely life, separation from her family and the death of almost everyone she loved. Her devoted loyalty to her husband and his interests survived his absences, neglect, infidelity and death and, though Frances was not always a likeable character, it is impossible not to admire her achievements in managing his estate and surviving the misfortunes of her family.

Not long after Frances' marriage to Thomas Balfour, he was negotiating for the lease of the Bu in the island of Burray, which he eventually took over at Martinmas 1778. It could hardly have been a more inauspicious time for a gentleman with expensive habits to take up farming. Orkney was again in the grip of famine because of the poor harvest the previous year. In April John Traill of Westness had written to Tom: *The great want of Fodder occasions the death of a number of the Horses and cattle and every day numbers are coming in for Bear* [i.e relief supplies of bere barley] *and meal and famine will appear every day more and more.*[9] Staying with her new in-laws in Surrey, Tom's sister Peggy wrote to her mother: *I am very sorry to hear by all accounts from Orkney of the very great want of bread that is likely to be felt there this summer – how the poor are to be supplied I know not.*[10] Four months later another devastating summer storm ruined almost all the crops throughout Orkney. That winter Patrick Graeme of Graemeshall imported four shipments of grain and meal from Caithness for his hungry tenants in Holm, so there must have been a similar dearth in nearby Burray in the Balfours' first winter.

The Bu, where James Stewart had made precocious attempts at introducing modern agricultural machinery and methods 50 years before, must have seemed a promising place to begin Balfour's own innovations. He started enthusiastically to rebuild the house and outbuildings (quarrying stone from the prehistoric broch to do so), make some enclosures and increase the sheep flock, but he was a proud and ambitious man who was never going to be satisfied with being a mere tenant farmer. He was desperate to become a landed proprietor with his own 'seat' and his opportunity came in 1783. The estate of Sound in Shapinsay came on the market – relatively cheaply as an interlude of peace had depressed grain prices – and, with the help of his family, he bought it and other lands on the island. The house had been destroyed by the Royal Navy in 1746 in reprisal for the Jacobite activities of its owner[11] (just as his own father's house of Trenaby had been) and the land was wholly 'unimproved', but flat and fertile, and only an hour's sail from Kirkwall.

1782 was a year of crop failure right across the country and in Europe. *I am informed of the state of your crop* wrote William to Elizabeth, *and of the state of all Scotland, England and abroad from which it is plain no human means can avert a famine ... I tremble at the thought of those miseries that await so many of the human race – God deliver them and inspire our hearts with pity to them.*[12] William may have trembled, but he was sharp to see the opportunities for stockpiling and then selling at inflated prices in time of shortage. *Nobody who has Salt and Cask can run any hazard by buying every Beast the people will sell,* he instructed his wife, *there being an absolute certainty that they will be glad to buy in 6 months at any price.*[13] Grain prices soared and deaths from famine would have been inevitable if the Government had not sent in 1,500 bolls of meal and peas to be distributed to those in most need.

The following years were little better. In 1786 William's brother, Thomas Balfour of Huip, was writing repeatedly to fellow-merchant William Watt to find hay or straw – at any price – to feed his animals. *I will give Money, Bent* [bent grass], *Iron or Salt for Straw deliverable in Kirkll ... I have two Horses and two Cows starving for want of it.* [14] In times of shortage, proprietors benefited from high prices, but rents became impossible to collect, and they still had to feed their own livestock, take some care of their tenants and foot the bills for famine relief when it was necessary. Thomas was evidently undaunted by the economic set-backs. He settled his young family on Shapinsay and by 1787 he had built a new house there which he called Cliffdale. He enthusiastically took on the role of an 'improving laird' on his estate and contemporaries (at least those who were not political opponents) were impressed.

In 1799 George Barry, the Shapinsay minister, wrote a sycophantic report of Thomas's agricultural improvements for the first *Statistical Account*. [Balfour] *has totally changed the face of that part of the island. Previous to his purchase, nothing was to be seen over its whole extent, but a dreary waste, interspersed with arable lands ill cultivated, a few miserable hovels thinly scattered over its surface ... which were not fit to shelter from the rigours of the climate a few ragged inhabitants, dirty thro indolence, lean with hunger, and torpid by despair. Everything on this estate now happily wears a very different and more pleasant aspect. An elegant house has been built, and an extensive garden laid out; the lands are substantially inclosed, and judiciously cultivated with the English plough ... and the soil, which formerly bore with reluctance coarse grass, and scanty heather, and puny oats and bear, now cheerfully produces oats, rye, barley, pease, wheat, potatoes, clover and turnip, in considerable quantity and of a good quality.* [15]

Barry's splendid prose has to be read with a good pinch of salt, especially regarding the wheat, which has not been successfully grown in Orkney since Neolithic times. He stressed the great advantage to the island of having a resident proprietor, but in fact Thomas was away from home a great deal, especially in the 1790s when Barry was writing. His trading concerns often required him – or gave him the excuse to – travel, and it has to be said that he increasingly felt that having a good time was not compatible with staying at home with a wife who was ten years older than himself. In 1793, war broke out with France and Thomas hastened to offer his services to the Crown in return for the pay, prestige and perquisites of raising a local defence regiment, the Orkney and Shetland Fencibles. He was rarely in Shapinsay thereafter. (Fencibles were full-time soldiers but enlisted only for the duration of the war and, initially, to serve only in Scotland. They were basically a local defence force with few pretensions to military effectiveness. *The government expected* [them] *to be raised by noblemen or gentlemen who were distinguished more for their rank, wealth and political loyalty than for their previous knowledge of army life: professional details could be delegated to inferiors.*)[16]

While Thomas undoubtedly enjoyed the kudos derived from his building schemes and enclosures and his superior cattle and sheep, and had plenty of intelligence to evaluate new ideas, he had no head for facts and figures, for the detail that makes a successful man of business. William Spence, his factor, complained that his books were *in great disorder*. Ten years after Tom's death, his brothers were still trying to sort out the inextricable muddle of his regimental accounts. Frances, on the other hand, was as meticulous at accounting for every item of estate or household expenditure as Thomas was careless. She kept every bill and receipt, whether it was for a cargo of timber or for hairpins and ribbons.

While Thomas was soldiering in Ireland, she sent him an exact account of the *Expenditure of Col Balfour's family at Cliffdale from Nov 12 1795 – Nov 12 1796* which gives some idea of the fare you could expect at the Colonel's – or his servants' – table.

4 barrels of beef containing 192 lb at 2d pp	£7	9	4
poorer quality Do for servants at 1 1/2d	£7	0	0
3 cattle from Kirkwall	£4	18	5
9 sheep @ 5/6	£2	9	6
4 fed calves @ 15/	£3	0	0
226 lb butter for the table @ 6d	£5	13	0
107 lb coarse butter for the servants	£1	16	1 ½
Garden seeds and onions	£1	9	0

There was also pork and poultry, oat meal and beremeal and 12 barrels of potatoes, and 224 lb candles @ 8d a lb, and linen for sheets and for making shirts for Colonel Balfour (and *some coarse stuff and linnen necessarily made for giving to the poor and others*).

Figure 4.4
Frances Balfour's letter to Thomas with the household accounts, several times redirected following Thomas' movements 'marching and countermarching' in Ireland, 4/12/1796. (OLA)

There were luxury items as well, Thomas's household did not stint on the liquor, but washed down their smoked beef or tongues and Westphalia hams with hogsheads of porter, ankers of whisky, rum, wine, brandy, Madeira, sherry, port, claret ... most of which would have been carried home from Leith or further south in his trading ships.

As well as the household expenditure, Frances itemised the wages for the domestic servants and regular farmworkers. James Reid earned £16 a year, but he must have been the foreman, for most of the farm-servants earned between £7 and £9 a year (21 men and boys *besides hoers, shearers and 2 herds*), and there were wages for the harvest workers, and *the expence of drink for the Peat Cutters.* At the end of her letter to Tom enclosing the accounts, she wrote: *If you think it worth examining I shall think my labour well paid, if not the paper may serve to light the candle ...*[17] Frances knew her husband. It is impossible to imagine Tom taking time out from more enjoyable activities to look over his household and farm accounts.

Even in good years, there was little profit to be made from farming. Wealth came from Balfour's kelp shores, his fishing boats (a government bounty paid on herring made them very profitable), and from trade. All Orkney lairds were merchants first and foremost at this time, with contraband often concealed in legitimate cargoes, and Thomas was a particularly successful one. He built up a fleet of eight brigs and sloops that traded all round the coast of Britain, and across the North Sea, even as far as St Petersburg. They carried Orkney bere to Norway and Russia, returned with timber, iron and flax, delivered his kelp to Newcastle and Leith and brought home coals and brandy and claret.

Trading journeys were always hazardous and, with Britain at war with France from 1793, the ships were endangered by enemy privateers as well as bad weather. In the stormy March of 1794, one of the Balfour ships, the *Swift*, was lost with its crew and cargo and, as Frances wrote to her sister-in-law Mary Craigie: *All our Fleet have been unlucky this year. The Fisher after taking in her cargo of herring took on board 16 sailers who had been wrecked in this country and was ordered to land them on the coast of Norway. By this means she lost her passage to London for she was blocked in by a Privateer till about a month ago, and then made her escape in the night. Contrary winds have detained her here till 3 days ago when she sailed for London. In the dreadful storm of the 25th Jan the Countess was driven to Whitby after losing most of her sails, her Boat and Cargo. She picked up 4 men at sea who were near perishing … The Pomona made a good voyage to and from* [?] *and is now gone to Gottenburgh with coals …*[18]

The income that could be made from farming the estate depended on trading the oats and barley – when the harvest was good enough that any could be spared – either as grain, or made into malt for brewing and distilling, or milled into oatmeal and beremeal. With Tom usually absent, and their correspondence frequently delayed by bad weather, Frances had to make the decisions as to what was the most practical or profitable course of action. In December 1796, she wrote to Tom for instructions: *we have a fine Oat crop and tho our bear* [bere] *is as good as anybody's, it is thought it will not turn out so well as to export it. If I thought you meant to export it, I wou'd keep it together, if not, I would dispose of it to the best advantage in meal and Malt. After all, I believe I must do the best I can without your advice, for I shou'd have time to eat it with my own teeth before I cou'd hear from you …*[19] Other estate produce was sold through Robert Bayne, merchant in Leith. In 1802 he received from Cliffdale: *9 cowhides, 7 doz and 3 rabbit skins, 13 calf skins, 53 spynals of yarn* … to offset the imports of necessities like vegetable seed and luxuries like whisky and sugar. *I should have charged a little Commission but as you was unlucky with your Goods last year I have not charged it …*[20]

A brief spell at home in the summer of 1796 was Thomas Balfour's last visit to Orkney and he died in Bath, aged only 47, in 1799. In all his long absences, and for seven years after his death, the management of his farms and tenants, the selling of his crops and cargoes, was left to his wife. Crop failure continued to be a recurrent nightmare. In 1800 supplies of grain had to be bought in for famine relief. 1801 saw a good harvest but it was a brief respite. Two years later, Mary Craigie in Westness wrote to her brother David Balfour in Edinburgh: *the Corn you sent home for a supply to the Poor tenants upon my Brother's and Nephews Estates was Shipped … such as has been and continues to be the uncommon severity of the Season that many people have been obliged to give the Corn they had reserved for Seed to their Cattle, and even the Bread they should have supported themselves and familys upon.*[21] In 1804 the Government sent £10,000 worth of meal to Orkney. In 1806 a severe storm on Christmas day destroyed houses, boats and cornstacks and there was no harvest the following season. Both the grain crop and the potato crop failed so yet again the precious seedcorn had to be fed to the animals to keep them alive. The proprietors were forced to organize famine relief again in 1808, and subscribed £1000 to buy meal to sell to the poor.

Frances stayed at Cliffdale running the estate until 1808 when her younger son, Captain William Balfour, (defying the strenuous attempts by all his family to dissuade him from abandoning his career) retired from the Navy and took over. Frances had always been criticized by Tom for any failings in her management and she frequently deprecated her own ignorance of matters relating to the estate, but this letter to William proves that in fact she acquired a highly practical, hands-on understanding of farming. *The unusual severity of the weather and 20 years experience, induces me to offer my advice unask'd ... there were never more than half the number of Horses upon your Farms than you now keep, we always found ourselves greatly difficulted to find subsistence for them even in the most forward of seasons till after the Meadow Hay was brought home ... I therefore earnestly recommend to you to sow 2 acres of Red Clover, to harvest green for your horses during the summer. Your meadow hay will succeed it after the Hay is got in, and by that time a second Crop of Red Clover will be ready for harvest ... At the West Hill, Tares will answer better in the soil than Clover ... The sooner the Clover is sown the better, at least 12 lb to any acre, 8 red and 4 white, and 3 bushels rye grass seed.*[22]

Elizabeth and Frances were of course wealthy by the standards of their tenantry but, if their husbands' activities gave them access to imported luxuries like sherry and gingerbread and contraband gin, no-one, after reading their letters, will ever have illusions that the wives of merchant-lairds led easy and leisured lives. These were women for whom the devastation of their harvest by appalling weather, food shortages, the shipwreck of their trading vessels and threat of invasion were their daily challenges.

A Visit to Court

In August 1777, two years after their marriage, Thomas and Frances Balfour travelled south to spend the winter with her brother, Earl Ligonier, and his wife at their home Cobham Park in Surrey. They took with them Tom's sister Peggy who had become Frances' close friend. Ligonier's letters to Frances are charming, humorous and affectionate; he must have been a delightful host. He was also a Lieutenant-General with a distinguished war record and he moved in the high society that Frances would have been used to before her marriage. The entire visit to England must have been an astonishing experience for 30-year-old Peggy, who had probably never been out of Orkney before, but the highlight was the invitation to be presented at court to King George III and Queen Charlotte. Breathless with excitement, Peggy rushed to describe the occasion to her sister Betty at home in Westray.

It is all over with me my dear Betty I have been at Court and done nothing and what have I recourse to now I know not heaven direct me and why not call heaven to aid it is a serious matter and the world can do no more for me. There was I dressed out in my best flowered silk sack [gown] *which I have not had above seven years with the plaits of the gown and petticoat took out to make it receive a hoop for nobody of rank (observe) goes without one my hair dressed out to such a size that I declare my head appeared to me almost as big as my whole body and lest it should not a good large cap on the top of all yet it was moderate to many I saw there with Lady Ligonier's jewels and some other things of hers which were better than I had of my own put on by her own hands which was more than she would have done for herself but she is one of the best natured women alive and free of that pride which is so common among people of her rank which they take every opportunity of showing to their inferiors. I hope you dont think me such a fool as really to appear even where I was a stranger in all the jewels that L Ligonier might appear in but her diamond earrings and necklace I had much against my inclination for fear of any accident happening to them but she would not be refused with all these advantages and Lord Ligonier told me I was a bonny lass tonight and I am sure his Lordship cant flatter ... it is in vain to attempt giving a description a very good way to get off say you not being very good at giving descriptions I can only tell you that it was a most brilliant assembly a great many very fine women elegantly dressed the men upon the whole very plain tho I heard of one suit being embroidered with french paste and other stones to resemble diamonds the King and Queen were very plain in their dress her Majesty is a very fine figure of a woman in my opinion and a sweet looking woman but not a good feature in her face the king is a good jolly looking man seems good natured easie and affable I think he is not unlike Tirlet* [neighbour in Westray] *we saw none of the young royal family ...*[23]

Figure 4.5
George III and Queen Charlotte with their six eldest children, painted by Johan Joseph Zoffany 1770. (Royal Collection Trust/© Her Majesty Queen Elizabeth II 2020)

"I Am His Property"

When the 22 year old Thomas Balfour met Frances Ligonier in Edinburgh, he had just graduated from Aberdeen University with a degree in medicine but was still without an appointment. Frances was ten years older than him and, by her own admission, no beauty, but she was the daughter and niece and sister of military heroes. Her uncle John Ligonier became a Field-Marshall, Commander-in-Chief of the British land forces and an earl, her brother Edward was then Viscount Ligonier and a Major General. Thomas was dazzled by her aristocratic connections and the potential of a marriage that would provide him with some much-needed income and a network of influential relations. Frances recorded the life-changing event in her terse diary of events: *went to Scotland, became acquainted with Mr Balfour, married him 19 Sept 1775.*[24]

Tom was handsome, sociable, well-educated and charming. Much better company than his more serious brothers John and David, he was doted on by his sisters, spoilt, vain, selfish and irresponsible. Frances was captivated by his charm and worshipped him on a pedestal for the rest of her life. 1775 was the year that the outbreak of the American Rebellion stirred a wave of patriotic fervour through Britain, (one imagines jingoistic headlines in the tabloids similar to those in the Falklands War). Men flocked to enlist to ensure that the colonies remained British, and Thomas quickly abandoned medicine for the glamour of a military uniform. His new brother-in-law obtained for him a commission as an ensign in his own regiment, the 9th Foot, a sinecure that entitled Tom to receive a small pay and to cut a fine figure in a red coat without risking any of the unpleasantness attendant on actually encountering an enemy.

The Balfours married in London and, after time in the capital and on the Ligoniers' estate at Cobham, sailed to Aberdeen where

154

they wintered. Tom's father William travelled from Orkney and lawyer brother David from Edinburgh to inspect the new bride, they were favourably impressed, and in the spring the couple tackled the rest of the strenuous journey to Westray – over two hundred and fifty miles on horseback. Thomas must have been relieved to find that Frances was quite undaunted by travel, but her brother knew that she had a tough constitution. *I am glad to find you safe after the Trials and Dangers of your long journey,* Ligonier wrote to Tom, *I was entirely convinced Mrs Balfour would be the last to suffer in such an Expedition, not excepting the hardiest of your horses. She is fortunately composed of such material, that she may safely set the Elements at defiance.*[25]

Figure 4.6
Artist's impression of the house of Trenaby, as rebuilt by William Balfour c.1750.

Meeting the rest of Tom's family and friends must have been a far more alarming ordeal to Frances, and nothing in her former life can have prepared her for the culture shock of landing in Kirkwall, a village with one filthy street and a large church which boasted boarded-up windows, slime-green interior walls, and a stench of mould, shallow graves and decay. After the gracious homes of the upper classes in 18th-century Surrey and Bath, her experience of Westray would have been similar to that of the first-time traveller to the third world today, precipitated from one age to another by jet aircraft. Apart from the other small lairds, most of the people shared their turf-roofed, earth-floored dwellings with their animals. The agriculture was primitive, totally untouched by the 'improvements' which had long been standard in the south, and the climate inhospitable. Frances must also have felt acutely aware that her social accomplishments, which had been admired in London, would cut no ice in a community based on farming and trade. There was not only no-one to be impressed by her fluency in French and Italian, but an almost impenetrable accent to be understood before she could converse at all. It says much for her that this first visit to Trenaby seems to have been a great success.

Entertaining letters to Frances from her sister-in-law, Lady Ligonier, full of gossip about their acquaintances and society scandal, give an idea of the aristocratic circles in which Frances had moved before her marriage.[26] When she married Thomas, and he was strutting around in his new red coat, she had almost certainly imagined that they would live in her familiar environment, with sojourns in Orkney confined to family visits, and never envisaged that her marriage would settle her there for the rest of her life. However, Tom had set his heart on becoming an Orkney landowner.

His determination is ironic and almost inexplicable given that his father's huge efforts to make enough money to educate his sons well were entirely directed to ensuring they got out, and stayed out, of Orkney. When he was trying to arrange Tom's career, William wrote to his lawyer with astonishing vehemence: *the thoughts of bringing him home, which is the same as to ruin him forever, will drive me to despair. I would bury him with less anguish.*[27] Later, William expressed the same attitude to his native land in a letter regarding his grandchildren in Edinburgh: [David's] *children are promising. To take them to Orkney, if I could, to ignorance and barbarity, would be most preposterous.*[28] Growing up with these sentiments, it is curious that Thomas chose to throw up the career opportunities open to him, either in medicine or the Army, for the uncertain prospects of an island farmer at a time when bad seasons and the failure of the crops followed each other with calamitous regularity.

Thomas gave laudable reasons: his filial duty to look after parents and sisters, but there just may have been an ingredient of wanting to be a big fish in a small pond rather than a small fish in a large one. It was certainly not a decision that Frances anticipated or relished, as is clear even in the title of her poem: *To Mr Balfour on his determination to go to Orkney. To Brother, Country, Friends I bid adieu* wrote Frances, resigning herself to move for ever to her husband's *Native Land ... pierced with northern blasts and drifting snow.*[29]

While Tom was busy with all the trading, political and social commitments that absorbed the time of an Orkney gentleman, Frances was expecting her first child, but the baby was still-born in May 1777. After her recovery, they returned to Cobham for another winter and their daughter Mary was born the following November, shortly after they had moved to the Bu in Burray. Frances' brother Edward Ligonier wrote to congratulate her and added: *I do not know but it is better than having a boy, as to your comfort, for few mothers see much of their sons after 5 years of age.*[30] In later years, Frances frequently stated how happy her first 15 years of married life were. A son, Edward John Ligonier, was born in January 1780 and William followed in December 1781. However, the years in which Frances could enjoy her children's company were indeed very short, with all the children being dispatched to boarding school at the age of nine or ten.

With her children and her husband away, Frances was desperately lonely. Her sharp, ironic wit, which had been entertaining in London, sounded acerbic, even hurtful in Orkney and her inevitable snobbery kept many of her husband's relations and acquaintance at bay. As she realized herself, her very education and accomplishments made it impossible for her to find anyone else with whom she had anything whatsoever in common. The one woman with whom she seems to have formed an affectionate friendship was Tom's sister Peggy, and the prospect of being separated from Peggy wrung from Frances one of her most agonized letters. *Her friendship has reconciled me to the dreary solitude of Orkney, and her company has sweetened a life that without her would have been insupportable. I cannot live without a Companion, without a friend. Tom is necessarily much from home and, out of your family, the females of this Country I must say are unfit for either.*[31]

After seeing so little of her children from the time they were very young, it is not surprising that Frances' relationship with them often sounds strained. She herself was illegitimate and an orphan and she had no experience of a happy childhood. When she was three years old, her father, Lieutenant Colonel Francis Ligonier, had died of pleurisy shortly after the battle of Falkirk. He had left his sickbed in Edinburgh to take command and, in falling snow, made a heroic attempt to rally his troops after their defeat by the Jacobite army. It was January 1746, (ironically, the same winter that her future father-in-law, William Balfour, was hiding from government troops in Westray). Materially, she was well provided for by her uncle but her own brief notes of biography show a pathetic lack of family life. *1753 My mother dyed, sent to school, remained there till 1758, 59 with Mrs Osgood ... Went to Bath, returned to London ... 70 My uncle dyed, went to France. Returned to England, went to board at Mildenhall ...*[32] Edward Ligonier was a very caring older brother, but he followed his father and uncle into the army at an early age. Frances must have suffered much from loneliness and the absence of mother or sisters in her childhood shows itself in her own failings as a mother.

In her letters she comes across as an insecure woman who found relationships difficult and made few firm friends, and was inhibited even with her own children. There was always a stiffness between her and them, in contrast to the relaxed and affectionate gaiety in the letters that pass between her sons and their aunts. Thomas had grown up with adoring older sisters, Betty and Peggy, and the much younger Mary. Perhaps it was because their father could not offer a dowry suitable to their station in life that they married so late, Betty at 42 and Mary when she was 34. Betty had one child but Mary remained childless and both doted on their niece and nephews as they had on their brother. Even with William, her favourite child, Frances never achieved an easy relationship and inevitably she was jealous of how much Mary was loved by both Thomas and their children.

If Frances was to some extent the victim of her own personality, she was also dealt many unkind blows by fate. Not only did her parents die when she was a child, but her brother Edward died at the age of 42. In all Frances' correspondence with her family, Ligonier emerges as the star character: brave, caring and witty. His letters contain fascinating snippets of news about the latest campaigns and the politics of the day, but they are also full of humour, affection for his sister, anxiety for her confinements (*I shall wait with impatience to hear you are safe from the matrimonial scrapes of producing nephews and nieces*),[33] and helpful advice for his importunate brother-in-law – whose irresponsible demands for income without effort he must have found infuriating. (*If Mr B were in full possession of every military book from the time of Julius Caesar to the present moment he might, for all I know, make a good general but ... he is totally unfit for an Adjutant*).[34]

As Tom spent more and more time away from home in the 1790s, he did not trouble to keep from Frances the fact that, with a fine family of three children growing up, he had lost interest in her and even regarded her as something of a social embarrassment. Pathetically she wrote to her husband: *I have long looked on myself as a burthen to you and am much mistaken if you have not been of the same opinion. for this reason I have ceased to live with you as a wife and that without ill humour for I am not such a fool as to suppose that a woman of my age can be an object of fondness to a man of yours.*[35] When John Balfour suggested that Tom might also find lucrative employment in India, her despair at the prospect of being totally abandoned in Orkney reached its height. A draft letter to John is a poignant comment on her sense of still being an outsider in an alien land. *On the north and winter shaded side of a bleak hill mischance has planted me, never to thrive, Child of another Soil, yet I am so firmly rooted that nothing but the hand of death can pluck me up. Perhaps the loss of my Husband and Children may ameliorate an event for which I confess I feel the utmost impatience.*[36] The India plan was dropped but Tom found plenty of excuses for being out of Shapinsay.

As the war with France grew more serious and the government demanded more men in arms, Major Balfour was promoted to Colonel with a commission to recruit a full-sized regiment, the North Lowland Fencibles. This meant that he had to take his military duties seriously for the first time and serve wherever in Britain or Ireland he was posted. (Fencibles were exempted from posting abroad). In 1795 he went to Ireland as commander of his regiment, a real soldier at last, to chase rumours of French landings and put down Irish revolts.

In the same year Frances nursed Peggy in Edinburgh through her last months of illness; her early death was one of Frances' many tragic losses. She returned to lonely isolation on Shapinsay, *in truth this is a most dreary abode, storms succeed each other, and there is not pleasant spot on which the wearied eye can rest. The violence of the weather has cut off all intercourse between us and the mainland for some days past ...*[37] When she did receive letters from Tom, they made clear his lack of interest in returning to her but not his plans. *I am still at a loss to know what is your plan for the future,* she wrote to him, *You told me you wish to reside some times at Cliffdale as a Bachelor. You speak also of purchasing a house or place in the neighbourhood of Edinburgh where you may occasionally live with me.*[38]

In 1798 Thomas was negotiating to buy a property in Caithness, but Frances still did not know whether he intended her to move there or stay in Shapinsay. Miserably, she wrote to his sister Mary Craigie: *I cannot help believing that he wishes me anywhere rather than here and that there is no human being that cares where I am, I shall therefore endeavour to make my wishes and my duty coincide. I am his property and he has a right to dispose of me wherever he pleases.* Frances often dramatizes in her letters but here she was, of course, just stating the bleak fact. In law she was effectively her husband's property.

In the early summer of 1798 Frances and her daughter Mary were at last reunited with Thomas and Edward for a few weeks in Caithness, but news of fresh insurrections in Ireland soon sent Colonel Balfour hurrying back to his regiment. Later it would emerge that he had rather more personal reasons for returning to Ireland that were unconnected with his sense of duty. He had already been ill for some months and that autumn Frances and Mary waited anxiously for his return in Edinburgh. Frances had a plan for her daughter. Her aristocratic sister-in-law Lady Wentworth, (Edward Ligonier's widow), [39] would open doors into London society and enable Mary to make her debut into the right circles and secure an appropriately fashionable marriage. Lady Wentworth was quite willing to co-operate; Mary was not. She had fallen in love with a young minister, Alexander Brunton, whom she had already met in Shapinsay, and with the prospect of *the quiet and privacy of a Scotch parsonage.* Brunton, a scholarly man who later held the chair of

Oriental languages in Edinburgh, did the surprisingly glamorous thing of eloping with Mary and saving her from Vanity Fair. Frances was furious and bitter at their deception; it took years for her to appreciate that Brunton had sterling qualities which made him an ideal husband for Mary despite his lack of social status. (Mary later won considerable acclaim for her novels *Self-Control* and *Discipline* but, tragically, died in childbirth in 1818).

Still reeling with fury at the Bruntons, Frances was finally allowed to rejoin Tom. He had returned to England in November a sick man and been advised to try the Bath waters; by the time Frances saw him in February 1799 he was clearly terminally ill. By March, he was bedridden. In May, while nursing the rapidly weakening husband whom she adored despite his treatment of her, a bundle of letters arrived at the house addressed to Col. Balfour. Into Frances' life erupted the person of Mary Montgomery, the married woman who was Tom's mistress: just arrived from Ireland, seven months pregnant, hysterical with anxiety and desperate to secure maintenance.

Mary Montgomery/Chute/Jackson/Clifford/Holland (she went by all of these names at different times) was the mistress from hell. Not only did she appear on the scene just when Tom was on his death-bed and Frances was already distraught, but after he died Frances had to field a torrent of incoherent, self-pitying letters, of which the main thrust was her demand for money. Mary's letters begin in a neat, educated hand but as she winds herself up to a frenzy of emotion her writing grows larger and wilder and she throws to the winds all inhibition, coherence and grammar. *(Oh what a wretched mother I am – My heart would drop blood if you knew my suffering ... on seeing me in a state of distraction – my frame in convulsions from agitation ... what can be charitably done for me but firing a pistol at my head ...)*[40] and much, much more in the same vein. Tom was just able to sign a paper settling an annuity of £50 on his mistress and Frances replied to her with dignified restraint, and even offered to raise the child herself.

Apart from her distress at her disgrace and her conviction that she would die in childbirth (or at any time thereafter), Mary's state of distraction stemmed from an unfortunate error on her part. When she first thought she was pregnant, Thomas had made arrangements for a just financial settlement. She then told him there was no child on the way after all and, thinking that she had finished their relationship, he returned her letters and destroyed the papers regarding the settlement. Somewhat late in the day, she seems to have realized her mistake and written to Balfour to reinstate the money he had promised her.

Thomas Balfour died in Bath on 9th August 1799 and Frances was back in Shapinsay in September, to take up the reins of the neglected estate, cope with yet another poor harvest and worry about her sons, now both on active service in war-time: William in the Royal Navy and Edward in the army. After a period of hanging around unemployed on half-pay, Edward had been reinstated to a regiment – the 9th Foot, formerly commanded by his uncle Ligonier. That summer it joined a combined British/Russian expeditionary force that attacked the French in the Netherlands. Ten days into his first action and six weeks after his father's death, Edward was killed at Alkmaar, less than four months before his twentieth birthday.

In her grief, Frances had to deal with yet more histrionic letters from Mary Montgomery. As always, she left her husband on his marble pedestal and refused to attach any blame to him. *I have the worst opinion of Mrs M* she wrote to her brother-in-law, *I very much suspect your poor Brother was the Dupe of artifice. She has uniformly endeavoured to claim money by every means in her power, and I do not even think it improbable that there is collusion between her and her Husband, for it is certainly very unlikely that she could remain on the spot with him till within 2 months of her delivery as was actually the case without his perceiving her condition, or that he should permit her to go to England alone upon the frivolous pretence she made use of. Poor Tom by your death you escaped disappointment, sorrow and disgrace, but of these you have left me the inheritance to their full extent.*[41]

What made Frances' situation particularly unenviable was the inevitable publicity surrounding the affair. After giving birth, Mary had been persuaded to return to Ireland, leaving her child in the care of a nurse, but her husband discovered the reason for her abrupt departure and sued for a divorce. Mary therefore came back to England, reclaimed her daughter, Charlotte, and settled in London. Frances was thus spared the need to bring up Tom's illegitimate child, but there was still the possibility that a claim for damages could be made on his heirs. She would have known exactly what a divorce involved and what major headlines it made in the newspapers of the day, for thirty years earlier she had been a witness in her brother's divorce case.

Ligonier had had the misfortune to marry a society belle, the appalling Penelope Pitt. (Twin portraits were commissioned from Gainsborough at the time of their marriage: Penelope is painted as a hard-faced beauty fashionably propped against a classical statue, Ligonier in military uniform, a much less arresting subject than his horse). Penelope relished the glare of publicity and flaunted a torrid affair with the flamboyant Count Vittorio Amadeo Alfieri, a left-wing playwright who dedicated a play about the heroic struggle against political tyranny to George Washington. Ligonier challenged Alfieri to a duel; neither gentleman was killed. Divorce was hard to obtain and could only be granted by a decree in the House of Lords. In order to provide grounds for one, the Ligoniers had to set up witnesses of the liaison: the lovers were seen to meet in Frances' London house, where they were alone for hours in the dark *and did not call for candles.* A divorce was granted but Alfieri then refused to marry Penelope, having discovered that she had already had an affair with her husband's postillion,[42] (she later married one of the soldiers in Ligonier's regiment, Private Smith). Frances had every reason to dread the publicity of Mary Mongomery's divorce case, and even the possibility of being cited to appear in the court, (*I would die 1000 deaths rather than do so*).[43]

Despite all the misery that Mary dragged Frances through, with the letters that swung between unctuous gratitude to *my beloved Mrs B* to weeping reproach that 'Mrs B' was not doing more for her, Frances took an interest in the education of Charlotte at her English boarding-school and sent the child presents, right to the end of her life. The little girl grew up knowing only that Mrs Balfour in Orkney was a kind friend of her father's, and she wrote back with thanks for the gifts. *I understand Geography and have read in it about Scotland and will thank you for a more particular account of it than my Geography Book gives me. I am Dear Madam, your obliged Charlotte Clifford.*[44] The Balfour family set up a trust fund for Charlotte who married a Dublin attorney, Mr Jones, in 1828.[45]

Frances loyally polished Tom's memory. *His frailties were such as are incident to humanity* she wrote to their daughter, *his virtues were those of an Angel ...*[46]

With one son already killed in action, Frances must have suffered acute anxiety for her second son, on active service all the time he was in the navy, but Frances refused to encourage him to return to Orkney. *From such a determination ... I would earnestly dissuade you. You can have no idea of what a set of wretches this country is inhabited. An honest man would almost stand alone in it, and I do most truly think that in such society neither morals nor manners can remain uncontaminated.*[47] It would seem the bitter remark of an outsider if one had not read the disparaging comments of the male Balfours on their native land.

However, despite his mother's protests, William resigned from the Navy in 1808 and came home to his inheritance. Until then, Frances continued live in solitude in Cliffdale and look after the house and estate for him. *In truth I have no attachment to this Country nor (with a few exceptions) to its Inhabitants,* she wrote to William, *but I shall not conceal that I am strongly attached to this place, the scene of many of my happiest hours, and the humble Monument of your Fathers taste as well as industry.*[48] She spent her last sad years in Kirkwall, the *vile place* she had always hated, until her death on 11th March 1813, aged 70.

Edinburgh Scandal

Thomas Balfour's younger brother, David, became a lawyer in Edinburgh and – luckily for Tom – looked after much of the family's business. His letters in their near-illegible handwriting feature frequently in the Balfour archive but, unfortunately, only a few survive from his gossipy wife Marion, whose letters are as entertaining as David's are dry and business-like. On this occasion Marion was writing to Frances, widowed three years earlier, to persuade her to come and visit them in Edinburgh. I imagine her to be kind and plump and very talkative, so different from Frances who is always serious and accustomed to solitude. Here Marion is gleefully distributing the latest scandals of the capital.

Am I to believe that you are serious when you flatter us with the prospect of seeing you here on your way to Bath – I know you are apt to lay Schemes which you never execute but in this case I hope you will remain steady – however I must apprise you of your danger before going amongst the gay and fashionable circles you will have occasion to meet with in the South – perhaps you think yourself secure against the arts of Seduction – no such thing you are just at the time of life which is most in vogue – if you get the Scandalous chronicle perhaps you are informed that the young Duke of M ... has left his young wife and eloped with Mrs Musters a Lady of fifty – the Duke of Manchester with Mrs Orby who has left Six Children – and to compleat the catalogue the Marquis of Blandford who lately disobliged his friends by making a love marriage has followed the example of the noble Dukes and gone off with a Mrs Sturt a Lady well stricken in years. These things will become so common that they will not even be spoken of.[49]

A Town of Numerous Widows

According to the *Old Statistical Account* of 1799, *the great disproportion of males to females in the village of Stromness is occasioned by the young men going abroad to various parts of the world; to the Greenland fishery, the coal trade, Hudson's Bay, and many are to be found in his Majesty's navy.*[50] In fact there were almost twice as many women as men. Many of them were paupers like Isobel Gunn, living in the poorest part of a town that was transforming itself from a small dirty village into a densely populated and very cosmopolitan port. As they walked its salt-drenched and fish-smelling streets and steep closes, selling knitted stockings and mittens to the sailors who caroused and brawled their way between the 'tippling houses', they must often have passed women leading very different lives at the other end of the social scale. Christian Robertson, perhaps, merchant and ship-owner, striding past at a brisk and businesslike pace, or Miss Maria Stewart, the daughter of a slave but brought home by her father to live a genteel life in the Whitehouse.

There was a huge economic gulf between the successful business women like Robertson, or Robina Flett who ran the Commercial Hotel while her husband skippered a trading vessel, and the *numerous widows (whose husbands have perished at sea), left with their large families helpless and dependent, unable to provide for their sustenance, far less to afford them a good education ...*[51] However, all faced the challenges of supporting their families single-handed, all of their lives were dependent on, enriched or destroyed by the sea, and all of them had to be tough and resourceful to find ways to provide for themselves and their families. Looking at just a few of the women who lived in Stromness in the 19th century, it is impossible not to be impressed by what strong and capable characters they were.

Christian Robertson was one of those feisty ladies who could have stepped straight out of the pages of *Orkneyinga Saga*: shrewd, forceful, with tongues sharp as their needles. Born in Birsay, she joined one of the foremost merchant dynasties of Stromness when she married John Robertson in 1795. At that time the harbour was crammed with shipping from all over the world – a few years earlier some 340 foreign vessels had called at Stromness (English, Dutch, Swedish, Prussian and American among them) – and a huge amount of shipping business flowed through the Robertsons' hands. They organised the freight of Orkney's exports, goods like kelp and linen, rabbit skins and geese; and her imports, essentials like coal and iron and timber, and luxuries such as wine and whisky and tea. They supplied provisions to outgoing ships like the whalers from Hull and Aberdeen and Dundee which stopped on their way north every year. They arranged their insurance *Anent Wind Seas and Weather,* engaged crews and paid wages and bounties to their dependants in Orkney.

However, Christian's life was not an easy one. She had four children of her own but she also brought up John's illegitimate son, born the same year that they married. In 1808 John died after a long illness, leaving her *a Disconsolate Widow with 5 children to provide for With the blessing of the Almighty to assist.* John also left her with a trail of bad debts, having been *very unfit for business* a long time before his death, and a number of impatient creditors. Christian was frightened that she might lose their property if she could not pay them quickly, and this at a time when the prices of all the necessities of life were rising rapidly due to poor seasons at home and the long war with France.[52] *The country is in a bad way,* she wrote to her cousins William and Nicol Leith, *people are hardly able to live ... Barley meal 2/9 st Butter 1/- lb eggs 6d doz Lamp oil 2/- pint ... and everything in proportion rising house rents etc.*[53]

Christian dealt with being single parent and breadwinner by being tough. She was not one to suffer fools lightly and fellow-merchant William Watt was one who often received a lashing from her acerbic tongue. *Sir, I am astonished at your behaviour to make fools of us altogether to pretend that you have ordered your kept man to attend your kelp, the Vessel is been down and obliged to come home again without the Kelp ... I can assure you that I can not afford to pay men and wadge and maintenance and a heavy Insurance to go dancing after your pleasure.*[54] Several other letters to Watt suggest that you annoyed Christian Robertson at your peril.

The final defeat of Napoleon in 1815 meant peace at last but not prosperity, especially not for those whose business lay in shipping. In harbours all over the country, unwanted ships rotted at anchor. The country was bankrupt, there was mass unemployment and, for all the ports which had thrived on building, repairing or provisioning naval vessels, it was a time of severe depression. Joshua Clouston wrote from London to Peter Leith in Stenness: *There hasn't been a ship in Shadwell Dock for a fortnight and no sign of any coming and some docks have had none for 2 months ... there is general stagnation in the place.*[55]

Fortunately for Stromness, the whaling fleets were still calling on their way to the Davis Straits and Christian invested her profits in the town. The population was growing but there was a shortage of housing and schools. She built six fine slated double houses on her pier at Ness, still her most visible legacy, and opened a school at Ness, Flett's Academy.[56] There was no bank in Stromness in her time, so every summer Christian had to order cash to be shipped from south so that she could pay the wages and bonuses of whaling crews. She lobbied for a bank, eventually provided in 1835. She raised a subscription for the widows of seven men who drowned in a pilot boat.

Figure 4.7
The double houses at Ness, Stromness built by Christian Robertson.

Perhaps most significantly, it was Christian's idea to invite Robert Stevenson to Stromness to design and tender for building a dry dock there. *This tract of coast,* wrote Stevenson, *lies in the direct course not only of the Greenland trade,* and *Hudsons Bay ships, but of the whole trade from Liverpool, the west of England and Scotland, and North of Ireland, to the Baltic etc, but also to the whole traffic of the kingdom, bound round the northern shores of Scotland.* Nonetheless, there was nowhere that ships could be repaired, not just in Stromness but anywhere between the Firths of Clyde and Forth, and Stevenson stressed the urgent need of building one, *having witnessed the total loss and destruction of many fine ships, from the mere want of a few days repair in a Dry Dock somewhere at the northern point of Scotland.*[57] Christian failed to get a government grant towards a dock and could not afford to build one herself, but it was due to her initiative that in 1836 John Stanger installed the slipway recommended by Stevenson at the Ness shipbuilding yard and the great days of Stromness shipbuilding and repair began.

Christian would have been on social terms with the wife of another Stromness shipowner, Margaret Login. (Later we will meet her son, Sir John Login, who left Stromness in the relatively humble role of ship's surgeon and became the official guardian of the Maharajah of the Punjab, Duleep Singh). In 1829 Margaret was a widow shouldering the huge financial losses caused by the shipwreck of her husband's uninsured vessels. With a young family to bring up, she set out to turn around the family fortunes and she made Login's Inn into a high-class establishment, catering for ships' officers and Orkney's lairds and merchants. One of her sons remembered her as *a woman of remarkable energy and courage,* [who] *struggled bravely on under great difficulties, winning the respect and admiration of all who came into contact with her ...*[58]

Much poorer than these women was widow Margaret Humphreys, one of many women whose children had emigrated or were working overseas. Struggling to make ends meet, she waited for the rare news that might come from her scattered sons: Thomas was an apothecary in Nova Scotia; John a sailor, gone to Archangel; James was working as a doctor in the war in Mexico; Robert Stewart and Alexander were in New Orleans and Charles was in the service of the Hudson's Bay Company.[59] Margaret had plenty of concerns with her family. Her daughter Mary died, leaving her to care for the orphaned grandchildren. News from her sons was intermittent, but she worried about Charles being attacked by natives at his Hudson's Bay Company base in Columbia. This was not unfounded, everyone in Orkney would have known about Edward Driver of Kirkwall who was killed when his party went ashore on Vancouver Island to get water.

Figure 4.8
Brown's Close, Stromness, photographed mid 19th century. (OLA)

The behaviour of some of her family had provided her with further anxiety for Charles' welfare. *Now My Dear Son doe not Spurn at a Mothers advice* she wrote to him in 1838, *be sober and Carefull keep good Company ... mind how some of your Brothers ruined themselves by their Extravigance and keeping Company with those how loved their Bottle Beware of this evil as it will soon Creep on and betray you into disgrace, and Sin and bring you to ane untimely end.*[60] Poor Charles was not ruined by the bottle but by the stress of his job as master of the *Beaver*, the Company's steamship on the coastal service. Given an impossible workload by the Company and huge responsibility at a very young age for dealing on his own with the natives as well as his crew, he suffered a mental breakdown, gave up his command and tried to commit suicide on the way home.

In 1836 and 1837 Margaret leased her house to make a hospital for the survivors of disastrous whaling seasons when ships became trapped in the ice in Baffin Bay for the whole winter, with terrible suffering and tragic loss of life. In the 1851 census she was in her late 70s and working as a midwife, still providing for her family in her own old age. Despite all her difficulties, and being often worn down with *a Life of Care and Woe,* Margaret's Christian faith was unshaken. *The present Crop all over England and Scotland is verry backward and provisions of every sort is on the rise but whey should we Complain God is ever kind and will bring about for our Comfort many unforeseen mercees.*[61]

In an island community, it was inevitable that a great many Orkney women spent their lives at home holding forts of one kind or another while their husbands were at sea. Some adventurous wives, however, refused to be left at home and accompanied their skipper husbands on their voyages, bringing a touch of late Victorian femininity to the rough life on a 19th-century sailing ship. In the 1870s Helen Ronaldson joined her husband Captain James Skinner who carried trade goods and emigrants to the colonies in the *SS Warwick*. Helen produced her fourth child on the voyage and *won the esteem of all on board.*[62]

Probably few women were as widely travelled as Marina Cromarty who married master mariner Captain Corrigall of Longhope and sailed all over the world with him for 15 years. *Over a great part of the Pacific she sailed, visiting many of the beautiful islands … and away north to Vladivostock in Siberia, before there were proper charts for that region. Japan, China and islands off that coast; India, S Africa, Australia, New Zealand, N and S America; the Mediterranean and the Baltic – scarcely a country bordering the sea but she had seen.* Marina kept goats and hens on board ship to provide fresh milk and eggs for the men and played the harmonium for Sunday service. Due to her influence, life was a great deal less brutal on the *SS Malta* than was normal at sea and Corrigall had men queuing to join his ship.

Souvenirs of the Corrigalls' remarkable travels survive in the possession of Marina's great-niece DeLille Diament. Among them are letters written to Captain Corrigall in 1869, welcoming him back to the Comoro Islands (between the East African coast and Madagascar) and signed *Sincere Friend, Sultan Abdallah, King of Johanna Comoro Islands*. The Sultan organised donkeys for the Captain and a 'moncera' or chair for Marina to transport them to his palace. *That is the way in which the ladies of this place are carried from place to place. By her coming in this manner, she would not be fatigued, so I hope she will come along with you ... Hoping to have the pleasure of a long talk with you and Mrs Corrigall.* Marina died in 1926 aged 91, *the last of her race*.[63]

Figure 4.9
Captain Corrigall's ship, SS Malta. (Courtesy of DeLille Diament, photograph by Rebecca Marr)

Crinolines in Papa Westray

Sometimes we can get a vivid impression of the personality of people from their letters, or letters about them, but can we also imagine how they looked? The gloomy 17th-century memorials in St Magnus Cathedral record the names and short lives of Orkney's 'Society', the well-to-do merchants and baillies of Kirkwall and their wives. Illustrations of their contemporaries in other parts of the country can give some idea of how they dressed, for they would have had access to the materials and the fashions of the day, even if they took a little while to percolate from Edinburgh to Kirkwall. Outside the circle of 'the gentry', the great majority of people in Orkney in the middle ages, and well into the 18th century, were too poor to dress in anything other than rather sombre clothes of undyed wool, home-spun and home-woven or knitted.

By the end of the century, however, most people had significantly more disposable income coming into their pockets from their work at kelp or the linen industry, or sent home by the men in Hudson Bay, and any spare money was quickly converted into smart apparel. It was the ministers who were best placed to see their congregations dressed in their Sunday best, and to comment on the fashions of the day. The observant eye of the Reverend George Low noticed the vanity of Orcadians in matters of dress. *The Gentry, and indeed all except the poorest sort,* he wrote in the 1770s, *do not content themselves with homespun but love to go very fine, and indeed here broadcloths, silks, velvets, cambricks, laces and other fineries are much more used than even in the richest shires of Scotland, in these articles our better sort of people affect to follow the fashions of their southern countrymen and often in these outdo them, without* [Low added wryly] *having their funds to support them.*[64]

Despite the wretched condition of the kirks – many of them semi-derelict by the late 18th century – Sundays were still an

173

occasion to dress up. Again it was George Low (an artist and naturalist as well as a minister) who painted a delightful picture of his Birsay congregation on their way to the kirk. *When I first came to the parish, there was not a piece of English cloth to be seen on a man's back; no figured waistcoats or velvet breeches; their stockings made of their own wool, their shoes of their own leather, tied with good strong sufficient points: Now the case differs; the young fellows, instead of bonnets, almost all wear hats; upon Sunday, a suit of decent S. country clothes, with cotton waistcoats, and corduroy breeches ... The women, on Sundays or holidays, come out neatly dressed in calicoes, calimancoes, or neat stuffs, with grey or brown cloaks, scarlet cloaks and a great number of beautiful scarlet plaids; their linen fine, clean and neat. The reason of the superior finery of late among the young people ... they have a good part of their own earning to themselves ... new methods of earning are daily occurring, and the price of their annual labour produces much more than it did 20 years ago. The old men and women are just in the style of their forefathers ... they still continue to wear good strong black clothes without dying ...*[65]

There is plenty of evidence that the Birsay folk were not atypical in the priority they gave to dress. Only a few years earlier, an elderly widow had died in Holm and her possessions had been auctioned off to pay her debts. The inventory of the wardrobe contained in Margaret Vedder's modest two-room home is astonishing:

One calico gown	10	6	
One tartan do	4	1	
One silk & worsted do	9	4	
do green do	6	6	
do Black & Orange do	6	0	
do Red & Blue do	6	1	
do Black & White			
Stamp'd Morning do	1	6	
+ 5 petticoats, quilted and woollen			
1 Scarlet Plaid	8	1	
1 Brown Cloak	11	9	
1 Blue Cloak	4	0	
+ 3 Linnen Aprons			
Total	£4	4	4

On what glamorous festive occasions did Margaret and her neighbours, living in poverty in the most basic housing conditions, require a Stamp'd Morning gown in order to receive visitors, or sally forth from their damp and sooty cottages in Tartan or Black and Orange silks? It must have been a glorious sight. The valuation of this finery, in comparison to the money she owed, is also thought-provoking. Sheena Wenham comments: *The range of clothes suggests that an extraordinary emphasis was placed upon fashion in a society where the housing was still primitive and the living precarious ... The proceeds from the sale of this flamboyant wardrobe would have paid Margaret Vedder's rent and bere multures for a quarter of a century, a second hand value which would seem inflated even to the customer of a Paris fashion house.*[66]

There is no reason to imagine that the folk in other parishes would have looked very different, or that their young women would not have walked out on Sundays in calimancoes and clean linen, and taken sly looks under their bonnets to see if they were making an appropriate impression on the young men in their cotton waistcoats and corduroy breeches.

From comments by 19th-century writers we know that fashionable clothes continued to be a priority for Orkney men and women. James Anderson, the Orphir minister, wrote disapprovingly in 1841: *There is a propensity among the young of both sexes to extravagance in dress. Umbrellas are in general use.*[67] Daniel Gorrie, visiting the islands in 1868, noticed that *the reign of fashion extends to the remotest islands, and crinoline is worn in its season by the daughters of Papa Westray.* He was also surprised by the incongruity between the standard of housing, which remained primitive at best for most of the population, and their clothing. *Some, who seem to care least about the condition of their dwelling houses, are very attentive to matters of dress, and rig out their families in Sunday finery. The visitor need not be surprised to see ample skirts and dainty hats, adorned with red and white feathers, emerging from the craziest cots, as he wends his way to the unpretending island kirks. The white woollen coverings for the head and shoulders ... still generally worn by grave and staid matrons, are now quite discarded by their young gipsies of daughters.*[68]

Figure 4.10
Un effet de crinoline au bord de la mer, lithograph by Honore Daumier 1857.
(Metropolitan Museum of Art, Wikimedia Commons)

As at all times and places, the girls loved to cut a sartorial dash. 18-year-old Anne Watters, a house-servant in Kirkwall, evidently did not receive enough education to inhibit her delightfully idiosyncratic spelling but she could afford to travel to Edinburgh and Glasgow, Dundee and Stirling *geten the fitthens of the bonnetes and the dresses*, as she wrote to her sweetheart Henry Horne, who went to Hudson's Bay in 1850. It is possible that she was working as a seamstress *up in the garret* and some of the purchased bonnets and dresses were intended for customers at home, but some were certainly for her own adornment. *You wold not know me now I ame so altered from what I wase*, she teased poor Henry, *i now sportes the veale and parsole and A gensen coulerd silk dres.*[69] I am not sure what colour her silk dress was [gentian?], but I love the image of Anne, consoling herself for the separation from her

176

Henry with a shopping trip to buy fashionable clothes. Henry came home early from the Bay in 1851, working his passage as a sailor, and the couple were married in 1852 and left Orkney. I hope that, wherever they went, Anne sometimes had the opportunity to sport her veil and parasol.

Chapter 4

1. William Balfour had also advanced 100 guineas to the Jacobite troops in Kirkwall on behalf of the North Isles lairds, Fereday 1980, 76. The lairds' Jacobite sympathies had rather more to do with enmity to their oppressive feudal superior, the pro-Hanoverian Earl of Morton, than with which king sat on the throne in London. The lairds who shared William's refuges in Westray were Archibald Stewart of Brugh (Westray), John Traill of Elsness (Sanday) and John Traill of Westness (Rousay).
2. Letter from William Balfour, Edinburgh to Elizabeth Balfour, Westray 1759, OLA D2/18/13.
3. Letter from Elizabeth Balfour, Westray to Thomas Balfour, Banff 3/9/1795, OLA D2/6/8.
4. Webster's Census of 1755 enumerated a total population of 23,381 in Orkney.
5. Letter from Thomas Traill, Papay to Elizabeth Balfour, Westray 4/6/1770, OLA D2/9/1.
6. MacGillivray 68-9.
7. Letter from William Balfour, Kirkwall to Elizabeth Balfour, Westray 14/5/1766, OLA D2/15/18; Fereday 1990, 23.
8. Letter from William Balfour, Edinburgh to Elizabeth Balfour, Westray 10/10/1767, OLA D2/12/19. Sadly this lurid piece of gossip is untrue, though the Hanoverian princes were frequently involved in scandals.
9. Letter from John Traill of Westness to Thomas Balfour 11/4/1778, OLA D2/5/3.
10. Letter from Peggy Balfour, Cobham to Elizabeth Balfour, Westray 15/4/1778, OLA D2/9/1.
11. James Fea of Clestran had actively assisted Prince Charles and the rebels. He was in hiding and his wife, Lady Janet Buchanan, was in their house of Sound when it was attacked by government troops in May 1746 and burnt to the ground. See Fereday 1980, ch.9.
12. Letter from William Balfour, Shetland, to Elizabeth Balfour, Westray 24/10/1782, OLA D2/19/8.
13. Letter from William Balfour, Shetland to Elizabeth Balfour, Westray 7/11/1782, OLA D2/19/8.
14. MacGillivray 69.
15. OSA (Shapinsay) 358-9.
16. '... the first Scotch fencibles were promised that their duty would be confined to Scotland unless the French invaded England. This geographical restriction was so inconvenient to the War Office that all later fencible regiments were raised ... to serve anywhere in the British Isles.' Fereday 1990, 144.
17. Letter from Frances Balfour, Shapinsay to Thomas Balfour, Ireland 4/12/1796, OLA D2/6/8.
18. Letter from Frances Balfour to Mary Craigie 3/1794, OLA D2/14/19. A letter from William Manson to his son William Manson jnr confirmed the tragic loss of the *Swift* with all its crew, and contained the news that the *Pomona* was also wrecked, 30/4/1794, O LA D2/34/16.
19. Letter from Frances Balfour, Shapinsay to Thomas Balfour, Ireland 12/1796, OLA D2/6/8.
20. Account from Robert Bayne, merchant, Leith to Frances Balfour 31/12/1802, OLA D2/ADDL/24. The yarn was probably flax for weaving linen.
21. Letter from Mary Craigie, Rousay to David Balfour, Edinburgh 31/5/1803, OLA D2/19/18.
22. Letter from Frances Balfour, Kirkwall to William Balfour, Shapinsay 25/4/1807, OLA D2/14/21.
23. Letter from Peggy Balfour, Cobham to Elizabeth Balfour, Westray, winter 1777/78, OLA D2/8/23. Thomas Traill of Tirlet was laird of another small estate in Westray.
24. Notebook of Frances Balfour, OLA D2/7/3.
25. Letter from Edward Ligonier, Cobham to Thomas Balfour 31/7/1776, OLA D2/4/12.

26   Letters from Lady Ligonier (later Lady Wentworth) to Frances Balfour OLA D2/23/10.
27   Letter from William Balfour to Samuel Mitchelson, Edinburgh 5/7/1773, OLA D2/15/18.
28   Letter from William Balfour, Edinburgh to Thomas Balfour of Huip 1786, OLA D2/23/4.
29   Frances Balfour, *Some Trifling Originals and some Selections written for the Amusement of a solitary hour*, OLA D2/119.
30   Letter from Edward Ligonier, Cobham to Frances Balfour, Burray 6/12/1778, OLA D2/4/12.
31   Letter from Frances Balfour to Elizabeth Balfour 1791, OLA D2/20/22.
32   Notebook of Frances Balfour OLA D2/7/3.
33   Letter from Edward Ligonier, Cobham to Frances Balfour, Burray 12/12/1781, OLA D2/4/12.
34   ibid.
35   Letter from Frances Balfour to Thomas Balfour c.1790, OLA D2/18/13.
36   Draft letter from Frances Balfour, Shapinsay to John Balfour c.1790, OLA D2/18/13.
37   Letter from Frances Balfour, Shapinsay to Thomas Balfour, Ireland 19/2/1797, OLA D2/6/8.
38   Letter from Frances Balfour, Shapinsay to Thomas Balfour, Ireland 1796, OLA D2/6/8.
39   Ligonier's wife Mary remarried after his death, to Lord Wentworth; she remained a loyal friend to Frances and her family.
40   Letter from Mary Montgomery to Frances Balfour 8/1799, OLA D2/27/11.
41   Letter from Frances Balfour to David Balfour, Edinburgh 1800, OLA D2/27/11.
42   Postilion, usually a liveried groom riding one of a team of carriage horses.
43   Letter from Frances Balfour to David Balfour, Edinburgh 1800, OLA D2/27/11.
44   Letter from Charlotte Clifford to Frances Balfour 1/10/1808, OLA D2/27/2.
45   John Balfour was Trustee of this fund which continued to be paid after her marriage, for in 1834 Charlotte asks John to pay the money from the fund to her daughter after her death. Letter from Charlotte Jones, Dublin to John Balfour, London 1834, OLA D2/23.
46   Copy letter from Frances Balfour to Mary Brunton 12/1801, OLA D2/ 53/20.
47   Letter from Frances Balfour to William Balfour 14/07/1805, OLA D2/7/3.
48   Letter from Frances Balfour to William Balfour 20/10/1803, OLA D2/5/6.
49   Letter from Marion Balfour, Edinburgh to Frances Balfour, Shapinsay 1/5/1801, OLA D2/ADDL/24. The names mentioned are hard to read and I have guessed at the spelling. Unfortunately I have been unable to verify any of these events. Trying to trace them, I noticed that the Duke of Manchester's wife, Lady Susan Gordon (the mother of eight children) caused a social scandal a few years later than this letter by eloping with one of her footmen. Penelope Ligonier came to mind. Marion Balfour would have loved the gossip.
50   OSA (Sandwick and Stromness) 113.
51   NSA (Stromness) 37.
52   Letter from Christian Robertson, Stromness to William and Nicol Leith, Stenness 2/10/1808, Robertson family; letter from Christian Robertson, Stromness to William and Nicol Leith, Stenness 17/10/08, Leith family.
53   Letter from Christian Robertson, Stromness to William and Nicol Leith 28/1/1810, Leith family.
54   Letter from Christian Robertson, Stromness to William Watt, Skaill 30/9/1809, OLA D3/27.
55   Letter from Joshua Clouston, London to Peter Leith, Stenness 4/1817, Leith family.
56   Wilson 222.
57   Printed report by Robert Stevenson, CE sent to Mrs Robertson & Son, Shipbrokers in Orkney 1817, OLA D2/36/1.
58   Lady Login 1890, 5 quoting Rev. William Login.
59   Beattie and Buss 103-115.
60   Letter from Margaret Humphreys, Stromness to Charles Humphreys 1837,

        Beattie and Buss 105.
61   ibid.
62   Wilson 142, quoting Testimonial from passengers on *SS Warwick* to Capt. James
        Skinner.
63   *The Orcadian Book of the 20th Century* vol.II (Kirkwall 2010), compiled by Howard
        Hazell, 49; DeLille Diament, pers.comm.
64   Low 1773, 53.
65   OSA (Birsay) 159-160.
66   Wenham 1996-7, 130-131.
67   NSA (Orphir) 20.
68   Gorrie 18, 327.
69   Letter from Anne Waters, Kirkwall to Henry Horne, Hudson's Bay 9/7/1850,
        Beattie and Buss 381-2. In the 1851 census Anne Waters is living in Main Street,
        Kirkwall, occupation house servant, with 90 year old Henrietta Moodie,
        annuitant teacher.

CHAPTER 5

Young Farstraers

Prologue

Growing up in the 18th century was a precarious business. Disease was endemic and no respecter of class and infant mortality was very high, even among the better off. In 1778 Barbara Baikie wrote to Elizabeth Balfour thanking her for sending some meal when her own crops had failed, and apologized for the lateness of her letter: 'but I had other work on hand. The fever came to us; poor Jamie was removed, but Jackie spared – and nothwithstanding of my great fatigue was safely delivered of a lovely daughter.'[1] Children were born and died, life had to go on.

For those who survived infancy, childhood was short. The children of the poor were working with their parents on their little farms or at their trades almost as soon as they could toddle, and farm- or house-servants before they reached their teens. The emigrant ships that left Kirkwall for Georgia carried whole families with children and unaccompanied boys as young as ten. Colonel Balfour's list of recruits to his Fencible regiment includes drummer boys aged 11. (We will pass over his six-month-old relative added to the payroll). The more fortunate could expect to be apprenticed to a trade or craft at 13 or 14, or sent to sea on a merchant ship like William Manson.

Even for the gentry, changing fashions had the effect of pushing children far from the islands at an early age. The lairds were increasingly distancing themselves from Orkney, desperate to get their sons out of what they saw as a dead-end into the world of opportunity, represented by Edinburgh or even the south of England. A Kirkwall education was considered quite good enough for Thomas Balfour and his brothers, born in the mid 18th century. A generation later, however, Thomas sent his own sons to a school in the far south of England, to ensure that Orkney was ironed out of their speech and they made the 'right connections'. The public school, with its rigorous timetable of Latin eight hours a day, was itself only a short stage before the boys were thrown into the adult world.

William Balfour went straight into battle at 13 as a midshipman in the Royal Navy.

The girls of the landed families were also more likely to be sent away to boarding school – even abroad – by the late 18th century, their education 'finishing' them at a much older age with social accomplishments like music and dancing as well as academic subjects. Little girls were not spared what we would consider a rigorous education from the age of four, as we can learn from Proud Parent letters between members of the Manson family.

For the young Billy Manson, born on board a fever-ridden emigrant ship and spending his first years in a country harrowed by war, his short life was a far-straying one with all the ingredients of tragedy. Deserted by his mother when he was three, crossing the Atlantic again and separated from his older sister at six, virtually abandoned in a boarding school by a father who had shifted all his attention to a new marriage and family, he died of fever in Antigua before he was 20.

Balfour Bairns

By the late 1700s the increase in money coming into the islands, from trade and from the many men working abroad, was generally improving the standard of living in Orkney. There were other signs of significant social change. Since the Union of 1707, Scots gentry had increasingly sought to improve their status by adopting English ways of speech, thought and dress. As the upper-crust of Orkney society became wealthier, they tended to disparage and distance themselves from Orkney, and even from Scotland, following their peers in the rest of country in believing that 'anglicizing' was the only way to 'get on' in the world.

We can see the change in language in their letters. William Balfour senior had a fine family of bairns; his sons had children. William was ambitious for his three boys: they were educated in Kirkwall and then sent to a tutor in Caithness to prepare them for Aberdeen University. *This agreeing with my own sentiments and yours,* he wrote to Elizabeth from Dunnet, *though I know it shall be censured by some people who will think the Scheme of a Colledge Education an unnecessary and extravagant Expence in my circumstances.*[2] Despite the strain on William's purse, his oldest sons John and Thomas were sent to Aberdeen in 1766 at the age of 14 and 16 respectively and the youngest, David, soon followed.

It would be interesting to know more about their university education. Thomas wrote to his father that he was being taught algebra and geometry and 'chronology'. His medical studies were sometimes enlivened by disturbance in the anatomy classes. *A few days ago the Doctors were mobed on account of a body they had got to dissect, which came to such a hight that they fired small shot on both sides and Mr William Sinclair received a good deal of shot in the hat and was a good deal hurt by stones (but had no bones broke so that at present he is very well) but it was soon quelled upon the doctors giving up the body.*[3] One can imagine Tom thoroughly enjoying the fracas.

William must have been proud of his sons' achievements: David becoming a lawyer, John entering the India East Company as a 'writer' and rising to high status and fortune, Thomas graduating in medicine. In comparison to Tom's sons, they seem to have had remarkably carefree teenage years. David started his apprenticeship as a lawyer at 16; John and Tom were still students in Edinburgh when they were nearly 20. By the time that Tom's own children were born, however, it seems that a Scottish education was no longer thought good enough. This was less to do with academic standards than with a wish to remove the influence of the Scots Kirk and to rub off what was now considered as embarrassing Scots accents and manners. An English education, with the opportunity for boys to make the 'right' contacts, was now considered essential, and Harrow, with its many links to the landed gentry, was the school preferred by many Scots lairds.

Tom's little boys were tutored at Elwick Lodge on Shapinsay by the Reverend Robert Yule at first, but when Edward was ten years old and William nine their father took them on the long journey to the south of England to settle them in a preparatory school in Walthamstow (now in north-east London). It's hard to imagine that they were not bewildered at the radical change and homesick, and it is unlikely that they would have been able to come home in holidays. *Hasten on things at Harrow School for your boys*, wrote Frances to Thomas when he was in London in the spring of 1793, *I suspect they will make no useful friendship at Walthamstow.*[4] At both schools the boys' educational diet consisted almost exclusively of Latin, eight hours a day. In large copy-book handwriting, 11-year-old Edward wrote home from Walthamstow: *Hon'd Father ... I am at the 31st book of Justin and the 2nd book of Ovid ... your most dutyful and affectionate son JE Lig. Balfour.*[5] Later, at Harrow: *during the day we do Ovid by turns ... On Sunday we do Latin testament.* A grasp of the language, literature and politics of the Roman Republic and Empire seems to have been the only learning thought necessary before the boys were hurled into their military careers in their early teens. Tom and Frances seem to have never considered giving their sons a university education.

Figure 5.1
Harrow School, with several classes being taught in one schoolroom, 1816. (Mary Evans Picture Library)

Even Mary was sent away at the age of nine for six years, to a boarding school in Edinburgh, to be schooled in music, French and Italian, which she had already learned from her mother, and cooking, which she probably had not. Frances *had been trained rather to the accomplishments which adorn a court, than to those which are useful in domestic life* as her son-in-law observed rather acidly.'[6] The Balfours clearly had an eye to Mary 'coming out' in a wider and more sophisticated society than Orkney. Mary at least had her uncle David and aunt and cousins in Edinburgh, who presumably provided some family life in between terms.

It is interesting to compare her education with that of her female cousins who were a generation older. The daughters of both William Balfour of Trenaby and his brother Thomas Balfour of Huip were sent to a dame school in Kirkwall run by a Miss Chrystie, where they were taught to sew so they could make their brothers' shirts and their own stockings and to embroider the inevitable sampler. Thomas' daughters were then sent to a convent school in Liège, the two older girls making the two-week journey by brig in 1777. *We read French with Arithmetic and play on the Harpsichord every day according to your desires,* wrote Elizabeth to her father, *we are to begin Geography after Christmas which will be very agreeable to us both.* At merchant Balfour's request, book-keeping was added to the curriculum.[7]

When she was 15 the youngest daughter Ann joined her sisters. Girls were allowed to address their parents more informally than boys and instead of *Honoured Father* she begins her letter *My Dear Papa ... I can't express my gratitude to you, for sending me where I have the Opportunity of learning everything necessary to render my Education compleat, and beg Dear Papa you will be persuaded that I will use all possible Endeavours, to make good use of the advantages afforded me for my improvement. There is nothing I find so entertaining as Geography, but the names of the Places are very hard to me ... I should be very glad if you would give me leave to learn to sing. I learn to play upon the Harpsichord and to Dance, and shall by my application to every Duty strive to repay yours and my friends solicitude for my good ... And I am, My Dear Papa your most dutiful and affectionate child Ann Balfour.*[8]

Despite the submissive language in the letters, daughters were not always dutiful. Mary Balfour, writing to their father to beg him not to send them to a boarding [finishing] school, sounds as meek as the sternest patriarch could wish ... *our Religion teaches us that a strict obedience to a Parents' commands shou'd overcome any avertion how great so ever ...*[9] However, it seems that a motivation for sending the girls to the convent was Thomas' anxiety at reports of Mary's wayward behaviour. In 1775 he wrote to his niece Elizabeth: *I observe by a letter from yr mother to Miss Chrystie that my Mary does not please her – I know not what to say about her or doe with her ... I intreat that you your Mother and Sisters will let me know the worst so I may doe all that now can be done for her reformation.*[10]

It was his sister-in-law Elizabeth Balfour of Trenaby who cared for his daughters after their mother's early death, but it was not a happy arrangement for the girls. From Liège, they wrote that Mrs Balfour was so mean with their allowance that they could not afford new clothes. *Mrs Balfour sounded very angry the last letter we had from her concerning our expences ... we have been in such Rags this last 3 months that we were ashamed to go into the choir amongst the nuns ... and we cannot buy Gowns and Petticoats such as we need ... Your ever Dutifull Daughters Elizabeth and Mary Balfour.*[11] We do not know what 'the worst' was but it seems hardly surprising to us if the 14-year-old girl, orphaned young and left in the care of an aunt who was perhaps ungenerous with both affection and money, became bored with sewing endless white seams with Miss Chrystie and rebelled. Despite Mary's teenage indiscretions, and then her wish to convert to Catholicism (a fairly predictable outcome of being sent to a convent school), a few years later she made an eminently acceptable marriage to one of the wealthiest Orkney lairds, Robert Baikie of Tankerness.

The Trenaby boys were not left in the Harrow schoolroom for long before they were considered ready for the professions chosen for them. The high-spirited and irrepressible Edward was destined for the army. He had been nominally an ensign in his father's regiment of Orkney and Shetland Fencibles since he was 14 and barely big enough for the duty. *Pray ask Mr Craigie if it is unprecedented to carry the colours on a wheelbarrow,* Frances wrote to her sister-in-law Mary Craigie, *for without some such assistance, I suspect he will not be able to carry them at all.*[12] At the age of 15½ his uncle John Balfour purchased him a commission and he was released from the Fourth Form into the captaincy of a regiment. Before he could see action, however, his classical studies were to be continued in Edinburgh where he was staying with his uncle David. Thomas had written a curriculum. *In addition to the elements of Mathematics, I wd wish that he be employed an hour or two daily in reading Greek and Latin with a good scholar – and one hour with a drill sergeant, who can instruct him in the Manual Exercise.*[13] However, judging from 'Injured Father' letters from Thomas to young Edward, it is evident that the teenager was enjoying a riotous time in the capital in disreputable company rather than studying Greek and Latin.[14]

Edward's very brief military career we will follow later in Ireland, where Thomas and quiet, scholarly Alexander Brunton, assigned the thankless task of being regimental chaplain and Edward's tutor, failed to keep *poor giddy Edward* out of scrapes and mischief.

William's dispatch into adult life was even more precipitate. At the age of 13, armed with the *Metamorphoses* and a dexterity in wielding Latin conjugations, he was appointed a midshipman on a naval frigate.[15] It is hard not to feel sorry for William, pushed into the notoriously brutal Royal Navy in war time, homesick and for a long time suffering from an unspecified illness, possibly a stress-related stomach condition. When he was not yet 15 he was serving on the *Irresistible,* one of the Channel fleet struggling against severe gales to blockade the French fleet in the port of Brest. Perpetually cold, wet and bullied, it is not surprising that he begged his father to be allowed to change his career. Thomas, at this time commanding a regiment in Ireland but enjoying the comforts of Dublin and his mistress while his officers were quartered in primitive hovels, wrote him a long letter sternly admonishing him to cheerfully endure the drawbacks of his profession.[16]

Figure 5.2
The Victory raking the Spanish Salvador del Mundi at the battle of Cape St Vincent, 14 February,1797. Painting by Robert Cleveley, 1798. William Balfour, a 15-year-old midshipman, was serving on HMS Irresistible in this battle. (National Maritime Museum, Greenwich, London)

William, *whose hardships are soon legend,*[17] in fact did well in the navy. His career was no sinecure such as his father had held. Britain was at war with France all the time he was in the service and he had experienced a large slice of both the ennui of blockades and the terror of naval battles, and been wounded twice, by the time he came of age. When he was 23 he was able to write home proudly with news of his early promotion. *The Admiralty have promoted me from 3rd Lt of the Amethyst to first of the Cleopatra a fine frigate. As I believe I am the youngest Lt who was ever apptd to a similar situation their Lordships approbation of my conduct is apparent.*

However, even in his success, William was wistfully thinking of domestic comforts rather than military glory. *I heard from Mrs Br[unton] some days ago ... Marriage has succeeded so well with her that I believe I shall try it myself in a day or two. Have you a good natured girl of your acquaintance – I except Miss Sinclair – who you could persuade to have me? If not I must bring a Wife , a Billiard Table and a Boat down with me when I come.* [18] Frances' reply was characteristic of her slightly acid wit. *Let it not raise your vanity if I tell you I believe you may throw your handkerchief at any Orkney belles. Men are scarce a competence still more scarce and a gentleman the scarcest of the 3.*[19]

In February 1805, Lieutenant Balfour was sailing home from the West Indies when *Cleopatra* sighted a larger French frigate, *La Ville de Milan,* chased her for 180 miles and engaged her off Bermuda. William did not spare his mother the details. *Our action was excessively warm,* he wrote to her afterwards, *almost every man on the quarter deck was wounded or killed.*[20] Both ships were badly damaged in the encounter and *Cleopatra* was finally forced to surrender, but she was recaptured by another British ship only two days later and the crew freed.[21] *He carried on the duty with great zeal as becoming a good officer,* wrote his captain, Sir Robert Laurie, *and at the action with the French Frigate La Ville de Milan he conducted himself with gallantry and spirit very much to my satisfaction.*[22]

A few months later, William was given his own command, the HMS *Bermuda,* to patrol the St Lawrence river, the coasts of Nova Scotia and Cape Breton and around the island of Bermuda. However, he was never enthusiastic about his career. In his letters home, his thoughts were always turning to Orkney, settling down and finding a wife. Uncle John Balfour's reaction was uncompromising. *If you resign your Commission you are afterwards without business, without pursuit, and in society but an Orkney Laird, which out of Orkney is to be nothing.*[23] William was not to be deterred. He came home on leave and threw his handkerchief no further than his first cousin Mary Manson, whom he married in August 1806.[24] John remained implacable in his opposition, his attitude to the islands of his birth closely echoing his father's when the future of himself and his brothers was under discussion. Only a month before the wedding he was writing: *This marriage will fix you in Orkney, which affords no suitable pursuits for a gentleman, where you must be idle, or uselessly employed, and where no young man of spirits ought to sit down.*[25]

Despite the family opposition, William retired from the navy in 1808 and settled down happily as landowner of a considerable Orkney estate and father of a large family. Mary died in 1820 shortly after the birth of her eighth child. Three years later William married his other cousin, Mary Baikie Craigie, (the adopted daughter of his adored aunt Mary Craigie) and they had another seven children.[26]

Figure 5.3
Lieutenant William Balfour's ship HMS Cleopatra

Betsy and Billy

We have seen William Manson's voyages take him many times round the world in the 30 years between leaving Kirkwall as a teenager and returning there for a comfortable retirement. What happened to his children after the mysterious disappearance of his first wife: the little girl who accompanied him on the ill-fated expedition to Georgia and back again, and the baby born on that appalling outward voyage in 1775? After their return from America, Betsy was left in London and Billy sent to a boarding school in Yorkshire. With Manson's marriage to Elizabeth Balfour, a great many letters to and from members of the Manson family found their way into the Balfour archive. Among them are poignant letters from William Manson's sadly neglected children and it is possible to follow young Billy through his lonely school years and the beginnings of his life as a mariner. A life, like so many 18th-century lives, cut tragically short.

Billy entered the world in the cramped cabin of a fever-ridden ship, as she battled her way through a stormy Atlantic on the last stages of a 14 week voyage between Britain and Georgia. It had been a horrible journey, several children had died and the conditions in which Margaret Manson gave birth must have been ghastly. However, she and her son survived and in December 1775 Billy was carried off the stinking *Georgia Packet* and into the port of Savannah with his parents, nine-year-old sister Betsy, a couple of aunts and an uncle.

Something of what the family went through over the next six years has already been told. The plantation that William had purchased in order to found a Quaker settlement – the Promised Land for the emigrants – had become a war zone and Billy's infancy was punctuated by episodes of being snatched up by one or other of his adult relations as they fled attacks by native

Americans or enemy soldiers. There cannot have been many peaceful family moments even when they were living in relative safety. The Manson's marriage was one of the casualties of war and fell apart under the strain. When Billy was three his mother disappeared, abandoning her husband and children. He never saw her again.

We lose sight of the family for a while, as the tide of war ebbed and flowed across the country and William tried to salvage something of his wrecked dream, but the situation grew so dangerous that eventually he decided to take the risk of returning to England. This was hardly an easy choice: with Britain and America at war, a ship crossing the Atlantic faced the hazard of being attacked or captured by enemy shipping, but in 1781 the Mansons arrived safely back in London. William had lost all the money he had invested in Georgia and urgently needed to find employment to support his family.

By February 1782 he had found a post as store-keeper to an agent supplying the plantations in Jamaica. A mundane job for an ambitious sea-captain, but it paid his children's school fees and soon he would be at sea again, skippering cargo ships taking coals and iron to Jamaica and hogsheads of sugar back to England for a wealthy plantation-owner, Simon Taylor. Letters between him and Taylor show how often his journeys were badly delayed by bad weather and his anxiety that he would be 'ruined' in consequence.[27] He was kicking his heels at Mrs Campbell's Lodging-House in Kingston, Jamaica, when he received a kind note from William Sutherland who was the overseer on the Blue Mountain Estate. *I have sent Trim* [presumably a slave] *with a Horse and Mule to attend upon you. I am very glad that you are now ready to sail. Perseverance will get the better of all difficulties.*[28]

Meanwhile Manson's children had been settled in boarding schools. *I have one great Consolation*, William wrote to his ex-mother-in-law Dinah Jackson, *that my daughter Betsy is grown up a woman, and is very Promising and Dutiful is at a boarding school near London and my son William is a fine strong boy about 6 years of age, he is also at Boarding school near London – Betsy is now turned 15 … In case of my Death, or being taken Prisoner by the Enemy, I hope thou will not neglect thy Grandchildren, poor Dear Creatures they cannot help what has happened.*[29]

Boarding school in a strange land seems a lonely destination for a little boy of six, but 18th-century children were expected to grow up quickly and little sentiment was wasted on them. His children bestowed in England, William returned to Kirkwall for good in 1787, married Elizabeth Balfour and settled into a comfortable domestic existence. His letters to his son and daughter are full of stern parental admonitions, pious hopes, and criticisms of the infrequency of their letters or their spelling but, despite protestations of affection, William seems to have paid them cruelly little attention. He did not even bother to inform them of his intended marriage and the hurt is too evident in a letter written by the ever-dutiful Betsy after she had heard the news and was *surprised to find that he had gone to Kirkwall and much more so when she knew his errand as he never did me the favor of mentioning it in the most distant manner which I marvel as he has taught me to believe for some time past that he looked upon me rather as a companion and one capable of sharing his confidence than merely as a Child.*[30]

Figure 5.4
Ackworth School, founded in 1779 for children of the Society of Friends.

Betsy spent the rest of her life working in a Quaker school in Wandsworth, a poor dependant. Billy was moved to the newly-opened Quaker school at Ackworth in Yorkshire, from where he wrote brief and totally uninformative letters to the father he rarely saw.[31] *Honoured Parents, It being the usual Time the Boys write Letters, I am now sat down just to inform you that I am favoured with good Health, a Blessing which I hope you are Partakers of. I should be pleased if you would send me a few lines as soon as you can make it convenient*

195

informing me of your Welfare. Having Nothing more to add at present but Duty to you, Grandmother, Uncles & Aunts and dear Love to Sisters, I conclude and remain your dutiful Son William Manson.[32]

Identical letters were written at the 'usual time', around every three or four months, in the following years. His father's letters were far less frequent and composed entirely of commands to Billy to improve his behaviour/writing/spelling, so it is not surprising that the boy's letters were uncommunicative. *Dear Father! Notwithstanding I have received no letter from thee since last year, yet it being the usual Time the Boys write Letters to their Parents ...* It is a bleak picture of teenage Billy seated at his desk, brow furrowed in concentration as he painstakingly penned his few lines in a large careful hand. We know nothing else of his life at Ackworth, there is no mention of holidays or visitors. It is unlikely that he saw any of his relations: one grandmother lived at a considerable distance in north Yorkshire, the other much further away in Kirkwall. Aunts and uncles were scattered far and wide, Betsy – who had been the only constant in his turbulent American childhood – was in London, struggling to live on the pittance she received from the school.

When William was given the post of Comptroller of Customs in Kirkwall, an undemanding post with a comfortable salary, Betsy's hopes were raised that he might finally remember her straitened circumstances. *I rejoice at thy new appointment and trust it will make thee to do something for me and my dear Brother, although my situation at Wandsworth is as agreeable as I can expect ...* [a] *dependant one has many disagreeables as well as uncertainty.* [33]

Sadly for poor Betsy, her father was too absorbed in enjoying the relative affluence that had come his way after his hardships in Georgia – his new wife had brought influential in-laws as well as domestic comforts and a baby daughter – to give thought let alone money to his older children. Betsy was embarrassed by demands for payment of Billy's school fees, her inability to pay for her own medical treatment, or even to dress suitably for her employment. *If my dear Father would send me a few pounds this spring it would be very acceptable as I want several things I shall not be able other ways to get, people in my situation are expected to make a genteel appearance neither gay nor plain.*[34] Evidently the few pounds never came, 17 months later Betsy was writing: *I am much disappointed at not receiving a trifle from thee,* and money promised to her by her Whitby grandmother seems also to have been indefinitely delayed.[35] On her cheerless 25th birthday she wrote to her father again. *This being the anniversary of my Natal day thou hast been much in my thoughts ... Pray hast thou heard anything of our Legacy since I heard last from thee, Cash runs very low with me father.*

While Billy took refuge in characteristically teenage non-communication, Betsy wrote at heart-rending length of her grief. *As it is my lot to be placed so far from you, letters frequently would in some sort make me forget the distance between us, but as I so seldom hear from you I am ready to conclude at times I am forgotten tho I trust this is not the case at the Idea I feel sensations too painful to be described.* Always her letters are full of expressions of devotion to her father and affection for the stepmother and little stepsister she was never allowed to meet. *Mary must by this time be very ingaging. I cannot express how much I want to see her, my Mother, Grandmother etc and of course most of all thyself.* [36] Only on occasional visits to her kind uncle Thomas Manson and his wife, busy running an insurance and merchant business and raising an ever-increasing brood of children in another part of London, did Betsy see family life at all.[37]

Meanwhile Billy in Ackworth was now 15 and, not having heard from his father for eight months, was wondering what plans had been made for his future. *I should be glad to receive a letter from thee, informing whether I am to go to London or the Orcades when my time expires, and by what Conveyance.* Like many school-leavers, Billy at first could not think what Trade he wanted to pursue, but he plucked up the courage to write to William that *[I] have since thought if it please thee [I] should like to be a Shop Keeper in London.*[38] His father had other ideas; instructions arrived that Billy should be forwarded via Darlington to Stockton, where an acquaintance would find a captain to take him in his care for the voyage to Kirkwall. At last he was to see Orkney, his father's homeland, and meet all the relations to whom he had been sending his 'best respects' for many years but never seen.

As there was no need for letters during the Kirkwall years, we lose sight of Billy. Presumably his father intended him to have 'work experience' on local boats until he was deemed ready to follow in his footsteps and start a serious apprenticeship as a ship's officer. We can hope it was a cheerful time for him in comparison to the bleak years in boarding school, and we know that he made friends among other young men crewing the many small trading vessels owned by Orkney's merchant lairds. Someone, probably his step-mother, Elizabeth Balfour, was concerned enough to draw up a list of clothing and equipment that should be packed in a sea-chest for the young William Manson when he left home for London.

Kirkwall Sept 8th 1792

Put in Mr Manson's Chest the Following Articles, Viz:

8 white shirts
6 check Do
6 pair linen Do
6 doz Woollen) Stockings
1 Pair cotton)
1 Green Great Coat
1 Brown close do
3 Waistcoats 3 pairs Breeches
3 pairs shoes 1 pair buckles
2 Silk Handkerchiefs 2 Cravats
3 Pair Worsted Mittens
5 Pocket Handkerchiefs

The following page lists further items which must be purchased. It is likely that Billy was despatched to his uncle Thomas in London so that he could be fitted out with the rest of his clothes and equipment before his ship was ready to sail.

To buy for Wm Manson at London and may be had cheapest, &
most suitable, at a slop shop [where ready-made clothes sold]
in Wapping

2 outside duffle jackets, lined in the body and sleeves with blue
Flannel at about 10/- to 12/ shillings each with horn buttons

2 Pair Canvas long trousers about 2/6 or 3/-
1 Pair blue Baize trousers do - ------------5/-
3 pair Woollen drawers at 2/- to 2/6
2 Under Waistcoats with sleeves 5/- to 6/-
Not lined & horn Buttons
1 Hammock bed of Flock)
2 Blankets and a Rug) @ 18/- to 21/-
1 pair Block Tin [i.e. solid tin not plate] *Buckles with Brass*
Chapes and Tongues @ 1/6
2 Sailors Frocks of Canvas to wear over all about 2/6 to 3/- each
1 French Grammar and Dictionary to be got second hand, and
any other small books he may chuse
One navigation book of Hamilton Moor's that has all tables used
in keeping a Ship's way at sea etc[39]
It is needless to buy a Quadrant for him the 1st Voyage, nor
Sea Charts. If Wm meets with John Paterson it will be
fortunate as he will know best what Things are most Necessary
for him either of Cloathing or other Things.
NB His Things must be very easy for him as Sea cloaths are
very apt to shrink and get past use in a little Time.[40]

Just a list, but it allows us to glimpse 16-year-old Billy, going down to the London docks with his sea-chest, probably feeling not a little apprehensive and over-conspicuous in his new clothes. The fact that he was equipped to be smartly dressed, in white shirts (how were they washed at sea?), silk handkerchiefs and cravats and buckled shoes, and armed with a textbook on navigation, tells us that Billy was to be trained as an officer like his father. The layers of clothes, including woollen drawers for exceptionally cold weather, with a duffle [woollen] coat and greatcoat on top, were some protection from the bitter conditions of a long winter voyage, but he would have had no oilskins to keep him dry. The French books were a thoughtful addition for a voyage to the Caribbean, where many of the islands were in French hands. With Britain on the verge of war with France yet again, some knowledge of the language could be useful to a sailor for communicating with captured prisoners of war, or even in the event of becoming a prisoner himself. It was an ever-present risk during the long years of conflict.

Billy was apprenticed to Captain Ross, sailing to the West Indies in the *Lady Jane Halliday* with cargo for the plantations and home again with sugar. When she docked in London, his father's characteristic letters would be waiting for him.

My Dear Son ... it contributes greatly to my happiness to find that you keep up at Sea and above all that you have a kind Master who favours you ... Now my dear Boy ... you are now at a time of life in which the allurments of Vice are often laid in your way to Dazzle your eyes with its Guilded Bait, in order to fetch you! ... Despise the mean practices of Swearing, Chewing of Tobacco and Drinking, which generally are the Forerunners of many other evils that befall seafaring men, and for the most part terminate in their Ruin ...

Your sister Betsy tells me you have grow much Stouter and Taller which I am glad to hear, I hope you have kept a Journall of the Voyage, and get grounded in the practical part of Navigation, and that you dont neglect your French of leisure hours ... from 4 to 6 Hours is time enough to Sleep in 24 Hours and I can assure you is sufficiently conducive to Health ... These injunctions, Dear William, may appear tedious to you but I can assure that by my reducing them to practice in myself at your time of Life, was the means of my being promoted, at the age of 19 to Chief Mate ...

I should like to know what kind of a Ship you are in, and how Equipped in this time of war ... Your little sister Mary has you in constant remembrance and speaks of you almost Dayly ... Fail not, my Dear William to write immediately to your affectionate Father William Manson

This time of war ... It is a refrain beating through all the letters written in the late 18th and early 19th centuries as, with slight fluctuations in intensity, conflict with France dragged on and on. Merchant vessels sailed to the West Indies in convoy, and armed, but Manson well knew that the risks of attack and capture were high. Nor was enemy shipping the only danger. Equally dreaded by merchantmen were the British naval ships that kidnapped their men for crew – a more certain death sentence than a French prison. William had advice to give for this eventuality too. *I have one thing more to Recommend to you, that if in the course of this War, you should be Imprest, dont run away from your Ship – it is a disgraceful thing for a Man to Flinch from his Colours, Should it so happen that you are Imprest, endeavour to win the favour of those amongst whom your lot may be cast, and all will be well.*[41]

It was not only the long-haul voyages that were dangerous. Ships risked wreck or capture even when sailing in home waters. In a letter from Orkney, Billy learned that his young friend John Sutherland was drowned with all the crew of Thomas Balfour's sloop *Swift*, wrecked on her passage from Shetland, and *the Pomona is wreckt on the S side of the Edinburgh Frith, the people all aboard, this is two Vessels belonging to Dr Balfour (now Major of the Fencible Corps) that have been lost in the course of four months, without one penny insurance on them, and the Fisher sailed from this port 6 weeks ago for London and no word of her yet which makes one doubtful she is taken by the French.*[42]

Wartime had brought the usual problems to the civilian population of Kirkwall, the unwelcome presence of large numbers of military quartered in the town. *Mary ... hopes you are quite unlike a parcel of Irish sailors (Volunteers in the Navy) who are going about this town at present, like great blackguards, swearing, and Chewing Tobacco and frightening the Women and Children, with Oliver Swinney the Bleacher [?] at their Head, a great Reprobate.*[43]

It is frustrating that, as so often, the correspondence is one-sided. One would give much to know what Billy thought about his shipboard life. Did he miss his family, or was he glad to get away from his domineering father? Did he take to his new role, or resent not being allowed to choose his own career and settle as a London shopkeeper? We will never know, for without a schoolmaster to enforce a *time when boys write letters to their parents*, Billy remained silent. In the last letter that has survived from William to his son, he crisply comments on the strange fact that all Billy's letters home seem to have gone astray, (his own never did!), but he is also solicitous. *You will desire your Uncle Thomas to buy for you, Four Check Shirts and Four or Five pairs of Coarse Stockings to keep you warm, as I imagine you are growing fast, to lay in many things at a time is only waste, and if your Captain and Uncle think it necessary, He may also purchase a Quadrant for you, before you go to sea again.* For once William seems to have been jolted by the grim news of another epidemic of fever in the Caribbean into an awareness of his only son's vulnerability and a genuine concern for Billy's welfare rather than his moral stature. With our hindsight, his last advice is tragically ironic. *I hope that by this time the dreadful ravages made by the Yellow Fever in the West Indies, has partly ceased, and I have to recommend to you to be easeful of your health as your situation will admit of.*[44]

It would be more than ten months before William Manson learned that Billy had become one of the many thousands to die in the lethal climate of the Indies. His uncle Thomas wrote to his sister in Kirkwall: *Our poor Brother has sustained an irreparable loss by the death of his son William at Antigua on the 13th of June last, of which I gave him the melancholy information in a letter yesterday ...*[45] Billy had died six months before his 20th birthday.

Child Prodigies

William Manson's mother, Marion Blaw, was one of the much-loved matriarchs of 18th-century Orkney. She outlived her husband (William Manson senior) by many years, but her widely-scattered children wrote to her regularly and it is evident that she was held in great affection by them all. While her sons wrote about voyages, wars and perils in distant lands, the girls kept her in touch with family news. In April 1793 her daughter Marion proudly described to her mother the scholastic progress of her own daughter, Henrietta, aged six. In a pious Quaker household like the Mansons, the emphasis was heavily on religious instruction.

My ever dear and Honred Mother

Henrietta has been at school these 18 months and comes on pretty well. She reads the Bible or any book very accurately, has by heart 10 or 12 Psalms ... and is between the commands and petitions of the Shorter Catechism, she was 6 years old in February.[46]

However, Marion's niece was evidently also a prodigy and in every way a match for her cousin. Despite his seemingly callous treatment of his older children, William Manson was evidently an adoring and proud father to the little daughter of his second marriage. He wrote to Billy in Antigua:

It will please you to hear that your little sister Mary is well in health and that although only 6 years old, she can read in the Bible or any English book very distinctly, a good Speller, and can play more than a Dozen different tunes on the Spinet or Piano Forte and is in every way a pleasant affable Child.[47]

Chapter 5 Notes

1   Letter from Barbara Baikie to Elizabeth Balfour, Westray 27/1/1778, OLA D2/8/3.
2   Letter from William Balfour, Dunnet to Elizabeth Balfour, Westray 2/5/1766, OLA D2/12/15.
3   Letter from Thomas Balfour, Aberdeen to William Balfour 29/12/1768, OLA D2/11/10.
4   Letter from Frances Balfour, Shapinsay to Thomas Balfour, London 4/1793, OLA D2/6/10.
5   Letter from Edward Balfour, Walthamstow to Thomas Balfour, Shapinsay 5/7/1792, OLA D2/5/3. The Roman poet Ovid (43 BC-17 AD) is best known for his *Metamorphoses*, one of the most important sources of classical mythology. The historian Justin (C3 AD) was the author of *Epitome*, an abridgement of *Philippic Histories* by a lost author Trogus. Both works were much read in the Middle Ages and, as here, standard texts in schools much later.
6   Comment by Frances' son-in-law Alexander Brunton in memoir of Mary, incl. in Brunton 1820, vii.
7   Letter from Elizabeth Balfour, Dunkirk to Thomas Balfour of Huip, Edinburgh 16/12/1777, OLA D2/7/13.
8   Letter from Ann Balfour, Liège to Thomas Balfour of Huip 7/1/1779, OLA D2/7/13.
9   Letter from Mary Balfour, Liège to Thomas Balfour of Huip 30/6/1780, OLA D2/7/13.
10 Letter from Thomas Balfour of Huip to Elizabeth Balfour of Trenaby, Westray 22/6/1775, OLA D2/8/23.
11 Letter from Elizabeth and Mary Balfour, Liège, to Thomas Balfour of Huip 7/7/1778, OLA D2/5/12.
12 Letter from Frances Balfour to Mary Craigie 3/1795, OLA D2/14/19.
13 Letter from Thomas Balfour, Ireland to David Balfour, Edinburgh 26/11/1795, OLA D2/8/25.
14 Draft letters from Thomas Balfour, Cork to Edward Balfour, Edinburgh 12/1/1796.
15 Midshipmen were the lowest-ranking officers in the Navy, and often as young as 13. In 1779 George III sent his third son William into the Navy when he was 14, as midshipman on HMS *Prince George,* with instructions that he was to be allowed no special privileges.
16 Letter from Thomas Balfour, Dublin to Midshipman William Balfour, HMS *Irresistible,* 9/12/1796, OLA D2/9/14.
17 Letter from David Balfour, Edinburgh to Mary Craigie, Rousay 1/1800, OLA D2/53/20.
18 Letter from William Balfour to Frances Balfour, Shapinsay 6/8/1804, OLA D2/8/9.
19 Letter from Frances Balfour, Shapinsay to William Balfour 20/8/1804, OLA D2/5/6.
20 Letter from William Balfour to Frances Balfour, Shapinsay 10/3/1805, OLA D2/13/7.
21 There were 22 men killed and 36 wounded on *Cleopatra.* After making repairs to both ships and transferring prisoners and a prize crew, both ships sailed again but two days later the HMS *Leander* recaptured *Cleopatra,* freed the crew and pursued and captured the badly damaged *La Ville de Milan.*
22 Reference for Lt. William Balfour signed Robt Laurie, 1805, OLA D2/17/2.
23 Letter from John Balfour, London to William Balfour 16/6/1804, OLA D2/8/29.
24 Mary was the daughter of William's aunt Elizabeth (Betty) Balfour and William Manson, born in 1788.
25 Letter from John Balfour to William Balfour 2/7/1806, OLA D2/5/6.
26 William and Mary Craigie, some of their children and other family members were buried in the kirkyard of St John the Evangelist in Edinburgh.
27 Letters from William Manson to Simon Taylor 3/12/1783, 13/4/1784,

27/12/1784, 14/6/1785, OLA D2/18/12.

28   Note to William Manson at Mrs Campbell's Lodging House, Kingston from William Sutherland, Blue Mountain Estate 13/7/1783, OLA D2/18/12. Sutherland was in charge of this sugar estate 1780-1804. He may well have been a fellow-Orcadian, like James Blaw, William Manson's uncle, overseer on Blue Mountain from 1766.

29   Letters from William Manson, London to William Jackson and Dinah Jackson, Whitby 23/2/1782, Letterbook OLA D2/60.

30   Letter from Betsy Manson, Wandsworth to William Manson, Kirkwall 23/11/1787, OLA D2/28/18. When Betsy is in Wandsworth she signs herself as Eliza, but her family address her and refer to her as Betsy.

31   Ackworth School near Pontefract was built 1757-59 as an appendage to the Foundling Hospital in London. It was purchased by Dr John Fothergill and three others who opened it in 1779 as a boarding school for children of the Society of Friends. It is still run as a coeducational school.

32   Letter from William Manson jnr (Billy), Ackworth to William Manson, Kirkwall March 1789, OLA D2/22/19. Almost identical letters were written on 31/3/90 and 19/11/1790.

33   Letter from Betsy Manson, Wandsworth to William Manson, Kirkwall 24/6/1790, OLA D2/22/19.

34   ibid.

35   Letter from Betsy Manson, Wandsworth to William Manson, Kirkwall 4/11/1791, OLA D2/22/19.

36   Letter from Betsy Manson, Wandsworth to William Manson, Kirkwall 13/1/1791, OLA D2/22/19.

37   Betsy died in Bath in 1838; presumably she never met her Orkney relations.

38   Letters from William Manson jnr (Billy), Ackworth to William Manson, Kirkwall 1/3/1791 and 31/3/1791, OLA D2/22/19.

39   John Hamilton Moor published his *New Practical Navigator and Daily Assistant* in 1772.

40   Letter from Elizabeth Manson [?] 8/9/1792, OLA D2/22/20.

41   Letter from William Manson, Kirkwall to William Manson jnr, London 30/9/1794, OLA D2/34/16.

42   Letter from William Manson, Kirkwall to William Manson jnr, apprentice to Capt. G.Ross, *Lady Jane Halliday*, Antigua 30/4/1794, OLA D2/334/16.

43   ibid.

44   Letter from William Manson, Kirkwall to William Manson jnr, London 30/9/1794, OLA D2/34/16.

45   Letter from Thomas Manson, London to his sister, Kirkwall 15/8/1795, OLA D2/9/15.

46   Letter from Marion Gibson to her mother Marion Manson, Kirkwall 21/4/1793, OLA D2/9/14.

47   Letter from William Manson, Kirkwall, to William Manson jnr, apprentice to Capt. G Ross of the *Lady Jane Halliday*, Antigua 30/4/1794; OLA D2/34/16. 14 years later, Mary married her cousin Captain William Balfour.

CHAPTER 6

Ireland: Invasion and Revolt

Prologue

The Seven Years War in the mid 18th century, followed by the American Revolution and the conflict in the Caribbean, took Orkney sailors and soldiers all over the world. By the end of the century, war with the new French Republic and the subsequent rise of Napoleon brought the battlegrounds much closer to home. It may seem that Orkney was safely distant from the scenes of military action, but every islander had friends or family at risk, abroad or at sea. Everyone, from one end of the country to the other, lived for years in fear of a French invasion.

We have already seen a few of the many Orcadians, military and civilian, whose lives were caught up in, transformed or destroyed by the wars. Letters from Lieutenant Sandy Watt to his family trace the movements of his regiment from Britain to the Caribbean, to India and North Africa fighting the French. The capture of the British West Indian islands also affected civilians like the young Mowat brothers from Kirkwall, overseers on sugar plantations. Merchant sailors like the two William Mansons risked attack, capture by the enemy or the press gang every time they sailed from a home port. At home, the requisition of foodstuffs to feed the enormous army and navy led to widespread shortages. The population suffered from the loss of their menfolk (whether volunteered or conscripted), from heavy taxation and a climate of constant anxiety. War and rumours of war are recurrent themes, occasionally triumphalist in tone after a major victory, but more often anxious and fearful as the armies of the French inflicted defeat after crushing defeat.

The war was fought on several different fronts at once, on sea and on land. In 1795 Colonel Thomas Balfour, commanding his own regiment of Fencibles, was posted to Ireland to resist French invasions and put down Irish revolts. With him was his older son Edward, soon to be killed in the Netherlands, while his younger son William was seeing action in the Mediterranean with the Royal Navy.

Figure 6.1

Colonel Balfour in Arms

In the 1770s Frances Balfour's brother, Earl Ligonier, followed international events with pained interest from his home in Surrey. His whole regiment had been taken prisoner in the American war and the men were in ghastly circumstances, and meanwhile both the French and the Spanish fleets were threatening the English coast. Ligonier himself, formerly a distinguished soldier but now an invalid, was frustrated by his own inability to serve and the incompetence of those now in command. *We are in hourly expectation of an Invasion ... a wide extended unfortified coast, a raw Militia, and Generals without experience, are great temptations to an enterprising enemy. Ireland I should think would be their first attempt, there the religion of the greatest part of the natives, joined to their poverty, and the love of novelty, may lead to expect a slack resistance, in short, we seem in a scrape.*[1] The threatened invasion did not happen as soon as he expected but by February 1793 Britain was again engaged in war with France, one that would drag on for the next 22 years.

Ligonier was proved right in thinking that the disturbed state of Ireland made it an open door for the enemy. The country was controlled by a tiny minority, the Anglican 'Protestant Ascendancy'. Under the Penal Laws, anyone who did not acknowledge the English king as head of their Church – impossible for Presbyterians as well as Roman Catholics – was debarred not only from Parliament but from the army or any position in public life. Catholics, the majority of the population, had no right to vote, neither did Protestant Dissenters or, in fact, most Protestants because they did not own sufficient property to qualify. Although Ireland was theoretically a sovereign kingdom, the English government had the right to legislate for it and to veto Irish legislation.[2] Resentment was inevitable, and not only among the disenfranchised. Even among the Irish ruling class there were liberals who pushed for reform and for greater autonomy for Ireland. The progress of the American War of Independence had been keenly watched in Europe, and other discontented subjects learned the lesson that colonies could successfully challenge Britain's authority.

In 1791 an Irish barrister, Theobald Wolfe Tone, and others founded the Society of United Irishmen. Its original aim was to unite Catholics and Protestants in lobbying for parliamentary reform and Catholic emancipation, and the society quickly gathered support across Ireland. In Parliament, the Irish Patriot Party, led by Henry Grattan, also lobbied for greater enfranchisement (but not for separation from England). They were successful to the extent that in 1793 new laws allowed some Catholics to vote, but only those with significant property, and they were still debarred from election to Parliament or any state office. For the United Irishmen, frustrated at their inability to bring about change by peaceful methods, the success of the French Revolution in overthrowing unpopular government came as further encouragement, and the war provided the opportunity. While they did not have the military strength to defy Britain on their own, a rebellion in Ireland backed by a simultaneous French invasion promised a good chance of success. However, the Society's secret negotiations with the government in Paris were betrayed and the leaders were forced to escape into exile.

The years 1794-95 were bleak ones for Britain and her allies. The French armies were victorious on all fronts, pushing the allied troops into rapid retreat in Flanders, taking Belgium, forcing the Austrians back across the Rhine and so clearing the way for their invasion of Italy. By the end of 1794 all hope that it would be the 'short war' promised by Prime Minister William Pitt had faded, and petitions from across Britain begged the government to seek peace. It was the worst winter weather for a hundred years. Ill-equipped British soldiers froze to death in northern Europe, where the frost was so intense in January 1795 that the French hussars were able to charge across the frozen Zuider Zee and capture an ice-bound Dutch fleet off the island of Texel.[3] The Republic of the United Netherlands, formerly an ally of Britain, surrendered to

France and was renamed the Batavian Republic. British attempts to land in France were a disaster and resulted in yet more catastrophic loss of life.

Apart from the financial and human cost of the war, anxiety over the threat of rebellion or invasion caused a mass paranoia which had a disastrous long-term effect on all social and political progress. Every call for improved working conditions or higher wages, let alone for extension of the franchise or the abolition of the slave trade, or any kind of political or social reform, was regarded as subversive. Calls of 'Treason' and 'Jacobinism' hustled peaceable citizens into prison, the gallows, or transportation. Mary Hardy, a Norfolk farmer, recorded in her diary: *May 23* [1794:] *the British Troops Defeated with great loss in France. Many people taken up in England for Sedition and Treason, the Habeas Corpus Act suspended.*[4]

At the outbreak of war, Thomas Balfour of Trenaby had seized the chance to enhance his own prestige and income by raising his own regiment, the Orkney and Shetland Fencibles. The mood in Britain in early 1793 was probably a little like that in August 1914 when it was thought that the war would soon be over, but, as the news from the fronts worsened, the government urgently needed recruits for the army, navy and local militias. In 1794 Thomas was promoted to Colonel and commissioned to raise a full-sized regiment, the North Lowland Fencibles, which would serve wherever in Britain or Ireland it was posted. Recruiting was not easy; Sir John Sinclair was raising his own Fencible regiment in Caithness, the navy was demanding quotas of men and, in the parish of Holm, Captain Alexander Graeme was raising men for his own ship. Other Orkney lairds were angry at being deprived of labour to work their kelp.

There were plus points for Thomas, however. Colonels of regiments were expected to provide their men with clothing and equipment and it was normal practice for them to enrich themselves with 'perquisites' on the side – the reason for thousands of poorly-clad soldiers dying of cold. Thomas could enjoy himself designing uniforms and running up bills at suppliers who were still trying to obtain payment years after his death. Another little bonus was that a name added to his list of recruits assured that person – or his relatives – a small wage. In this way Thomas was able to act the benefactor to his poor cousin Ann de Monti at no expense to himself.[5] Presumably no-one noticed, or drew attention to the fact, that Ensign Charles de Monti was only six months old when he was enlisted in the regiment.

Figure 6.2
Colonel Thomas Balfour in the uniform of the North Lowland Fencibles, by Henry Raeburn 1795. Photograph by Annan, Glasgow of painting formerly in Balfour Castle. (OLA)

Alerted to the danger of both rebellion and French invasion, the government dispatched more troops to Ireland and, in the late summer of 1795, the North Lowland Fencibles were on their way to Cork to join them. Colonel Thomas Balfour, for the first time in his life compelled to go soldiering in earnest, went with them but, for the moment, the country seemed quiet and he left them doing garrison duty while he returned to Orkney. In his absence, the troops were reviewed in their summer camp by Lieutenant General Rowley, who was unimpressed by Balfour's regiment. *Their Appearance in the Field Yesterday determined me no longer to defer doing my Duty* he wrote to the Commander in Chief. *They were so badly cloth'd as to prejudice their health last Winter, and must be a derision to the Regiments on the Right and Left.*[6] Although Thomas had been assiduous in ordering yards of silver lace for his Sergeant Major's hats and silk cockades, the money that should have been spent on warm clothes for his men had clearly gone into his own pocket.

In October 1796 news reached Britain of a French army assembling on the Brittany coast and Thomas was obliged to return to duty in Ireland. His older son, the irrepressibly exuberant 16-year-old Edward, joined the regiment. Edward, whom Tom always refers to as *a giddy fellow*, was evidently full of high spirits and mischief and he found plenty of time between marches to fall into scrapes. News of his escapades found its way back to his mother in Orkney. *I understand our Edward has commenced an intimacy with a very improper person, Capt Frasers son. He is a drunken idle profligate and he has more than once been near laying his Father in jail for his debts.*[7]

When the plotting of the United Irishmen was discovered, Wolfe Tone fled to the United States, from where (thoroughly disillusioned with the Americans' lack of democracy), he travelled to Paris to persuade the government that Ireland was ripe for rebellion. At the same time, other exiled leaders such as the young Lord Edward Fitzgerald, a former member of the Irish Parliament, negotiated with the French Directory, (the Republican government), from Hamburg. Their joint approaches convinced the French that a general rising of the Irish people would quickly follow a French invasion. They agreed to send a fleet of forty-five ships with an army of 15,000 men under the command of General Louis Lazare Hoche. In mid December 1796 the fleet set a stormy course from Brest, dodged the gale-battered British ships and with Tone, alias Adjutant-general Smith, and a large supply of munitions on board, sailed into the long inlet of Bantry Bay in south-west Ireland.

Everything but the weather was on the side of the French. Castlereagh, Lieutenant Colonel of the Londonderry militia, was appalled at the lack of British intelligence and organization. The fleet sailed to Ireland without seeing an English ship. Hoche was a brilliant, experienced and ruthless general, whereas the British troops in Ireland were described as *scabby, beggar fencible regiments, which had more the appearance of Falstaff's recruits than of soldiers to whom the defence of the country was to be entrusted.*[8] (How mortified Balfour would have been to hear this cutting appraisal!) If Hoche had landed there is no doubt that he would have mown down the unprepared and massively outnumbered troops like Balfour's shivering Fencibles, who struggled south through blizzards to meet him. He would have occupied Ireland and realised Britain's worst fears. If. Instead, after days of waiting in vain for the storm to ease enough for them to land, the French fleet turned back to Brest. Only 15 of the original 43 ships of the invasion force made it back to port. Bitterly disappointed, Tone wrote: *England has not had such an escape since the Spanish Armada.*[9]

The government in Dublin responded with brutal repression. Habeas corpus had already been suspended. Government troops set out to terrorise potential rebels with a campaign of burning Catholic houses and churches, torture and summary executions. Rumours flew about French landings or Irish revolts and Balfour's weary regiment was kept in constant motion. The men marched from Carrick to Tipperary, back to Roscrea, then to Gort in Galway, south again to Ennis in County Clare, to Limerick, then north to Athlone. In a letter to his sister Mary Craigie, Thomas grumbled: *We have been marching and countermarching for the last 3 weeks hunting every idle and lying report of French ships on the coast. It is believed that they are now all off for ever without landing a man so that all our toil is to go for nothing.*[10]

The failure of the Bantry Bay invasion was by no means the end of attempts to defeat the British with combined Irish and French forces. Hoche's attack was intended to be supported by diversionary landings in England; one aimed at Newcastle (prevented by the weather), and a third fleet, commanded by Irish-American Colonel Tate, which sailed to attack Bristol. Again the elements were on the side of the British. Strong tides defended the

Somerset coast and Tate's ships, flying British flags, attempted a landing near Fishguard in Wales. The only opposition was the local militia, civilians brandishing pitchforks, and women in red flannel petticoats whom the invaders mistook for soldiers. Unluckily for Tate, his ships were recognized as French and his troops, almost all recruited from convicts, deserted as soon as they landed. Tate surrendered, his 'invasion' a complete debacle, but it proved to the nervous British public that a French landing *was* possible. It was fuel to the government propaganda machine, which used all the media available to promote fear of 'Jacobins' and revolutionaries and so win support for continuing a deeply unpopular war.

Even without French invasions, Ireland was thoroughly unsettled. For some years a Catholic secret society, the Defenders, had been arming themselves by raiding the houses and farms of wealthy Protestants and local rebellions broke out in 1793 and 1795. By early 1797 Ulster, in particular, was so disturbed that the army was ordered to disarm the people and Balfour's Fencibles were occupied attempting to confiscate weapons. First Lieutenant John Buchanan wrote to his colonel that his troop had *since their being embroiled exerted every power to repress the Rebbels of this Country, which is almost innumerable ... our Country is infested with treators* [traitors]. *The number of arms we have taken in is 2 Guns 10 Bayonets 1 sword 2 pistols. We are in great want of a Drummer to instruct the one we have ...*[11]

It is clear from a number of other letters on the subject that the Irish were out-manoeuvering Balfour's officers by handing in *bayonets, blunderbusses, Fowling Pieces, Firelocks etc etc* that were well past their sell-by date. In June 1797 Captain Ker reported that he had collected:

1-	*Guns that are serviceable*	160
2-	*Do that are not serviceable*	100
3-	*swords*	20
4-	*Case of Pistols serviceable*	8
	Do not	4
5-	*Spears*	8
6-	*Pike heads*	1
7-	*Bayonets* *half serv*	20

If they were not admitting as much to Balfour, it must have been obvious to Ker and the other officers that the rusted relics that were being handed in were not the effective weapons the rebels had seized in raids.[12] However, with the hatred simmering between British and Irish, and between Irish Catholics and Irish Protestants, there was enough action to keep even young Edward Balfour occupied. *They are both well,* wrote Frances to her sister-in-law, *but in a very turbulent part of the country where they are kept in constant alarm by the united Irish devils. The barracks have been willfully set fire to, the very morning our Reg'mt was to have occupied them.*[13]

Meanwhile, the ill-fated Wolfe Tone was busy raising a fleet in the Netherlands for another attempt at invasion. Yet again, contrary winds delayed the expedition and it did not leave Texel until October, only to be immediately crushed by the British navy.[14] In Ireland the situation was becoming increasingly grim for the rebels and for the civilian population as a whole. More British troops were arriving in the country and torturing and killing anyone suspected of rebel sympathies. When General Abercromby (recently returned from the campaign in the West Indies) took up the post of Commander in Chief in Ireland, he was appalled at their atrocities, but his attempts to control the army and protect civilians from their excesses had no support from the Irish government and he resigned. His successor, General Lake, had no qualms over the tactics used to punish and terrorise. Informants amongst the 500,000 strong United Irish betrayed the leaders, most were arrested and martial law was brutally imposed over most of the country in March 1798. The remaining leaders felt they could no longer wait for French help and they planned a general uprising in May.

Again, they were betrayed. The planned seizure of Dublin was a rout but revolts broke out in many parts of the country and initially the rebels had considerable success. However, the British troops had the advantage of numbers and far better arms and, in one battle after another, the United Irish forces were defeated. By the end of June the last major rebel force had been crushed.[15] On the Continent, Wolfe Tone had not given up trying to persuade the French to invade in support of the Irish but Napoleon's sights were set on an expedition to Egypt not to Ireland. When a small

French force finally sailed for the Irish coast, their help was far too little and too late. At the end of August 1798, General Humbert succeeded in landing a thousand men in Killala in County Mayo, put the British garrison to ignominious flight and proclaimed the Irish Republic. It lasted only 12 days until British reinforcements arrived and defeated Humbert at the battle of Ballinamuck. The French troops who surrendered were repatriated but hundreds of Irish rebels were captured and executed. Thomas Balfour wrote to Frances of the invasion and his hope that the people would not be encouraged to rebel again, *the horrors of their late revolt being still before their eyes and their leaders in custody or put to death.*[16]

Not realizing the fate of Humbert and the short-lived republic, a larger French squadron sailed for Ireland in October with Wolfe Tone and 3,000 men and attempted to land on the Donegal coast. They were intercepted by British ships in Lough Swilly and forced to surrender. Tone was arrested on the captured French flagship and tried for treason. Refused death by firing squad, he committed suicide in prison in Dublin before he could be hanged.[17] His death and the savage reprisals ended the Society of United Irishmen and all hope of French help. The expeditions had cost France scores of wrecked ships and thousands of men drowned without advancing either her own cause or that of Irish independence. Tens of thousands of Irish had died in battle or by execution and the United Irishmen's Utopian goal of a secular, non-sectarian society based on universal male suffrage had been defeated by sectarian atrocities on both sides as well as by loyalist troops. Two years later, the Irish Parliament, which had existed since the 13th century, was abolished under the Act of Union and from then until 1922 Ireland was ruled directly from London.

If the Irish Rising was thoroughly crushed, the fear of a French invasion in another part of Britain still dominated people's thoughts. For people in coastal communities, normal civilian life – travelling from one island to another, or dealing in merchant shipping – was almost impossible due to the threats from French and Spanish naval ships, or prowling privateers. Frances Balfour in Orkney, trying to look after the family's merchant interests while her husband was in Ireland, wrote to brother-in-law David: *I beg leave to acquaint you with the loss of our Brig the Edinburgh which I understand has been captured by the Spanish ... The enclosed will inform you of the suppos'd destination of the Pomona and as it seems to everybody a voyage replete with danger, I am advised to insure her and her freight, particularly if she is charter'd to sail without convoy.*[18]

The Defence of the Realm Act in 1798 put the whole of Britain on a war footing. Officials in every country and parish had to provide lists of all men capable of assisting the war effort in any capacity. There were emergency plans for livestock wagons carrying flour to be moved to the armies. Companies of pioneers were formed to repair roads and bridges or destroy them before an invading army and beacons and wooden signaling stations were built along the coast. With handbills, plays and songs, the people were bombarded with warnings relating to Napoleon's designs on Britain. In the climate of fear, every stranger was taken for a spy or an enemy alien. The country rang with rumours. Robert Baikie wrote from England to Mary Craigie in Rousay: *No particular Public news – every day looking for Bonaparte – some Irish fishing smacks having taken shelter in Milford Haven were mistaken for Frenchmen, as they spoke Irish, & hence a report that a part of the immense host preparing to arrive had landed.*[19]

Letters from Orkney allow one a glimpse of the impact that the long years of war had not only on men at the battlefront but on their families at home. Faced with the more immediate danger posed by yet another failed harvest in Orkney, Frances Balfour was less anxious about the French. *The Invasion is much spoken of but little fear'd here. Our poverty is our defence, and indeed we have none other, either naval or military. This poor Country is so far from being an object of plunder, it wou'd not even afford existence to an Enemy while they passed thro it, for I am sorry to say we are threaten'd with another year of famine by failure of the Crop.*[20] Dearth was coupled with rampant inflation caused by the war. *Everything is very dear,* William Leith wrote from Stenness to his sons in 1808, *Oatmeal 5/- per st, Beremeal 3/6, malt 4/6 and none to be got but what is brought from the south country ... Many great houses could not sow their ground and it lies unsown.*[21]

As in all wars at all times, the focus shifts from brutality and corruption to heroic patriotism or patient resignation. There are stories of appalling adversity, of military ineptitude, of brief moments of glory and long days of grief. There was sabre-rattling bravado from young men like Sandy Watt. *We have received Orders to hold ourselves in readiness to March at a Moments Notice but where cannot say as Bonoparty is expected verry soon and the sooner he makes his appearance so much the better as we are almost in readiness to receive him which will be a verry warme one. I hope he will come himself.*[22] There was the controlled, dignified grief of Edward Balfour's family when the 19-year-old died in his first action. *He died honourably, and we must console ourselves with the belief that all is ordered for the best.*[23] There was the mingled stoicism and anxiety of Mary Craigie in Rousay. *The present Alarm of an Invasion creates in my mind much anxiety and uneasiness for my friends who are in exposed situations. For myself, I have not a fear. Our Poverty will preserve us from French visitors, and for more remote Evils I trust in God and our Brave Defenders.*[24]

Chapter 6 Notes

1   Letter from Edward Ligonier, Cobham to Thomas Balfour, Orkney 18/7/1779, OLA D2/4/12.
2   Poynings Law 1494 gave England the power of veto over Irish legislation; the Declaratory Act 1719 gave Britain the right to legislate for Ireland.
3   'One of the few times in recorded military history wherein cavalry captured a fleet' is the French version of the story. Less glamorously, Dutch historian Johannes Cornelis de Jonge states that the a few French hussars crossed the ice to negotiate the terms of the surrender of the Dutch fleet.
4   Uglow, ch.12.
5   Ann, the youngest daughter of Thomas Balfour of Huip, shocked her relatives and friends by marrying a Hungarian/Italian music master, Hurka de Monti, in 1793. Marion Balfour called it a 'disgraceful connection'. Letter from Marion Balfour, Edinburgh to Elizabeth Balfour of Trenaby 27/6/1793, OLA D2/11/1.
6   Letter from Lt.Gen. William Rowley to Gen. Cunninghame 31/8/1796, OLA D2/5/11.
7   Letter from Frances Balfour, Shapinsay to Thomas Balfour, Cork 4/12/1796, OLA D2/6/8.
8   Elliott 329, quoting John Fitzgibbon, Lord Chancellor.
9   Elliott 327-8.
10   Letter from Thomas Balfour, Ireland to Mary Craigie, Rousay 12/1/1797, OLA D2/19/3.
11   Letter from 1st Lt. John Buchanan, Fintona to Col. Thomas Balfour, Monaghan 4/6/1797, OLA D2/18/10.
12   Letter and return of arms from Capt. Ker to Col. Thomas Balfour 24/6/1797, OLA D2/18/10.
13   Letter from Frances Balfour, Edinburgh to Elizabeth Manson, Kirkwall 27/4/1797, OLA D2/11/12.
14   The Dutch Vice-Admiral Jan de Winter was defeated at the battle of Camperdown by a British fleet under Admiral Adam Duncan.
15   The battle of Vinegar Hill in Co. Wexford on 21 June 1798.
16   Letter from Thomas Balfour, Ireland to Frances Balfour 3/9/1798, OLA D2/19/3.
17   Wolfe Tone died on 19th November 1798, aged 35.
18   Letter from Frances Balfour, Kirkwall to David Balfour, Edinburgh 21/12/1796, OLA D2/44/27.
19   Letter from Robert Baikie to Mary Craigie, Rousay 12/11/1803, OLA D2/16/6.
20   Letter from Frances Balfour, Shapinsay, to William Balfour 20/10/1803, OLA D2/5/6.
21   Letter from William Leith, Stenness to his sons William and Nicol 5/6/1808, Leith family.
22   Letter from Lt. Alexander Watt, Hastings to his family in Orkney 10/7/1803, OLA D3/267.
23   Letter from John Balfour, London to Mary Craigie, Rousay 28/12/1799, OLA D2/4/17.
24   Letter from Mary Craigie, Rousay to David Balfour, Edinburgh 12/9/1803, OLA D2/19/18.

CHAPTER 7

The Lure of the Nor'Wast

Prologue

It would be hard to overstate the importance of the Hudson's Bay Company to Orkney, especially in the later 18th and early 19th centuries. From 1702, when the Company sent a ship to Stromness for the first time, the number of Orcadians on its payroll steadily increased, until by 1800 almost 80% of the workforce in the Bay came from Orkney. The money that they earned enabled a distinct improvement in the standard of living at home. Culturally, the Nor'Wast entered the islands' bloodstream.

At home, women played significant social and economic roles, their menfolk often absent farstraers working in very masculine environments where women had little place, or none at all. It would be hard to imagine a harsher or more physically demanding place than Hudson Bay, but it is here that we find one of the strangest and saddest stories of an Orkney woman, Isobel Gunn.

No woman could have strayed further, geographically and morally, than Isobel, who leapt over all the boundaries set by custom and Kirk, society and biology to follow her dream and 'sign on for Hudson Bay', disguised as a man. It is true that Isobel wrote no letters and contemporaries wrote little about her, but her story is so remarkable, and has so often been fictionalised and romanticised, that I could not resist weaving it into the wider story of the Bay. I have tried to imagine something of the world that she knew, both in the Orkney parish that she left in 1806 and in the wide lands of the Nor'Wast. Her stranger-than-fiction adventure allows us a sideways look not only into the life of the fur-traders but into the many anomalies in their attitudes towards issues of race and gender.

The majority of Orkney men who went out to Hudson Bay signed on as labourers for a fixed contract and came back after a few years. Some, however, settled permanently with their Indian wives and children, and the Red River valley in what is now Manitoba became home to the mixed-race descendants of retired Company men. The letters from James Sutherland to his brother in South Ronaldsay vividly describe both the disasters and

225

dangers that beset the Red River colony and its times of prosperity. They also give a poignant picture of a man always torn between loyalties to families on both sides of the Atlantic, to the old world and the new.

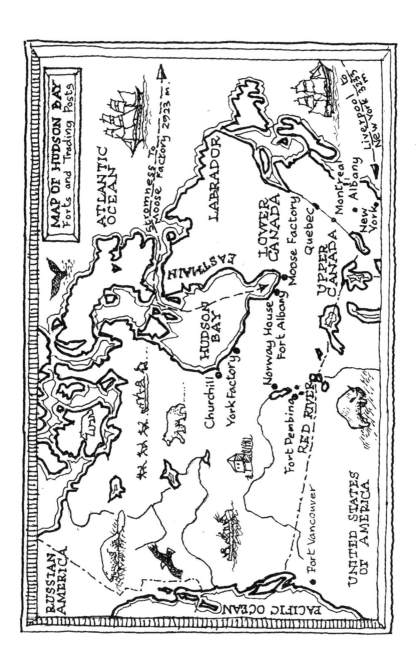

Figure 7.1

Hudson Bay and the Strange Story of Isobel Gunn

On 29th October 1809 the Hudson's Bay Company ship the *Prince of Wales* was sighted sailing into Stromness. The return of the Company ship was always an occasion for considerable excitement in the town. Parents, wives and sweethearts, who had waited for long years for their men to return home, eagerly watched the approaching sails. The 'tippling houses' prepared for a run of business. On board, returning Company servants leaned over the rails watching the strip of grey houses grow larger. Most of them had been away from home for at least 3 years – the basic term of a contract – and some for much longer. Letters from home had been infrequent, and frequently never caught up with their travels between trading posts at all. They must have been wondering what they would find: were parents still alive, the girl still waiting? Among all the men impatiently watching Stromness grow nearer, one woman stood, a little apart. She held by the hand a small child, a little boy not two years old. She watched as the ship passed between the hills of Hoy and the Black Craig above Outertoun, past the strips of green and yellow fields sloping down to the sea, but hers was the only face that held no excitement in it. She was probably the only one on the ship that had not wanted to leave Rupert's Land and had no expectation of a happy reunion with family. Stromness presented grey stone walls to the sea. For Isobel, the ship sailed into a grey stone wall of condemnation.

I have imagined Isobel Gunn's return to Stromness. So little is known about her that one can do little but imagine. The verifiable facts of her story can be gleaned from a few entries in Orkney parish registers, censuses and the Hudson's Bay Company (HBC) archives, and told in a few sentences. She was born in 1780 and grew up in the Mainland parish of Orphir. In 1806 she disguised herself as a man and signed on with the Company's agent in Stromness as

John Fubbister. She worked as a labourer and canoeman in Rupert's Land, her sex kept a secret until the moment when she gave birth to a baby in December 1807. She was sent back to Fort Albany to work as a washerwoman and nurse to the schoolchildren and, in 1809, shipped back to Orkney with her child. In 1821 Isobel and her son were living in Stromness; there is no trace of her in the 1841 census but she appears, living alone and very poor, in the Stromness census for 1851 and again in 1861. Later in that year she died, a pauper, at the age of 81.

That is about the limit of our certain knowledge of this remarkable Orkney woman, who dared to jump over the rigid boundaries imposed by her society on what was or was not permissible or possible for a woman; for a little over a year succeeded in that leap, and spent the next 50 years of her life in poverty and obscurity, apparently unforgiven by her family or community. The outline of her story is well-known; it was embroidered in the telling from the beginning, it inspired poems and novels and has become an essential item of the literature of Hudson Bay; yet it remains just a tantalizing glimpse of a brave and adventurous woman whose own voice is silent and whose face entirely unseen. Isobel left no letters or diaries; there is not a word that tells us what she thought and felt, nor even a description by an acquaintance.

When I first read the story of Isobel Gunn, I was sceptical that a woman could pose as a man while living with a large number of men in the total lack of privacy afforded by an 18th-century sailing ship or labourers' barracks. However, I discovered that in fact Isobel was one of an extraordinarily large number of women who successfully worked in male employment in disguise, occasionally for romance and adventure but more often to escape the suffocating tedium of the work that was available to them as women, and to access the higher wages and better social status and conditions that were available to working men. Christian Davies fought for years in the Duke of Marlborough's campaigns until she was wounded at the battle of Ramelies in 1705 and her disguise discovered. Around the time of Isobel's birth, Deborah Sampson, alias Robert Shurtleff, was in action in the American War of Independence and became aide-de-camp to General Paterson in 1783. When she later made a profitable lecture tour out of her adventures, she stressed her patriotic motive, but admitted that she first enlisted *to have a little frolic and to see how it would seem to put on a man's clothing but chiefly for the purpose of procuring a more ample supply of money*.[1]

At the same time as Isobel was growing up in Orkney, women from several European countries were fighting in the Napoleonic wars. Mary Anne Talbot, alias drummer boy John Taylor, excelled as a sailor and was twice wounded in naval battles in the 1790s. A number of women died fighting at Waterloo. It is alleged there were as many as 400 women serving in regiments on both sides in the American Civil War. Among them was Emma Edmonds who joined up aged 19 and *followed through hard-fought battles, never flinched from duty, and was never suspected of being else than what she seemed*.[2] The sheer number of female sailors who worked on British ships in the 19th century is astonishing. Mary Anne Arnold worked for four years as an able seaman before her discovery in 1839. *I have seen Miss Arnold among the first aloft to reef the mizzen-top-gallant sail during a heavy gale in the Bay of Biscayne,* her Captain wrote, *she has well done her work as a strong active boy in this ship*.[3]

Less romantically, many working class women found employment as navvies, miners or dockers: often these were widows or wives who had been abandoned by their husbands and had children to support. The hard physical work was no worse than was the normal lot of a female farm labourer, or of a girl growing up on an Orkney croft, like Isobel Gunn. The interesting thing about these stories is the common thread running through them. The women longed for liberation from the constraints of their smothering clothing, from the powerlessness and poverty, the lack of adventure and opportunity that custom and culture forced upon them. For a time at least, they were perfectly successful in their disguise and proved themselves equally competent as, or even excelled, their male colleagues in performing their work, even when it required heavy labour, the agility to climb a ship's rigging in a storm, or bravery under fire. As soon as their disguise was discovered, they were dismissed from their employment, treated with scorn, forced into female dress and 'female work,' suffered a humiliating financial and social loss and, in most cases, died in poverty. *Happy endings are all too rare in these stories*.[4] The story of Isobel Gunn is not just the strange adventure of an Orkney girl, but the story of the anomalous attitudes to working women who were often obliged to support themselves and their families by the hardest and heaviest physical labour, yet debarred from the better paid 'masculine roles' that were regarded as 'unfeminine' and 'unsuitable'.

We know enough about the Orkney that Isobel grew up in to imagine the world she left in 1806, and the possible reasons that motivated her attempt to escape to Hudson Bay. On the 3rd of September 1780 it was recorded in the Baptismal Register for the parish of Orphir that *John Gun in Kirbister had by his spouse Isobel Leask a child Baptized named Isobel*.[5] John and Isobel had already baptized a son, George, and three daughters, and a fifth daughter would be born in 1784. We have no information about the Gunns other than the brief entries in the parish registers, but it is likely that John and Isobel struggled to bring up their young family through the lean years of the 1770s and 1780s, and a ratio of five girls to one boy cannot have been seen as a blessing. According to the *Old Statistical Account*, the majority of Orphir men could be described as farmers or cottagers in 1795. Among those who had a trade were five wrights, six shoemakers, six weavers, five tailors, six masons, three millers and one smith in the parish,[6] but many would also have a small plot of land on which they tried to grow crops to pay the rent and feed themselves and their few animals.

That at least was the hope that carried people through the back-breaking toil of cultivating their few peaty acres beneath the Orphir hills. Most farms were very small, and entirely 'unimproved' in the sense that enclosures or drainage or crop rotation or crops for winter fodder were still virtually unheard of. John and Isobel and their children would have carried seaweed from the shore for manure in creels on their own backs and sown their crops of black oats and a few potatoes, but again and again seen the cruel Orkney climate destroy their efforts.

The winters of the 1770s were long and hungry. By the spring of 1778 animals were dying of starvation and disease, and only the relief supplies bought in by some of the landowners prevented their tenants from dying as well. That summer yet another devastating storm ruined almost all the crops throughout the islands. When Isobel was two years old, the savage weather destroyed the crops

Figure 7.2
The Orphir hills, a familiar sight to Isobel Gunn as she grew up. The farm of Naversdale, bought by her brother George Gunn, can just be seen in the distance.

not only in Orkney but all over Scotland, England and even abroad so that grain could only be bought at an exorbitant price. If Isobel did not remember that time herself, she would certainly have heard stories of it, and hunger must have been a regular companion of her childhood, though the newly-introduced potatoes helped families avoid starvation. Even in good years, the small tenant farms offered scant livelihood for large families. Boys and girls worked as herds when they were only 9 or 10 years old; by the time they were in their teens most boys had left their cramped homes to find work as labourers on the big farms or joined the Merchant or Royal Navy or the whaling fleets that headed to the Davis Straits. In increasing numbers throughout the 18th century, they sailed to Hudson Bay.

The discovery that valuable furs could be obtained in the interior of North America and sold for stupendous profits in Europe had been made by two Frenchmen, Médard Chouart des Groseilliers and Pierre-Esprit Radisson, in the mid 17th century.[7] They failed, however, to interest the governments or merchants of France or America in backing a trading enterprise, and so they turned to Britain. They might well have been equally unsuccessful there if it were not for Prince Rupert of the Rhine, cousin to King Charles II, soldier, scientist and entrepreneur. Persuaded by the prince, in May 1670 Charles granted a Royal Charter to the *Governor and Company of Adventurers of England* giving them a monopoly of trading privileges in all *those Seas Streights Bayes Lakes Creeks ... together with all the Landes and Territoryes ...* accessible via the huge inland sea that is Hudson Bay. No other European power appeared to have claimed it, so Charles felt quite entitled to annex 'Rupert's Land' as his own. The Governor (Rupert was the first) and Adventurers were made *true and absolute Lordes and Proprietors* of this vast and vaguely defined territory, on payment of two elks and two black beaver a year whenever the King or his successors should visit the territory.[8] Despite the general ignorance of geography and of the fur-trade, and of the hostile rivalry from French traders in the Bay, the investors made staggering profits. In 1690 the Company was able to report that *our returns in Beaver this year (by God's blessing) are modestly expected to be worth £20,000.*[9]

Rupert's Land of course had native populations: human, of many different tribes, and animals in great numbers clad in luxuriant fur coats for the savagely cold winters. The pelts of arctic fox, otter, marten and muskrat were all highly prized, but above all it was the *harmless and civilized Beaver*[10] whose misfortune it was to have a waterproof coat that was the ideal material for European gentlemen's hats. While beavers were still plentiful, HBC ships brought home 80,000 to 100,000 pelts a year, which gives some idea of the number of these animals before the traders arrived. The harmless Beaver not only drew many hundreds of Orkney men to the 'Nor'Wast', but made a huge impact, socially and economically, on the impoverished islands that they left.

The HBC was run by a Committee based in London, but England's almost constant state of war made such a drain on her manpower that it was hard to recruit servants for the Rupert's Land posts. In the 1690s there was conflict with France, swiftly followed by Marlborough's campaigns in the War of Spanish Succession in the first years of the 18th century. The Londoners that the Navy had not already pressed or recruited, the Committee found unsuitable: they had a poor physique, a poor work ethic

Figure 7.3
Prince Rupert of the Rhine, Count Palatine 1619-82. Painting by Simon Pietersz Verelst in Petworth House. Rupert was cousin to King Charles II and soldier, explorer, scientist and founder of the Hudson's Bay Company. (© National Trust Images/ Derrick E. Witty)

and they drank. They turned to Scots, who they perceived to be more sober and accustomed to deprivation, *for that countrie is a hard country to live in* as Governor John Nixon observed in 1682, and the Scots were *a hardy people ... To enduyre hunger.*[11] In 1702 they sent a ship to Stromness for the first time, to hire *ten or twelve stout able young men*. The Company found Orkney men ideal servants: so poor that they were willing to work for low wages, *submissive and industrious*,[12] and *more sober and tractable than the Irish*,[13] used to hard work outdoors and to managing boats. It was also convenient that they spoke a version of English, unlike the Gaelic-speaking servants from the west of Scotland and the Hebrides. For the men, the Company offered more stability than fishing or whaling and, despite all the hazards, a higher chance of survival than in the Royal Navy, and at least twice the wages that they could earn as labourers at home.

For the first century of its existence, the Company operated from a few forts scattered around the shores of Hudson Bay, each manned by an Officer or Chief Trader, a few craftsmen for the skilled jobs of boat-building or tool making, and unskilled labourers for all the heavy manual work. Every summer two or three ships sailed to the Bay with fresh supplies and men and returned in the early autumn before the Bay froze, carrying furs and retired employees who had finished their contract. The Company servants did not trap animals themselves, but traded for them with native trappers; the unit of exchange was Made Beaver, one good (cured) adult beaver pelt, and all furs and imported goods were priced in this currency. In the spring, Cree, Chipewyan and Assiniboine trappers canoed to the posts with furs (sometimes acting as middlemen for more distant tribes such as the Blackfoot) and returned to their settlements with manufactured goods: knives, kettles, axes, beads, needles and blankets. Iron tools and utensils such as cooking kettles were highly prized. Other imports, such as alcohol and guns, had a far more unfortunate effect on native society.

After a hundred years of ruthless exploitation, however, the decline of the luckless beaver in the accessible hunting grounds, and competition from the rival fur trading company, the North-West Company (NWC),[14] was forcing the HBC to expand into the interior. A string of forts and trading posts was established along the river networks, where the modern cities of Winnipeg, Calgary and Edmonton evolved. There was therefore a constant need to recruit new servants, especially as most men worked a fixed contract, usually three to five years, and then returned home.

Figure 7.4
Trapping for beaver. Hand-coloured woodcut. (North Wind Picture Archives)

Britain was at war with France again in the late 18th century, so there was every reason for British shipping to avoid encountering French privateers in the English Channel. A safer sea-route from London to the 'Nor'Wast' followed the east coast to the north of Scotland, and Stromness provided a convenient harbour to take on fresh water, supplies and men before heading across the Atlantic.

A few weeks before the ships were due to arrive, the local agent advertised recruitment with handbills posted on church doors. The wages offered must have seemed enticing to anyone with any sense of adventure. In the 1790s a man might earn £3 or £4 a year drudging as a farm-servant, with miserable living conditions and little hope of improvement or promotion. As an unskilled labourer in Company employment he could earn £8, and there was the potential for him to move rapidly up the hierarchy as he learned the skills of canoeman or steersman or canoe-builder. Craftsmen such as blacksmiths and carpenters and boat builders could earn twice the basic wage. There were other routes up the ladder too. Some illiterate men, such as Orcadian Magnus Spence, who was engaged as a labourer in 1783, proved to be exceptionally good linguists and so were prized as interpreters. Another incentive was that, as board and lodging were provided, the men could send much of their income home to their families, or save towards the hope of buying their own farm when they returned home. By 1800, 418 out of a total of 524 employees in the HBC's pay were Orcadians.

The landowning class regarded the drain of labourers from the land with dismay. 18th-century ministers were often the mouthpiece of the 'gentry', who were their close relations, and the Reverend Francis Liddell of Orphir parish put the full weight of his powers of oratory behind his diatribe against emigration. *Many young men ... enter into the service of the Hudson's Bay company; and ... hire themselves out for slaves in a savage land where, in the language of Scripture, they are literally employed as hewers of wood and drawers of water; or ... in dragging along large loads of timber, yoked in the team, like beasts of burden. My God! Shall man, formed in the image of his Creator, desert the human species; and, for the paltry sum of £6 a year, assume the manners and habits of the brutes that perish? Fy be on the man, who would rather be the slave of a Company of private merchants, than enter into the fleets and armies of Great Britain, and bravely fight for his King and country, our religion, our liberties and our laws.*[15]

Liddell's outburst of patriotism conveniently overlooked the fact that *honourable service to King and country* took more young men out of Orkney than the HBC. His objection that emigration *scarce leaves hands to cultivate the ground* was based less on a concern for agriculture than the landowners' anxiety that labour shortage would push up wages.

Isobel's brother George, 12 years her senior, went away to the Bay in 1791 and did not return for eight years. Possibly her older sisters Jean and Marjory were married by this time, or in service in one of the big houses, but the younger girls would still have attended the parochial school. However, there may have been no school at all for some of Isobel's school years. Although a schoolmaster was appointed in 1792, the heritors (landowners) were, as so often, reluctant to pay their share of building a school or schoolhouse or the schoolmaster's salary.[16]

Even when a parish school was functioning, it was a common complaint of the teachers that their pupils were often kept at home to help with the farmwork at busy times of year, and for many children in outlying areas of the extensive parishes one central school was just too far away to reach. All the ministers writing their *Statistical Account* in the 1790s voiced the crying need for additional schools – a need underscored by the fact that most HBC employees from Orkney were illiterate and so debarred from the higher paid clerical posts. Most of the men who rose to high positions in the Company were those lucky enough to come from wealthier backgrounds and receive a reasonable education. Isobel could probably read, that she could write more than her name is unlikely, but her younger sister Helen may have benefited from the school which ex-HBC man Magnus Twatt founded in Kirbister (in Orphir) in 1796. He was one of the few Orcadians who rose from the lower ranks of the Company to make a considerable fortune and, like William Tomison from South Ronaldsay, he left a bequest to fund a school in his native parish.

It is not difficult to imagine the house that Isobel grew up in. The *Old Statistical Account* makes little mention of housing, presumably because it was so standard that the ministers did not think it worth commenting on, but by the time their successors wrote the *New Statistical Account* 50 years later, they clearly thought that living conditions *should* have moved on from one or two rooms with a central hearth and no chimney. The basic design of stone-built house, usually unplastered inside and out, and thatched with turf and simmons (twisted straw rope) had changed little in generations. *Most of them are wretched hovels,* wrote the Reverend Charles Clouston of Sandwick, *with holes in the roof instead of chimneys, which permit that part of the smoke to escape, that is knowing enough to find it; but most of the soot attaches itself to the roof and rafters, whence it descends again on the inmates. Another hole in the roof, about six inches square, and often without glass, is the substitute for a window; and cows, calves, pigs, geese, and fowls share the benefit of the peat fire, placed on the middle of the floor for the accommodation of all.*[17] In Isobel's time, sleeping space for large families in very small houses was provided by neuk beds – alcoves built either in the thickness of the stone walls or as outshots – with a covering of straw or heather on the earth floor. The hardiness of Scots in hostile environments is understandable when we remember the degree of cold, damp and discomfort to which people were accustomed at home.

The one day of the week that was not spent in hard labour was not spent in rest or any form of recreation. On Sundays all the Gunn family would have put on their one set of good clothes and walked to the kirk at the Bu' to be harangued by Mr Liddell. Perhaps the undoubted oratorical skills of the minister (who also earned himself a reputation for his outrageous behaviour when very drunk) made the long services less tedious than they might have been, and occasionally they were enlivened by arguments and even fights among his flock. There were no standard rows of pews in the kirks then; people brought their own stools, or built their own seats, and quarrels over seat-rights often feature in the minutes of Orphir Kirk Session meetings. The floor was of earth, and seats had to be removed at regular intervals to allow for someone to be buried in their ancestral plot within the kirk, so there was a strong and unpleasant smell of damp and human remains.

Whatever the weather, it was not permissible to be seen outdoors on a Sunday other than on the way to morning or afternoon service. Non-attenders were hauled before the Kirk Session to be rebuked and fined. Those whose sexual transgressions had come to light were 'examined' and it was not just unmarried girls and young men who got into trouble; most meetings were dealing out 'admonishment' to married couples whose first child had arrived rather earlier than was acceptable. In October 1790 *William Miller in the island of Cava confessed that he had been guilty of antenuptial fornication with his wife Jannet Loutit was rebuked and admonished ...* Helen Leask was similarly rebuked in February 1797 for sinning with her husband William Leask, but as he had gone to Hudson Bay he could not be absolved.[18] William must have signed on with the HBC immediately after marriage, which was not at all uncommon.

Isobel would have witnessed the public confessions and rebukings at Sunday service and had no doubt as to the Kirk's zero tolerance of anyone defying its authority. For spirited young men, another motive for emigration must have been the desire to escape from the stifling dual control of Laird and Kirk. The promise that there were no ministers at the Bay and considerable sexual freedom to be enjoyed with the women at the trading posts, unaccompanied by retribution, was undoubtedly attractive.

The society in which Isobel grew up was overwhelmingly female. Almost every family she knew had a husband, son or brother working at sea or abroad as economic migrants and, by the mid 1790s, the population of many parishes had dropped significantly since the Webster census in 1755. There were almost a hundred more females than males in Orphir, a parish of 855 souls. In the village of Stromness there were 851 females to 493 males and the number of women in Birsay was almost double that of men. At the best of times, Orkney wives and daughters were accustomed to the heavy physical tasks of carrying water from the well, peats from the hill and ware from the shore. Women milked the cow and cared for the cattle in the byre, ground grain in the quern and cooked over an open fire, and produced children. Men usually ploughed – horses were traditionally a male domain – and cut peats and fished and went to the marts for buying and selling beasts. With so many of the able-bodied (and more enterprising) men absent, much of their share of the work fell to the women.

All Isobel's life she must have heard tales of the Nor'Wast, first from the men who came home to neighbouring families and then from her own brother George who spent three years as a labourer at York factory from 1791, and a further five seasons as a canoeman at 'York inland.' Setting fox traps in Saskatchewan, he accidentally shot himself in the leg and was invalided home. George's accident was not unusual, and there were few doctors and very little medicine at the trading posts. Orcadians were hardy and accustomed to handling small fishing boats in all weathers, but they had no experience of enduring sub-arctic winters with temperatures that plunged to minus 50 degrees, or of steering laden birchbark canoes through rapids, living off the land far from friendly shelter, or handling rifles with frostbitten fingers. Deaths from wounds, drowning or exposure were not uncommon.

The Committee in London had no idea of the conditions in the distant territory they administered: of how dangerous the rivers were or how long it took to train a skilled canoeman. They expected their servants to be frugal with their rations because food was expensive at home in wartime, not appreciating that they were often starving. The supplies that the Company sent out were inadequate and often rotten; local game and fish were sometimes plentiful, sometimes non-existent, so men suffered from malnutrition and scurvy. Some were attacked by hostile tribes and some, even more seriously, attacked by fellow Scots employed in the North-West Company. Orkney man John Crear and William Plowman from Wick, for example, were beaten and stabbed by Alex MacDonnell and his men.[19]

Isobel could not have underestimated the dangers of life in the Bay. She saw the men who stepped – or were carried – off the ships in the autumn: cripples like Joseph Johnston who was totally disabled by a gunshot wound at Moose Factory in 1800.[20] Some came home with their health broken by the rigours of their journeys, some with frostbitten feet or hands which had to be amputated, or maimed by a shooting accident. But she would also have heard, from George and many others, stories of long journeys in canoes or on snowshoes through deep snow, of firelit camps with friendly Indians or astonishing encounters with wild animals, of great forests and frozen rivers, of vast spaces and great silences. There were some who spoke with nostalgia for a life of adventure in a new land, free from the conventions and constraints of Orkney society and family. Some, after a winter of rain-laden skies and mud, of low wages and hunger after another failed harvest, of exacting lairds and disapproving ministers, returned to the agent's house in Stromness when the ships called again in early summer. Some had native women and mixed-race children to return to, and a wage (for those who already had experience and a good record in the Bay, like John Scarth, steersman) four times that of a young man's first contract.

When Isobel was in her teens, there were 120 unmarried women above the age of 20 in Orphir, so it is not surprising that she was still a spinster at the age of 25 when she took her great decision. In the spring of 1806 the HBC ship *Prince of Wales* lay in Stromness harbour to take on new supplies and recruits. David Geddes, a wealthy merchant, was the Company agent, with a quota to fill. Recruitment had been difficult: due to the war with France many of the men in their prime had already enlisted or been press-ganged into the army or the navy; the NWC were also starting to recruit in Orkney. Perhaps Geddes did not look at the recruits who came to his office in Stromness with too critical an eye and, in a society where only men wore trousers, anyone wearing trousers would be assumed to be a man.

Figure 7.5
Coat-of-arms of the Hudson's Bay Company. (Photograph by Rebecca Marr © Stromness Museum)

It is not hard to imagine Isobel passing for a man in her brother's clothes. After a life of hard physical graft, outdoors in all weathers, she would have had a thoroughly weather-beaten complexion; if we had met her we would probably have taken her for much older than her 25 years. She may have been well-built for a woman, and certainly was muscular after a life of lifting heavy creels of peat or sea-ware, steering a plough through heather and rock, carrying stones to mend a dyke or a byre. Her hands were coarsened with work, ingrained with dirt, just like those of the other recruits who picked up the unfamiliar tool on Geddes' desk and fumbled their way through a signature or made an unsteady cross beside their name. Isobel Gunn of Orphir disappeared and John Fubbister from St Andrews parish appeared on the books of the HBC.

The name was carefully chosen: Fubbister was a common name in St Andrews and Isobel was familiar with St Andrews from visiting her mother's relatives there, and so would have been able to speak about the place and its inhabitants if she was questioned. She perhaps knew that there were no other recruits from that parish that year, who would have questioned the appearance of a man they did not know. Other aspects of her transformation into John Fubbister are harder to understand. If her family were not party to her plot, was there no hue and cry at her sudden disappearance? And did no-one comment on the strangeness of a stranger in Stromness who spoke with an Orphir accent but whom nobody recognised? There must have been few men in Orphir who were not seen in Stromness, only a few miles distant, at least on market-days.

Women had been banned from Hudson Bay since the 1680s, when the Company allowed Governor Sergeant to bring out his wife and a female companion. The sufferings from which they had to be extricated – (from the cruel climate, primitive conditions, attacks by French, their ship lost in the ice ...) – caused the Committee to recall Sergeant and his *parcell of women* and pass a resolution forbidding any female a passage to Hudson Bay.[21] From that time till Isobel's arrival virtually no white woman had set foot in Rupert's Land.

Almost all the accounts of Isobel Gunn assume that the motivation for her disguise was to follow her lover. A man, John Scarth from Firth, 17 years older than Isobel, had entered the Company's service in 1789, come home on leave in 1796 (did he meet and impress the 16 year old Isobel then?) and signed on again for another eight years in 1797. He came home on leave in September 1805 and travelled back out to the Bay on the *Prince of Wales* with Isobel in the summer of 1806. When her child was born in December 1807 she gave Scarth's name as the father. Some at least of her colleagues assumed that she had joined the Company to follow Scarth. *She hired with Mr Geddes in Stromness as a man, in Men's Clothing 1806* wrote surveyor Peter Fidler, *remained at Albany one winter and her sex was not known till delivery except to one John Scarth her paramour on whose account she came out.*[22] In the Stromness baptismal register Isobel's son was *begot by John Scarth,*[23] and in the HBC archives it is noted that John Scarth had a son, James Scarth, whose mother was *Isabel Gunn.*

All the evidence, therefore, points to Isobel claiming, and Scarth accepting, his paternity of her child, but even if he had been *her paramour* in Orkney, I am unconvinced that he would have encouraged her to follow him to the Bay. The men went there to earn money, to help their impoverished families and to work their own way to a less impoverished future. No man would willingly have risked disgrace or demotion by smuggling a mistress onto the ship or their quarters at one of the forts. It is inconceivable that Isobel and Scarth (who had 16 years of experience of life in the Bay) could have had any illusions about enjoying a romantic relationship there. They would have known the likelihood that they would be sent to different posts and that, even if they were working in the same place, Isobel's disguise and her survival in the Bay depended on her being indistinguishable from the other labourers.

I find it hard to believe that a woman as tough, brave and resourceful as Isobel would have run away to Hudson Bay from purely romantic motives. She staked everything on this adventure. She knew that, unlike the men, she was going out on a one-way ticket: her action in masquerading as a man was so flagrantly immoral in the eyes of her contemporaries there was no way that she would ever be able to pick up the threads of her former life in Orkney again. To become the lover of Scarth – or anyone else – and risk pregnancy would obviously destroy not only her life in the Bay but her whole future. Did Rupert's Land offer an escape from the drab drudgery of her life in Orphir, a life of constant heavy toil with so little reward but ruined harvests and hunger, little prospect of marriage or of any improvement in her circumstances? Brother George and many other HBC men had come home with tales of their exploits – some horrific, but some exciting – and with money in their pockets. Is it impossible to imagine that Isobel took the great risks she took for Adventure? Morag MacInnes conjectures this version of the story in her poem *Alias Isobel*.

> *Why pit a man in me tale?*
> *Mibee*
> *I jist upped*
> *and went fur the romp …*
> *Beasts that weak*
> *they canna walk*
> *Fower bad harvests.*
> *Trowshot, fur aal the saucers*
> *o sippans we set on the howe.*
> *… Time*
> *tae lowp.* [24]

Did Isobel just decide there was nothing at home to keep her, nothing to lose even if she failed, that it was just time tae lowp?

Many of the women who adopted male dress initially for economic motives found it immensely liberating to step out of the constraints that society imposed on women. *To change from the cumbersome, unhealthy attire of a woman to the more convenient, healthful habiliments of a man*, wrote Elsa Guerin (alias 'Mountain Charley'), was to be instantly transformed into a state more physically comfortable as well as better paid.[25] There were many ballads written and sung about the women who made their great escape and, for a time at least, enjoyed their liberty; perhaps they reached Orkney. Whatever the truth, Isobel sailed out of Stromness on the *Prince of Wales* on 29th June 1806, with about 40 other Orcadians, new recruits like herself and returning old hands like Scarth. Five weeks later, the ship dropped anchor at Moose Factory and, on 27 August, John Fubbister and John Scarth were sent to the fort at Albany.

Summer in the Bay was short, and as soon as the ship landed the men were at work unloading the stores and preparing for the long winter by fishing, hunting, trapping and brewing, salting down partridge, geese, rabbits and deer and packing the provisions in sawdust or in ice-houses for their preservation. There was firewood to be cut and also timber for new buildings or repairing old ones; there were the few cows and pigs they had brought with them to be cared for, and hay made for their fodder. The labourers had to do all this in the relentlessly insect-ridden heat, driven mad by mosquitoes and flies. The new recruits soon learned that the climate of Rupert's Land was savagely inhospitable in all seasons.

Figure 7.6
A South East View of Albany Factory: A Winter View, watercolour by William Richards 1804-11. Richards was employed as a cooper and canoeman by the HBC and noted as an amateur artist. He may well have been at Albany at the same time as 'John Fubbister'. He died in the Bay at the age of 27. (Hudson's Bay Company Archives, Archives of Manitoba)

When the winter set in, there were still plenty of tasks to keep the Company servants employed. The decline of the beaver in areas easily accessible from the Bay was driving them further inland in the search for furs so stores had to be repacked for canoe transport to the interior the following summer. There were guns and ammunition to prepare for hunting, sleds and snowshoes to make for travelling, skins to dry and stretch for clothing, iron kettles and hatchets to beat out for trading. In the spring, when canoe-loads of furs started to arrive at the trading posts, they had to be packed and stored ready to be sent to England when the Company boats arrived.

The HBC archives have a record of all their employees and the expeditions they undertook. Early in September 1806, John Hodgson, the Chief at Albany, sent a party to canoe up the Albany River to Henley House with provisions and trading goods and return with timber for building new boats. The party included Fubbister and Steersman Scarth who knew the river well for he had spent eight seasons on it during his second contract. There were no complaints about Fubbister's performance. As HBC man Peter Fidler later said, she *worked at anything and well like the rest of the men.*[26]

In the early days of the Company, the Committee had tried to enforce a monastic state on their servants, keeping native women away from the forts, but it was only with the help of the women that their British employees were able to carry out their work, or even survive. The HBC men arrived totally without the skills or experience to survive in a sub-arctic environment. While the First Nations men were the main hunters, they too were dependent on the support of their wives. They ground the corn, made the essential moccasins (which the Europeans soon found to be the only suitable footwear) and the intricate netting of snowshoes, chopped firewood, skinned buffalo, dried the hides and sewed them into bags and made their meat into pemmican to store in them. The women on Lake Athabasca were skilled at fishing and salting fish; around the Bay they dried or salted geese. They snared small game, such as hares and partridges, collected berries and in some areas harvested wild rice and maple sugar. Often they saved traders from starvation.

In British colonial fashion, London Committees and chief officers were slow to understand the total dependence of their enterprises on native women. Samuel Hearne was prevented by the Governor at Churchill from taking Chipewyan women with him on his first attempts to reach the Coppermine river. To Matonabbee, the Chipewyan guide of the third and successful expedition of 1771-72, it was obvious that an expedition without women was doomed to failure. *When all the men are heavy laden, they can neither hunt nor travel to any considerable distance; and in case they meet with success in hunting, who is to carry the produce of their labour? Women ... also pitch our tents, make and mend our clothing, keep us warm at night; and in fact there is no such thing as travelling any considerable distance, or for any lengths of time, in this country, without their assistance. Women ... though they do everything, are maintained at a trifling expense; ... the very licking of their fingers in scarce times is sufficient for their subsistence.*[27]

Figure 7.7
Hudson Bay pipe. (Photograph by Rebecca Marr © Stromness Museum)

Women also made a huge contribution to the fur trade by dressing furs; the Council at York factory told the Committee that they *clean and put into a state of preservation all Beaver and Otter skins brought by the Indians undried and in bad condition.*[28] It was also their job to collect the wattappe, the roots of the spruce tree, which they split into fibres for sewing the birchbark canoes, and the spruce gum with which they caulked the seams. As the HBC moved inland, the men were increasingly dependent on women to help paddle and repair the canoes. (The irony cannot have escaped Isobel, that as soon as she was known to be a white woman, she was no longer allowed to paddle a canoe). As an intermediary between the native trappers and the white traders they were also invaluable, many could interpret between English and several First Nations' languages and they often played a diplomatic and peace-making role. It was only with the help of their wives that some of the more senior officers, such as William Tomison, were able to adapt so well to life in the interior.

It was fortunate for the traders that, for a start, the very different attitudes to sexual morality among the local people made it easy for them to acquire partners – whom they often married 'a la facon du pays' – and that the women found advantages in living at the forts. Life was easier for them, as they were not expected to do the hewing of wood and carrying of water which was their usual role, and European trade goods were more readily available. The down side was that they traded a great deal of their independence. In their own communities, a wife's children remained hers even if their father left her. As the wife of a white trader, a woman was subject to the rules of British patriarchal society and her mixed-race children were automatically the property of her husband. This was the cause of many harrowing separations as it was increasingly common for officers to send very young children, especially if they were boys, back to Britain to receive a 'civilised' education. There were other disadvantages in being a 'country wife'. The women who lived at the forts were more exposed to European diseases and to their most harmful import, alcohol and, living outside the taboos that guarded sexual behaviour in their own tribes, they tended to have far more children.

The traders were astonished by the strength of the native women, which seemed to justify Matonabee's statement: *Women were made for labour; one of them can carry, or haul, as much as two men can do,* and appalled at the way they were treated as beasts of burden. The lot of Cree women was: *an uninterrupted succession of toil and pain* according to Alexander Mackenzie.[29] Isobel must have listened to many conversations around the table or the camp fire when her companions discussed these attitudes, seemingly oblivious of the fact that their own mothers and sisters were little more than beasts of burden in Orkney. She herself had toiled under heavy loads at home in Kirbister and seen the other women of the parish wear into premature old age after a life of hard physical labour, often on an inadequate diet. George

Low had watched people at work gathering seaweed in Birsay. *This is their favourite manure and is carried up immediately as the tide leaves it, or they have use for it, in creels thro very narrow passages often cut thro the rock. This is performed by men and women, horses being useless in these dangerous footways. I have often seen 60 or 70 of these poor people hard at work in this slavish employment from morning to night, scarce allowing themselves time for eating, one part employed in filling the creels, and these mostly men, while the patient females lent their shoulders to the burden. This was continued for as long as any was to be had or they had use for it, without intermission, a most fatiguing work and fitter for asses than women, who indeed are here very much of burden ...*[30]

The senior officers, who usually came from better-off families, were amazed by the native women's no-fuss attitude towards childbirth in comparison to that of the pampered white women of the middle classes. *I can affirm*, wrote Alexander Graham, *that women have been taken in travail while on a journey; and they only drop behind the company, bring forth the little stranger, tie it up in a cradle and, carrying it on their backs, proceed as if nothing had happened.*[31] A delightful description of a two week old baby comes from J.H. Lefroy, who had obviously suffered at home the embarrassment of a young man presented with an infant relative for his admiration. *It ... was packed up in that peculiar Indian fashion which I think so excellent. It was so neat and compact, about fourteen inches long, unlike an ordinary baby, which may be put in ones arms, and one does not know which end one had hold of, or which is baby and which is petticoat. It was made to hang up or set upright ... The outside case is made of cloth ... and embroidery; the inside stuffing is a soft silky moss, very abundant in this country, so that nothing can be so economical.*[32]

Isobel must have been intrigued by the behaviour and skills of the First Nations' women and, coming from a family of girls and a community in which women greatly outnumbered men, it is hard to imagine that she did not feel the loneliness of being cut off from female company. A loneliness greatly accentuated when she realized that she was pregnant. However the only facts we know of her life in Rupert's Land come from the HBC records for John Fubbister. We know that she spent her first winter in Albany fort, and the following May was sent on another three-week canoe expedition taking inland cargo to Martin Falls on the Albany river and returning with furs, again with Scarth in the team. After a couple of days back in Albany, Fubbister was one of the crew of several boats which returned to Martin Falls with more cargo. In the fall 'his' brigade travelled up the Winnipeg and Red Rivers to the fort at Pembina. Hugh Heney arrived to take charge of the post in mid September; one of his men, David Spence, had drowned in rapids on the way. December was bitterly cold and stormy but buffalo had been plentiful so there was a good supply of food. The men visited the North-West Company post of Alexander Henry to share the Christmas celebrations.

Henry's journal entry for 29 December has often been quoted. The young HBC men returned to their post that morning but Fubbister asked to be allowed to stay behind.

I was surprised at the fellow's demand; however, I told him to sit down and warm himself. I returned to my own room, where I had not been long before he sent one of my people, requesting the favor of speaking with me. Accordingly I stepped down to him, and was much surprised to find him extended on the hearth, uttering dreadful lamentations; he stretched out his hands towards me, and in piteous tones begged me to be kind to a poor, helpless, abandoned wretch, who was not of the sex I had supposed, but an unfortunate Orkney girl, pregnant, and actually in childbirth. In saying this she opened her jacket, and displayed a pair of beautiful, round, white breasts ... In about an hour she was safely delivered of a fine boy, and that same day she was conveyed home in my cariole, where she soon recovered.[33]

Isobel named John Scarth as the man by whom she had been 'debauch'd' and called her child James Scarth. Was Scarth indeed the lover she had followed from Orkney in a romantic dream? Or was she the victim of rape or blackmail? Whatever the truth, they had no further relationship. He came home to Orkney on leave once more in 1812, while she was living in poverty with the five year old James (did they meet, did he have any remorse for her situation?) The following year he returned to Rupert's Land for good, retiring to the Red River colony in 1815 and seven years later he married Nelly Saunderson, the Cree widow of a white trader and the mother of his two daughters. The only other information about Scarth in the HBC archives is a list of his purchases in the colony store: tobacco, alcohol, playing cards, powder and ball and an English New Testament ...

Strangely enough, James Scarth was not the first white baby born at Pembina. He was beaten to it by almost a year by the child of a French-Canadian trapper Jean-Baptiste Lagimodière and his wife, Marie-Anne Gaboury. She was the first European woman to travel and settle in western Canada and her life was even more adventurous than that of Isobel and ended much more happily. Following her husband's nomadic hunting life, she had her first baby at the HBC post at Pembina in January 1807 and left by canoe that spring for Fort des Prairies with three other trappers and their Cree wives. In 1808 her horse was chased by buffalo. After a hair-breadth escape, she gave birth the same night and was riding back to Edmonton three days later. The couple were the first Europeans to settle at the Red River in 1812 but the following years saw the colony repeatedly harried and destroyed in the savage conflict between the two rival fur-trading companies. The fur-trade life was not for the faint-hearted.

With the dramatically sudden revelation of her sex, Isobel's days of wearing man's clothes and doing a man's work were over. Like all the other women who worked in male disguise and were eventually discovered, she was in disgrace, back in European women's dress and only allowed to perform the kind of menial jobs that were thought suitable for a female. Now that she could no longer enjoy even the camaraderie among her former colleagues, her loneliness must have been acute. In the spring, when the rivers melted and canoe travel was possible again, 'Mary Fubbister' was sent back to Albany. (Did she choose not to resume the name Isobel, or was Mary thrust upon her? It was the name commonly given to native women whose own names the Europeans could not be bothered to learn). No matter that she had canoed and portaged all the way there, even though heavily pregnant, or that First Nations' women paddled canoes just as much as their men. She had to sit (resentfully I am sure) and be paddled. Peter Fidler heard that Hugh Heney's party had gone down the Red River below Pembina on May 21st, *the woman Mary Fubbester who was delivered of a Boy* with them, he wrote in his journal.[34]

252

Grim as her situation might be in Hudson Bay, Isobel knew it would be far worse back in Orkney, and she managed to resist being sent home with the Company ships that summer of 1808. She was found a job as a washerwoman, and 'nurse' to the children at the Fort. The number of mixed-race children at the trading posts was growing. By the end of the 18th century, the Company had made a grudging admission that it should take some responsibility for their education and sent out a number of reading books and spelling primers to the Bay. It was 1808, however, before a serious attempt was made to establish schools and, with some difficulty, four schoolmasters were hired and sent to different posts. The move was welcomed by many of the officers, who wanted their daughters to have as European an education as possible and to be estranged from their mothers' culture. It was the beginning of the racist attitudes (which grew much worse as European women started to come out to Rupert's Land as officers' wives), which were to drive a wedge between the native peoples and the white settlers.

There were many anomalies in European attitudes to race and culture. Although the survival of the HBC employees had depended on the help of the native women and their traditional skills, the same men wanted their daughters to grow up as Europeans, isolated from their mothers' society which *would keep alive the Indian language and with it, its native superstition which ought to be obliterated with all possible care*.[35] All children were admitted to the schools on condition that they were baptized with a European name, and the education was designed to drown native 'superstition' with a thorough dose of British-style Christianity. The children learned to read from Trimmer's *Sacred History,* to recite the Church catechism and to sing Dr Watt's *Divine Songs for Children.* John Best at Albany ordered *Duties of Woman* to be sent from England for the edification of the little girls at the fort.[36] Sylvia Van Kirk has pointed out how vulnerable this white education made the girls. When their fathers or husbands died, or abandoned them when they retired or took a European wife, they had no skills to support themselves. When European women increasingly became part of trader society, the mixed-race women were automatically seen as of lower social status, but they did not have the support of a native kinship network either.

William Harper's school at Fort Albany was the largest, with 23 children in 1808. In September he wrote home, not unsympathetically, about Isobel to his patron in Orkney, William Watt of Breckness: *I have to inform your Honr that we have got an Orkney woman here, she came out for the sake of a Sweetheart ... she has been Inland 1500 miles and has had a Child to one of the men that was in Company with her and was never known to be a Woman till the very hour she was Delivered ... she is now at the factory and her Child, and her chief employment is washing for all hands, which indeed she is no Witch at, as I think, as she has been washing for me, the Governor intends to make her a nurse for the Scholars, as she seems not inclined to go home, and I believe he feels more for her misfortune than she is sensible of doing herself.*[37] Harper's last comment is interesting. Much as she hated being a laundrywoman, Isobel was not wallowing in self-pity. On 16th October 1808 the schoolmaster conducted divine service at Albany and afterwards *he Baptized the Son of Isabel Gun ... which performances was afterwards duly registered.* [38]

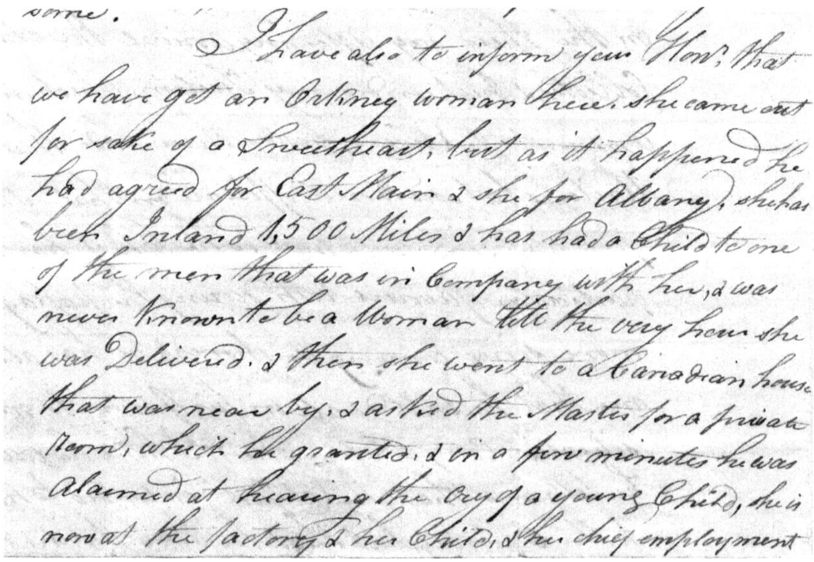
come.
I have also to inform your Honr that we have got an Orkney woman here, she came out for sake of a Sweetheart, but as it happened he had agreed for East Main & she for Albany, she has been Inland 1,500 Miles & has had a Child to one of the men that was in Company with her, & was never Known to be a Woman till the very hour she was Delivered. & then she went to a Canadian house that was near by, & asked the Master for a private Room, which he granted, & in a few minutes he was alarmed at hearing the Cry of a young Child, she is now at the factory & her Child, & her chief employment

Figure 7.8

Extract from letter from William Harper, schoolmaster, Albany to William Watt, Breckness, Orkney, 5/9/1808. (OLA D31/35/3/2)

It is unlikely that Isobel received any letters from her own family – we do not know if they even knew where she was – but she would have heard news of Orkney from the other servants when the Company ships arrived in the summer with the annual mail drop. The weather and farming prospects had not improved at home. On Christmas day in 1806, the worst storm that anyone in Orkney remembered had wreaked havoc in the islands, flattening cornstacks and even houses in a whirlwind of destruction. Two ships were lost off South Ronaldsay with nearly all their men. The famines of the following years have already been mentioned.[39] Whatever Isobel felt about going home, the Company had no intention of allowing her to stay for another year. On 14th September 1809 the Albany Fort Journal reported her as *discharged from your Honours Service ... We cannot think of keeping this Woman any longer, as she is of bad Character and has not answered the intentions for which she was detained.*[40] On 20th September *Isabella Gun and her Son* were marked on the passenger list of the *Prince of Wales,* and on 29th October they disembarked in Stromness. It was exactly three years and four months after 'John Fubbister's' departure.

Kirk records should have been the place to discover what happened to Isobel when she came home. One would expect that the Kirk Session of her parish would have summoned her to appear before them for 'Discipline', on account of her illegitimate child and the deception and immorality of cross-dressing. It was rare for anyone to refuse Discipline, however humiliating, for to defy the Kirk would be to place oneself altogether outside the community and become a social outcast. However there is no reference to Isobel in the Orphir Kirk Session minutes and, very sadly, the minute books for the Stromness Kirk Session for the years 1763-1812 have been lost, so we will never know what was said to – or about – her. However, only two weeks after Isobel's return, the Stromness Parish Register of Baptisms for 1809 records: *Nov 12th Isabella Gunn had a child begot in Hudsons Bay by John Scarth born the 29th Dec 1807 and baptized the 12th day of Nov 1809 by the Revd Mr William Clouston named James.* The fact that Clouston was willing to baptize the child so soon after their arrival – before Isobel had time to be Disciplined – suggests that James had become seriously ill on the long voyage home and Isobel was worried that he might not live. Also, that she –

or the minister – did not think that the baptism by the schoolmaster in Albany would have been effective if the worst happened.

In 1810 Isobel received the balance of her wages, £13:0:11d, from David Geddes and the page in the Company accounts *for Dr* [debtor] *Jn Fubbister Labourer alias Isabella Gun* (the last words added in another hand) was closed. It is unfortunate that we do not know what was said at their meeting! Her account had been debited twice for goods she had bought at the factory (tobacco, knives, clothes) and the sum of £1: 4 shillings paid to one James Brown, but the largest sum, £6:0:0, a considerable proportion of her total wages, had been paid to Catherine Oman. In 1821, the earliest available census, there is no-one of this name in Orphir or St Andrews, where most of Isobel's family lived, but a Catherine Oman is living in Stromness, *age: 58, occupation: Old Maid*. Presumably this older friend or relative had known Isobel's secret from the beginning and if, as seems likely, Isobel was ostracized by her family and most of the community on her return, Catherine would have been a good reason for her to find a home for herself and James in Stromness.

Figure 7.9
The Hudson's Bay Company Ships Prince of Wales and Eddystone bartering with Inuit off the Upper Savage Islands, Hudson Strait, watercolour by Robert Hood 1819. (Library and Archives Canada)

She must have often seen the men waiting outside the agent's house on the harbour to sign on for Hudson Bay. Geddes had evidently been reduced to scraping the barrel for recruits for in 1810 the Committee complained: *For some time past they have had cause to lament the very inefficient Men who have been sent from the Orknies to the Compys Settlements ... Of late many men have been sent out who, on their arrival were found totally unfit for the Service. The Board will not consider themselves bound by any Agreement, you may make, unless the Men engaged by you are Stout able and active ...*[41] 'Fubbister' may have been in their mind, but it seems that, until the moment her baby was born, Isobel was probably rather more *stout able and active* than many of the men employed. The problem was not only finding suitable recruits but persuading them to stay for more than the minimum period.

A memo of 1812 headed *Suggestions for the Consideration of the Honourable Hudson's Bay Company* reveals that, although Orcadians had for so long been the backbone of the HBC, they were not regarded as ideal employees. *One great obstacle to your inland commerce is a want of men and even those you employ are but ill calculated for the country. When an Orkneyman engages in your service it is more from necessity than inclination; he can find employment nowhere else, and when he has accomplished his darling object of gathering a few pounds, he bids farewell to a country that affords him no pleasure; this often obliges you to abandon Posts until a supply of men arrives from those Islands, so that when you reestablish these Posts, you find yourselves Strangers to the country and almost forgot by the Natives. Another thing Orkney men are unacquainted with the manner of voyaging in Canoes, by which the Northern business is conducted.*[42] Increasingly, the HBC was able to recruit native-born (often mixed-race) Canadians and the proportion of Orkney men on their books fell.

However, Company ships continued to call at Stromness and young men continued to sail away on them, leaving behind broken-hearted sweethearts and brand-new brides who wrote them letters full of loss and longing and the fear that their lover might take *some indinen wife.*[43] Anne Waters wrote to her sweetheart in the Bay in 1850: *my Brother hast got mared to Betsy Tealur and he is Away to Hudson beay Abut sex Wekes after he mared and John Fleat hase got mared to A strums* [Stromness] *girl five wekes Agoe and he is away to*

Hudson beay.)[44] Letters to relations in the Bay are also eloquent of the poverty and unemployment in Orkney which had driven the men away. *The work in this Country is farely done there is Nothing to do at all* wrote William Ross from Kirkwall to his son on Vancouver Island. [45]

Figure 7.10
'The Great Traders of the Great West', recruitment poster (detail) for the Hudson's Bay Company. Signed A.H. Hider (1870-1952). (Photograph by Rebecca Marr © Stromness Museum)

Isobel lived in Orkney for another 52 years after her return, in poverty and obscurity. According to the 1821 census, *Isoble Gunn*, aged 48 (she would actually have been 40, but ages are often very inaccurately recorded in the early censuses), was living in the Outertown district of Stromness with her son James Scarth, aged 14, and Nelly Craig, aged 8, who were both at school. Nelly may have been the daughter of Isobel's sister Janet Craig and, if so, she had contact with some of her family at least. There is nothing to suggest that she received any help from her brother George, who was relatively well off by this time but supporting a large family. Ten years after being invalided home in 1799, George married Margaret, one of his Leask relations from St Andrews and 16 years younger than him. In the 1821 census, they appear living comfortably at Naversdale in Orphir, with eight children and 24 black cattle, 4 sheep, 24 geese, 6 swine, a plough and a cart to their name – a substantial farm for the time.[46] George may have felt that Isobel had totally disgraced herself and her family and wanted nothing to do with her.

After 1821 there is a gap of fully 30 years in which we have no information about her at all. There was no census in 1831 and in the first general census in 1841 her name does not occur in the records of any of the Orkney parishes. This gives some weight to the tradition that she became a vagrant; if she was sleeping in barns or under haystacks at this time she would have avoided the house-to-house count of the enumerator.

What we do know, from the *New Statistical Account* of 1841 and contemporary letters, is how little farming and living conditions had improved in the previous 50 years. Orkney continued to be dogged by cycles of atrocious weather. Isobel was one of many single females living in poverty, some of them trying to eke out a living at plaiting straw (an industry that had once been a considerable source of female employment, but declined as straw bonnets went out of fashion) or knitting, some of them simply labelled as paupers. According to the *Account* for Stromness, there were over 500 persons over the age of 50 in the parish and 85 on the poor roll, *in general 2s or 2s 6d is the sum allotted quarterly ... some allowance is made during winter for fuel.* (Male day labourers were earning a shilling a day at this time and females 6d, while two shillings a day would pay a skilled craftsman; paupers had to survive on two shillings **for 90 days**, in a time of rising prices). Collections taken at the kirk door, from congregations that were mostly struggling to keep themselves off the poor roll, and fees charged for marriage banns and the hire of the mortcloth for funerals,[47] were the only source of poor relief. These were very small sums that had to be thinly spread. *In general the people are so very poor, that they evince no reluctance to seek parochial relief.* [48] In the worst years, deaths from starvation were only avoided by the actions of a few of the landowning class, like Thomas Balfour, Member of Parliament, who worked hard to organize relief during the famine of 1837.[49]

Wherever Isobel wandered to in the thirty lost years, by 1851 she had returned to Stromness and was living on her own at Hellyhole and giving her occupation as a Stocking Knitter. It is intriguing to wonder whether she knew any of the women who were brought to Orkney from Hudson Bay by Orcadian fathers or husbands. In the same year Letitia Hargrave, the wife of Chief Factor James Hargrave, wrote of *a widow from Orkney her name Mrs Flett who came out by the ship and set up in Red Rivers as a dress maker ... She is a 'native' but has been in Orkney for 30 years.*[50]

In the 1861 census, Isobel was still in Stromness but had moved again, to Main Street, and was working as a 'Spinner and Mitten Maker'. Later that same year, two months after her 81st birthday, William Rendall, Inspector of the Poor, registered her death on 7th November *of natural decay.* Enough of her fame, or notoriety, was remembered for the death of a pauper to feature in the Deaths column of *The Orcadian* on 23rd November. *At Stromness, a few days ago, Isabella Gunn, at an advanced age. Isabel in her youthful days dressed herself in male attire and went out to Hudsons Bay in search of her lover and lived there for sometime till her sex was discovered.*[51]

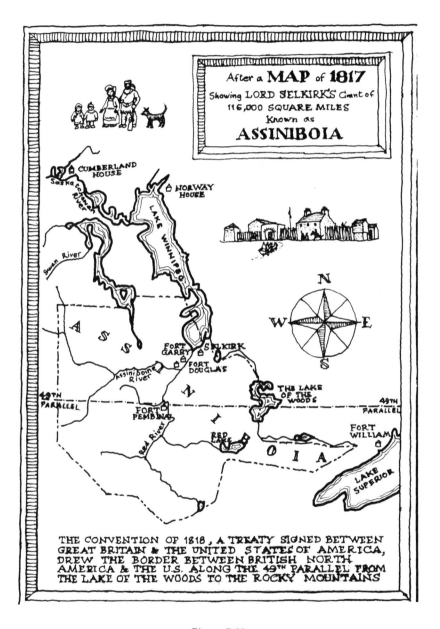

After a **MAP** of **1817**
Showing LORD SELKIRK'S Grant of
116,000 SQUARE MILES
Known as
ASSINIBOIA

CUMBERLAND HOUSE
Saskatchewan River
NORWAY HOUSE
LAKE WINNIPEG
Swan River
ASSINIBOIA
Assiniboine River
FORT GARRY
SELKIRK
FORT DOUGLAS
THE LAKE OF THE WOODS
49TH PARALLEL
FORT PEMBINA
Red River
RED LAKE
49TH PARALLEL
FORT WILLIAM
LAKE SUPERIOR
N W E S

THE CONVENTION OF 1818, A TREATY SIGNED BETWEEN
GREAT BRITAIN & THE UNITED STATES OF AMERICA,
DREW THE BORDER BETWEEN BRITISH NORTH
AMERICA & THE U.S. ALONG THE 49TH PARALLEL FROM
THE LAKE OF THE WOODS TO THE ROCKY MOUNTAINS

Figure 7.11

Red River Letters

James Sutherland was one of a number of Orkney men, mostly employees of the HBC like himself, who chose to retire in Rupert's Land and never return home. In 1831 he wrote from the Red River Settlement (later part of the Canadian province of Manitoba) to his brother John at home in Knarston in South Ronaldsay. The picture of abundance and prosperity that James paints gives no idea of the violence and disasters which had attended the birth of the settlement only a few years earlier. *I have every comfort within my Grasp. I see my family rising about me ... My Farm produces more wheat that we can consume ... I can sport a change of Horses, my Cattle, Pigs and poultry breed faster than I can eat them, the dairy gives me more butter than we use – the river at my door affords abundance of Fish in Variety, what can man wish for more ...*[52]

The Red River colony was created by Thomas Douglas, the 5th earl of Selkirk, to provide a home for some of his impoverished countrymen who had been dispossessed by the Clearances and left without homes or livelihood. From 1799, when he inherited his title and estates, Selkirk devoted his wealth and connections to purchasing land in the territory then known as British North America. He hoped to create self-sustaining agricultural colonies but two attempts at establishing Highland families in Prince Edward Island and at Baldoon in Upper Canada failed, and his requests for a grant of land from the HBC were at first refused. The Company's territory was vast, stretching from the Atlantic Ocean westward to the Rocky Mountains and from the central prairies to the Arctic Circle, but it was an exclusive commercial domain, jealously guarded against any competition in the fur trade. By 1810, however, the Selkirk family owned sufficient shares in the HBC to have a controlling interest and the Company saw the advantage in having a settled farming population that could produce food for their traders and reduce their dependence on imports from Britain. In return for a grant of 116,000 square miles – an area about five times the size of Scotland – Selkirk had to guarantee that the colony would provide 200 men annually to the HBC and keep out of the fur trade.

Selkirk's new settlement was based where the city of Winnipeg now stands, at the confluence of the Red and Assiniboine rivers, and he called it Assiniboia. The place had long been a trading rendezvous and was already home to native Assiniboine, Cree and Ojibwe traders as well as Métis, French-speaking people of mixed descent. In July 1811 a working party of 36 Scots and Irish under Miles Macdonnell sailed from Stornoway to prepare the settlement but, after a hideous 61 day passage on an ill-equipped ship, they only reached the HBC post at York Factory that year. Illness and desertion thinned their ranks over the winter and it was not until August 1812 that the remnant completed the 700 mile journey to take possession of Selkirk's domain.

By that time it was too late in the season to plant crops as well as building houses and a fort. It was fortunate for the early settlers from Britain that a French family of experienced pioneers also made their home in Red River in 1812. Jean-Baptiste Lagimodière, a hunter and trapper (and father of the child who had pipped Isobel Gunn's son to the post five years earlier by being the first white baby born in Pembina) was hired by Macdonnell, the first governor, to supply the settlers with food.

The first group of colonists from Ireland and the Hebrides reached Red River in May 1813 and a second group set out that June. These were mostly families from Kildonan and Helmsdale in Sutherland, lands which had just been granted to Patrick Sellar to 'improve' by evicting all the tenants to make a vast sheep farm. They were not destitute people but once-prosperous farmers who had paid £10 a head for their passage and the promise of an allotment of 100 acres of land at five shillings an acre, with a year's provisions until their first crops could be harvested. Ninety-seven settlers gathered in Stromness and embarked on the HBC ship, the *Prince of Wales* – the same ship that had taken Isobel Gunn out to the Bay and back again. It was another disastrous journey. Not only did the settlers endure two months of rough passage but typhus broke out on board. In panic, the captain hastily set them ashore at Fort Churchill, 150 miles from York Factory where accommodation and supplies were waiting for them. Frozen, sick and starving all winter, a party of 31 men and 20 women set out on snowshoes in April and reached York after three weeks. Finally, in August 1814, fourteen months after leaving Stromness, the survivors of the party reached the Red River.

From the beginning the settlers were beset by all the disasters that man and nature could throw at them: war, epidemics, crop failure, prairie fires and catastrophic floods. The first harvests were poor and there was little sign of the promised land of peace and plenty for the wretched immigrants. Macdonnell attempted to conserve food stocks by forbidding buffalo-hunting from horseback and the export of pemmican from the colony. It was a disastrous public-relations blunder; the livelihood of the Métis depended on hunting buffalo and trading pemmican with the NWC traders who in turn depended on these provisions to supply their canoe brigades. Both were infuriated by this threat and retaliated by enticing many of the settlers to desert to Canada and harrying those who remained.

The next few years must have been terrifying ones for the settler families. In 1815 the NWC set fire to the settlement and captured Macdonnell and 150 of his people. He was replaced as governor by Robert Semple who repopulated the colony the following year with some new settlers. There were more violent clashes, ending in the 'Massacre of Sevenoaks' in which Semple and 20 others were killed by Métis soldiers. Again, the houses were burnt down and the settlement abandoned. Lagimodière was captured when he was away carrying dispatches to Lord Selkirk in Montreal and in captivity heard reports of a massacre at the HBC post where he had left his wife Marie-Anne and their four children. In fact, they had fled down the river and taken refuge with friendly First Nations' people, and the Lagimodières survived to become one of the most prosperous and successful of the River families and play a significant rôle in the area's history.[53] Another settler family that must have been caught up in the fighting was that of John Scarth, supposed father of Isobel Gunn's child, who was last seen retiring to the Red River in 1815 with his wife and children.

About the same date, James Sutherland was in Montreal and writing to his father and younger brother in South Ronaldsay with a much more positive view of immigration. *I was four days coming to this place by Coach* [from Quebec] *which enabled me to see the Country and a very fine Country it is – what a Contrast between the laboring people in Scotland and this; here they seem to enjoy every comfort of Life with little labour even the lowest classes have everything ... I have seen several scotch and Orkney people who are settled in this Country and one and all of them Bless the day they left their native Country.*[54] James had joined the HBC at the age of 19 in 1797 and had a very successful career. By 25 he was in charge of the major trading post Cumberland House, in 1814 he controlled all the Red River trading posts, by 1821 he was a Chief Factor in Saskatchewan and the following year a Councillor of the Governors of the HBC Territories. He survived being attacked and taken prisoner by NWC. After a lifetime of travelling in the Territories and two journeys back to Britain, he retired to the Red River where he died, surrounded by several generations of his large family.

The majority of Orkney men in the service of the HBC were illiterate labourers who served their contract and returned home. Men like Sutherland, his friend Alexander Kennedy and William Tomison (all natives of South Ronaldsay) owed their administrative posts in the HBC to the fact that they were educated men. All settled in Rupert's Land, made permanent marriages and raised mixed-race families. James was well aware of the advantage of literacy. As he wrote to John: *Of all the blessings bestowed upon man no one distinguished more from the brute Creation than that of having the Power to impress on a blank Sheet of Paper our Hopes and fears our Ideas and Sentiments ... to hold conversations with friends millions of miles from us, and you and I ought to be particularly grateful to our Maker and not forget that we are greatly indebted to our earthly Parent for enabling us to possess that Power.*[55] We can also be grateful that Sutherland had that Power and did commit many of his Ideas and Sentiments to paper in long letters to his brother, and that many of those letters have survived. We know from the HBC archives where Orkney men worked and when and in what capacity, but it is rare to know, from their own words, what they thought and felt.

Figure 7.12
Fort Garry, a trading post on the Red River, early 1800s. Hand-coloured woodcut.
(North Wind Picture Archives)

Many of them, especially those who chose to stay permanently in Rupert's Land, must have struggled (as Sutherland certainly did) with the conflicting pulls of homes and families in the old world and the new. James was a man of strong attachments. For nearly fifty years he was torn between his love for his Orkney family and his love and sense of duty towards his own children and dependants in America, between the tug to go home to his native island and his dread of the long journey and that island's *Dreary Climate*. He swings between contentment and depression, at one time proud of his affluence and at another complaining of hardship and his *great expences*. He takes the Hudson Bay story a stage further, into the world of the settler rather than the trader, and into the Company's legacy of mixed-blood people, a great many of them with Orkney names and genes.

It has been my lot to have a large family in a savage country and I consider it to be my duty to Provide for them in this world and put them in a way to prepare themselves for the happiness Promised in the world to come – to accomplish this I make a great sacrifice in separating myself from Friends, Relations and Country but as the intention is good I hope that God will prosper it and my Relations forgive me. The thought of being separated from yourself in the evening of life is the only thing that hangs heavy on my mind ...[56]

Anxiety for his family is the main theme of James' letters, always he is trying to gather them together under his roof and the worst anguish he experiences is when he takes his son William to Orkney and leaves him there for several years' schooling. *I never regretted anything I ever did in my lifetime as the bringing my Boy home the thought of being so far separated from him has given me a great deal of anxiety ever since I left him but I hope it will be for the good of both his soul and body to get a little Education ...*[57]

When Lord Selkirk heard the news of the disaster at Sevenoaks he was leading a band of new settlers he had recruited to Red River. His men were DeMeurons, Swiss ex-mercenary soldiers, who swiftly retaliated by seizing the NWC's Fort William and recapturing their own Fort Douglas. The settlement was re-established, Selkirk distributed land and succeeded in making treaties with the local tribes and restoring confidence, but the colony that he had created with so much hope and altruism destroyed him. Exhausted by lengthy litigation in Canada with the NWC, he left for Britain in 1818 but he never saw Scotland or the Red River again. He died of consumption in Pau in France in 1820, aged only 48.

The following year, 1821, the Hudson's Bay and North-West Companies merged and the long decades of violence and deaths caused by their rivalries finally ended. However, the settlers still had to battle with their environment for survival. In 1818 and 1819, plagues of locusts devastated their crops. In 1826 the river flooded to the greatest extent ever known and virtually destroyed the settlement. There were less tangible plagues: schools and clergy had been promised; to the annoyance of the Presbyterian Scots, the first churchmen to arrive were Roman Catholic priests (the Métis were Catholic) and, when a Protestant missionary finally reached them in 1820, he was an Anglican.

Selkirk's executors cut expenses by refusing to recruit new European immigrants but the population grew rapidly with the influx of retired fur traders and their native families and they were impressively resilient to the setbacks. By 1827 there were over 1,000 farmers in the colony with their dependants. In August that year

Sutherland was on his way back from Britain to the HBC post at Norway House. *On my voyage here I visited Red River and certainly was unexpectedly surprised to find the people there so contented and comfortable for nevertheless that they had a Poor crop last year owing to the Flood of the preceding spring they had not felt the want of Food, fish they got in abundance which with Potatoes a little bread Plenty of Butter and Cheese and a good deal of fresh Beef of their own rearing they lived well.*[58]

James must have crossed the Atlantic at least five times. In 1813 he came home with his son William who he left in John's care, returning to the Bay in 1814. There is a gap in the letters between 1817 and 1826, when he retired from the Company, came to Britain in October and met John in Edinburgh. In March 1827 he wrote from Liverpool while waiting for his ship back to America and there is little homesickness for Orkney in his letter. *The Country I am going to is a rising Country and in course of time will be a great country. Great Britain and Orkney in Particular is on the decline and many thousands of them that now inhabit it will have to [?] for another country.*[59]

The length of the journey varied considerably. The unfortunate first group of Red River settlers were storm-tossed for two months; Sutherland made the reverse sailing from York Factory in only 26 days in 1826, but the Atlantic crossing was only part of the ordeal. His description of his return journey stretches the imagination to picture the immense distances these men covered, both in connecting the outposts of the HBC and in their heroic efforts to link and keep in touch with their sundered families. It started with a *tedious passage* of 42 days due to contrary winds, then, after two days in New York, *start with a steam boat came up a river 160 miles against a rapid Current in 12 hours this is reckoned the fastest Boat afloat in any country, next day I took Coach from a Place called Albany and came across country through a very rugged country and bad roads and came only about 60 miles in 14 hours and next morning start again in a steam Boat remained in her all day and all night and came through a lake about 120 miles we again landed and took coach for about 18 miles at the end of which we arrived safe at this place* [Montreal] *... found all our canoes for Hudsons Bay had taken their Departure ...*[60]

To continue to Norway House, Sutherland had to buy a canoe and hire a crew. *The voyage was the longest and most tiresome I ever performed, I was solitary at times having no Companion and did not even perfectly understand the men that was with me as they all spoke French ... I suffered much from constant exposure to extreme Heat and alternately cold, and the incessant torment from mosquitoes exceeded anything I had before seen ...*[61] He had left England in March, reached Montreal early in May, and did not expect to reach his family at Red River until mid July.

He spent the winter there, intending a temporary stay. For years he had complained of severe bouts of illness, but he wrote to John that due to *the Salubrity of the Climate* and the constant exercise since he had taken up farming and gardening, *my health recovered so much that I determined on remaining in a country and with an employment that seemed to agree with me so well ... In fact I do not see what I have to go in search of in another country; here I have everything that man requires for the good of both soul and body – Religion in its purity, the best of Climates, a soil that Produces all the Productions of the earth in Perfection and with very little labour, the society is not extensive but agreeable. My children I can get them educated sufficient to enable them to serve their God and enable them to perform all the duties of life, and if they are brought up to Industry, they will be as happy and independent as they can be in any other country.*[62]

While James was *dashing about in* [his] *carriage* and enjoying plentiful food and agreeable society, poor John (whose letters have not survived) was at home in South Ronaldsay, dealing with an ageing father, a grasping stepmother, wrangles over property and Orkney's perennial problems of failed crops and shortage of money. *I am sorry to hear of the distresses in my native country,*[63] wrote James, but he refused to encourage his brother to follow him. Even for a man with some education, it was hard to get a rung on the administrative ladder of the HBC. *I think it would be a wild plan of yours to go to America you hardly can expect to earn a livelihood by any other means than that of hard labour ... you will have the chance of being a slave all your life and earn little or nothing.*[64] John accepted the advice and stayed in Orkney to toil over Knarston's small farm and receive James' annual letters describing his prosperity, his *800 acres of the best of Country,* his multiplying flocks and herds and progeny.

James formally married his 'country wife', Jane Flett, and remained at Red River with most of his numerous descendants for the rest of his life, but his letters show him still torn between attachment to his roots and to his River family. John sent him out parcels of Orkney stockings and gloves and the *Edinburgh Weekly Journal* or *The Scotsman* so that he could keep abreast of Scottish news. It was a particularly sad moment when his good friend and fellow-islander Alexander Kennedy left Red River to return to Britain for good. He had *enjoyed so much of Mr Kennedys cheerful company, and nothing would have given me greater Pleasure than to have accompanied him home were it at all Practicable, but I dread a Voyage home by Hudsons Bay and still more the climate of Orkney or any Part of great Britain.*[65] He was also held back by the knowledge that his family were still dependent on him, although he was able to report good progress in settling his daughters. *I have now got all my daughters married, the last two, on one day, to an Orkney Man and a Half-Breed native of this country both of the name of James Inkster – the first is from Orphar and a boatbuilder to trade, the second is the son of an industrious good man has a good farm well stocked ...*[66] Inkster is a distinctively Orcadian name, particularly associated with the parish of Orphir; the marriage link with the two James Inksters suggests how close-knit was the Orkney community within the settlement.

My grandchildren increase rapidly he wrote a year later, in 1832, *... so that when I get all my Sons, Sons in law, Daughters and Daughters in law with already Nine Grandchildren around me I consider myself as one of the Patriarchs of Old, and my Roots and Branches have taken so firm a hold of this Soil that it will be impossible for me to leave it, for all depend upon my advice and the greater part on my Purse ...*[67]

As Patriarch of a large family, James had heavy responsibilities, and the colony was heading for more difficult times. In 1836 the Selkirk family transferred Assiniboia to the HBC, which ruled it solely for its own economic advantage. Its monopoly of trade stifled any economic development and the lack of opportunity for an increasingly literate population led to an exodus of young people. After two poor harvests, James' annual letter home painted a very different picture of Red River from his earlier glowing reports. *Red River is getting quite an altered place for the last 2 years we have had very bad crops. Few in the settlement raised enough Bread for themselves and many was at Starvation. I fortunately had in the House about 100 Bushels of Wheat from Crop 1835 so that I felt no want. Our present crop is poor and late so that if we have early frosts we will not have Bread.*[68] In 1841 one of his grandchildren joined a gruelling trek to find a new home. *This last summer a kind of mania got in the people here to go to the Columbia River on the NE coast of the continent and on 1st June 100 souls started to go there on horses oxen and carts ... some is of opinion that the winter will set in before they reach their destination if so they will have their trials if they should escape with their life.*[69]

Figure 7.13
Birch-bark canoes in rapids on the Red River. Hand-coloured woodcut. (North Wind Picture Archives)

James was aware that the colony's problems were not only uncertain harvests but the perennial ones of changing expectations. The standard of living that had seemed good to the early pioneers (many of them fleeing destitution in Scotland) was no longer adequate for the new generation of settlers, and James admitted he could not resist trying to keep up with the new life style himself. *We have here now some rich old fellows that has acquired large fortunes in the service have got married to European females and cut a dash and have introduced a system of extravagance within the place that is followed by*

271

all that cant afford it, and I to keep up a little respectability have followed it in a small way.[70]

Finding suitable employment for his sons was a constant source of worry. Brother John had evidently offered to take care of a younger son so that he could have a Scottish education. James' response is interesting, given his anguish when he left William in Orkney out of a sense of duty to do the best for him. *I feel obliged for your kind offer towards your namesake but I perceive that the Children of this Country do the best that is brought up in this Country, all those that have been educated in Europe acquire a Pride that unfits them for the customs and habits of this Country and the greater part of them turn out to be blackguards or unfit to do for themselves.*[71] Was he already aware that his adored William, about to be married to a girl of extravagant tastes, was turning out to be a wastrel?

His sons had received a good education in the colony but it was turning out to be a double-edged blessing as there was only manual work available in the settlement and, outside of it, the Red River children were finding that growing racial prejudice was blocking their way. Under the governorship of Sir George Simpson, who was virtually the British viceroy of all Rupert's Land from 1820 to 1860,[72] attitudes hardened towards mixed-race people. In the Rupert's Land that Isobel Gunn's knew, in the first years of the 19th century, white women did not exist and friendships and intermarriage between the European fur-traders and native people had been common. As Victorian Britain grew into an Empire, so did racial arrogance and assumptions of white superiority and 'right to rule'. A new generation of upper-class officers brought their wives and daughters to the Bay and with them came considerable baggage in the form of the snobberies of European society.

I have still 3 of my sons with me, wrote James in 1840, *George the first is a hearty robust chap and can do several things in the carpentering line, and is a tolerable farmer. The second is a good scholar, has a better education than ever I had, but how can he apply it. I could get him in the Company's service but halfbreeds as they are called has no chance there nor are they respected whatever their abilities may be, by a parcel of upstart Scotchmen who hold the power and control in the concern.*[73]

There is plenty of evidence that Sutherland's experience of prejudice against mixed-race people was common. Obsessions with rank and race and protocol in Britain were exaggerated amongst the ex-patriate community, exactly as they were amongst the British in India during the Raj. In fact mixed-race people from both continents faced far less discrimination in Britain than they did at home, as is illustrated by the career of Alexander Kennedy Isbister. A grandson of James' friend Kennedy by his Cree wife, Isbister was sent back to South Ronaldsay for four years of schooling, but he returned to the Bay and joined the HBC at the age of 16. He wrote scientific papers based on his journeys in the Company's most northerly districts and soon proved himself to be a young man of exceptional intelligence and ability. However, promotion within the Company was impossible because of his ancestry and he returned to Scotland in 1842. Study at both Aberdeen and Edinburgh Universities was followed by a remarkable career as a teacher, author and educator in London, but he also campaigned constantly on behalf of his countrymen, lobbying the British government for free trade rights in Red River and for the welfare of the native peoples. Somehow he had time to earn an LLB from the University of London and become a barrister of the Middle Temple.[74]

James died in Red River in September 1844, aged 66. Appropriately, it was another Orkney man, Robert Clouston of Orphir, who conducted his funeral. For some years, James' sons kept up the correspondence with their uncle in Orkney and reported on the ups and down of Red River. In 1845 there was a plan to build a distillery to cut down smuggling. *There were 100 stills in daily use in the settlement during the winter,* wrote nephew Roderick. The HBC wanted to sell their whisky in quantities of not less than half a gallon, *which doesn't do much for temperance ... a great many of the Canadian half breeds have taken the pledge – all through the influence of their Bishop – not the same as the Clergy of our denomination as they are rather fond of sipping wine and brandy and water.*[75]

Roderick took a pessimistic view of other changes. *Red River is going to the background fast ... property will not be very safe soon, as all the buffalo hunters have again returned empty, the buffalos being driven off by the Indians. It is imagined they will turn free booter and take from them that has.* The following year it was a terrible epidemic of dysentery that was *making dreadful rages on the inhabitants, it is the most awful disease that has visited us yet ... it is no uncommon thing to see 6 or even 9 burials in 2 days ...*[76]

The Red River people could survive periodic visitations of poor harvests or disease, but increasingly they were battered by the politics of the outside world. In 1867 the provinces of Ontario and Quebec (formerly known as Upper and Lower Canada) united with New Brunswick and Nova Scotia to form the Confederation of Canada. In the same year the United States purchased Alaska from Russia.[77] The Canadian government, nervous that the US would attempt to annex Rupert's Land as well, opened negotiations with the HBC to obtain its vast territory and, under pressure from the British government, the Company surrendered its 200-year-old charter to Canada.[78] The Métis people of the Red River area were furious that the government arranged this transfer with no consultation with the inhabitants and no guarantees to respect their land or political rights. *All these poor people know,* wrote Prime Minister John Macdonald, *is that Canada has bought the country from the Hudson's Bay Company and that they are handed over like a flock of sheep to us.*[79]

It was a grandson of the Lagimodières, Louis Riel, who led the Red River Rebellion and forced an acknowledgement of Métis' rights and cultural identity. It was largely through Riel that in 1870 Red River was admitted to the Confederation as the Province of Manitoba, but it was not a happy ending. The Canadian government reneged on many of its treaty promises to both native and mixed-race people, opening their lands to an influx of white settlers and deliberately redrawing the boundaries of Manitoba to limit the power of the Métis people. Many of them left the province and trekked further west in search of greater freedoms.[80]

Red River was not the Promised Land that Lord Selkirk had dreamt of providing for his countrymen and it failed to become the multi-cultural land of equal opportunity that many of its founders and leaders had hoped and worked for, yet surely he would have been proud at the contribution that so many of its people made to the evolution of Canada. The Red River settlers and their descendants, the Sutherlands, Kennedys, Isbisters, Fletts, Inksters, Drevers and so many more with Orkney names and First Nations blood, the Kildonan families from Sutherland and the

French-speaking pioneers like the Lagimodières, not only survived the many disasters that befell the young settlement but left a remarkable heritage: a fusion of the energies and resourcefulness, the skills and traditions and spirituality of both the old world and the new.

Chapter 7 Notes

1   Wheelwright 133.
2   ibid 137.
3   ibid 84-5, quoting 'Extract of a letter from an officer of the *Robert Small* off the Cape of Good Hope', *The Times* 28/12/1839,p.7.
4   Wheelwright 19.
5   Baptismal register for Parish of Orphir, OLA (microfilm).
6   OSA (Orphir) 74.
7   Des Groseillers 1618-96) and his brother-in-law Radisson were French explorers and fur traders who mapped many of the Great Lakes and trading routes. Having failed to get backing in France for investing in the fur trade, they travelled to England. Captured by Dutch privateers on the way and set ashore in Spain, they eventually reached London and convinced Prince Rupert and Charles II that it was worth sending an expedition to Hudson Bay. Two ships set out in 1668; the *Nonsuch*, with Des Groseillers, reached the Bay and returned to England in 1669 with a rich cargo of furs.
8   Rich 30.
9   Innis 120, quoting *Papers presented to the Committee Appointed to Inquire into the State and Condition of the Counties adjoining to Hudson Bay and of the Trade carried on there* 1749, f26.
10   OSA (Sandwick and Stromness) 122.
11   John Nixon was Governor of the HBC settlements 1679-83. His letter of 1682 is the first detailed account of conditions in the Bay and the only 17th-century governor's dispatch to survive.
12   OSA (St Andrews and Deerness) 13.
13   OSA (Sandwick and Stromness) 121.
14   The North-West Company was established a century later than the HBC, in 1779. It was managed primarily by immigrant Highland Scots from a headquarters in Montreal, and employed French Canadians as labourers and canoemen. Rivalry between the companies became fierce and often violent until pressure from the British government brought about a merger in 1821.
15   OSA (Orphir) 75.
16   Pogue 1956, 50. The heritors in each parish were liable to pay a share of the costs of building and maintaining the parish kirk and the parish school and paying the schoolmaster's (meagre) salary. The heritors were invariably reluctant to accept their responsibility.
17   NSA (Sandwick) 59.
18   Minutes of Orphir Kirk Session, OLA, OCR 16/2.
19   Rigg 95.
20   ibid 86.
21   Van Kirk 173.
22   Journal of Peter Fidler, HBCA.
23   Stromness Baptismal Register in OLA (microfilm).
24   MacInnes 3.
25   Elsa, a widow left penniless with two children, lived undetected for 13 years in North America as prospector, soldier and cabin boy, Wheelwright 69.
26   Journal of Peter Fidler, HBCA.
27   Van Kirk 63.
28   ibid 61.
29   ibid 18.
30   Cuthbert 70.
31   Van Kirk 19.
32   ibid 21, quoting J.H. Lefroy, *In Search of the Magnetic North: A Soldier-Surveyors Letters from the North West 1843-44*, G. Stanley ed., (Toronto 1955) 130.
33   ibid 175-6, quoting Elliot Coues, ed., 1965, *New Light on the early history of the greater Northwest: the manuscript journals of Alexander Henry and of David Thompson 1799-1814* (Minneapolis), 426.
34   Journal of Peter Fidler, HBCA.

| 35 | Van Kirk 104, quoting HBCA B239/b/79 fo. 53d. |

35   Van Kirk 104, quoting HBCA B239/b/79 fo. 53d.

36   ibid 104-6.

37   Letter from William Harper, Albany to William Watt, Breckness 5/9/1808, OLA D31/35/3/2.

38   Bolus 25, quoting HBCA.

39   See chap.4, *Merchant Ladies* pp.150-1.

40   HBCA.

41   Bolus 26, quoting HBCA.

42   Innis 161, quoting Colin Robertson, *Suggestions for the Consideration of the Honourable Hudson's Bay Company* 1812.

43   See e.g. letters of Isabella Simpson of Kirkwall to George Horne and Anne Watters of Kirkwall to Henry Horne 1850, Beattie and Buss 378-386.

44   ibid 381.

45   ibid 389.

46   Orphir Parish Census 1821.

47   The parish mortcloth was hired out to wrap the bodies of those whose family could not afford a coffin.

48   NSA (Stromness) 38.

49   Tragically, Thomas Balfour MP (2nd son of Captain William Balfour of Trenaby) had a nervous breakdown and died in an asylum in 1838.

50   Beattie and Buss 47. Mrs Flett's age is given as 37 when she remarried in Hudson Bay, so she would have come to Orkney as a child of seven.

51   *The Orcadian* 23/11/1861.

52   Unless otherwise stated, all letters quoted in *Red River Letters* are from James Sutherland to his brother John Sutherland in Knarston, South Ronaldsay. The originals were transferred to the HBC archives, copies are in OLA D112/Y1/1. Letter from Red River 8/8/1831.

53   Van Kirk 177-78.

54   Letter from Montreal 29/6/1814.

55   Letter from Red River 8/8/1831.

56   Letter from Liverpool 15/3/1827.

57   Letter from Montreal 29/6/1814.

58   Letter from Norway House 13/8/1827.

59   Letter from *Prince of Wales* off Land's End 15 /10/1826; letter from Liverpool 15/3/1827.

60   Letter from Montreal 9/5/1827.

61   Letter from Norway House 13/8/1827.

62   Letter from Red River 10/8/1828.

63   Letter from Red River 10/8/1832.

64   Letter from Norway House 24/8/1817.

65   Letter from Red River 8/8/1831.

66   ibid. There are still Inksters from Orphir living in Orkney. At this time the Anglophone mixed-race people were usually referred to as Half-Breeds, with no pejorative intent. Later, as racist attitudes hardened among the white people, the word was used contemptuously.

67   Letter from Red River 6/8/1832.

68   Letter from Red River 7/7/1838.

69   Letter from Red River 10/8/1841.

70   Letter from Red River 10/8/1832.

71   Letter from Red River, 8/8/1831.

72   Simpson was a brother-in-law of Lord Selkirk.

73   Letter from Red River 10/8/1840.

74   For the remarkable career of Alexander Kennedy Isbister, see online Dictionary of Canadian Biography, www.biographi.ca

75   Letter from Roderick Sutherland, Red River to John Sutherland 5/8/1845.

76   ibid 6/8/1846.

77   The US purchased Alaska from Russia in 1867 for $7.2 million.

78   Canada did not 'buy' Rupert's Land, as the HBC did not technically 'own' it, but in 1870 the Company transferred its charter of monopoly to the Canadian government (retaining some forts and settlement areas) for compensation of

$1.5 million.

79   Prime Minister John Macdonald to George-Etienna Cartier, 1869, www.cbc.ca
80   Louis Riel, 1844-85, was forced to flee into exile in the United States but continued to champion the cause of the Métis. Asked by the Métis people of Saskatchewan to present their grievances to the Canadian government, he organised resistance which turned into a military confrontation – the North-West Rebellion of 1885. The rebellion was crushed and Riel hanged for treason after a show trial.

CHAPTER 8

India

Prologue

Britain's colonies opened doors to impecunious Scots all over the world. In India, there were opportunities for both the very poor and the rich and well-connected: in trade, in the service of the East India Company and in the Indian Army. In 1771, just a few years before the teenage Hugh and Robert Mowat set out for the Caribbean, John Balfour from Westray sailed for Madras (Chennai)[1], where he would spend the next 18 years of his life working for the Company, marry an heiress and eventually return to Britain with a fortune.

While John was in Madras, the Company was undergoing its transformation from a commercial trading company to a belligerent occupying power, opportunistically acquiring control of Indian territories and wealth. Company interests were secured, not only by the legion of civil servants like Balfour but also by its own large standing army. It would be another hundred years before Queen Victoria styled herself 'Empress of India', but the imperialist land-grab was already under way. We can glimpse in John's letters the transition between the era when British men often became comfortably 'Indianised', adopting Indian customs, wives and friends, and the different world of the Raj, where the British rulers lived aloof and separate lives, as insulated as possible from cultural contact with the native peoples, rather like ex-pat retirees on the Costa del Sol.

John's letters to his family reveal little of his personal life. When he left India, letters written to him by a former colleague colour in a little of the gossip and atmosphere of the Company offices in which they had worked together, and we also learn the news of the siege of Seringapatam which would bring the powerful and wealthy state of Mysore into the avaricious hands of 'John Company'.

Sixty years after John Balfour arrived in Madras, John Login from Stromness set out for India as a ship's doctor and, in a remarkable and meteoric career, rose to become the British Resident in Lahore and guardian of the deposed Maharajah of the Punjab, Duleep Singh. In 1849,

281

after victory in the Sikh wars, the East India Company 'annexed' the Maharajah's kingdom (a somewhat euphemistic term for taking possession of, also defined in the dictionary as purloined or appropriated). A few years later, the 93rd Sutherland Highlanders regiment was sent to India to reinforce the troops putting down the Mutiny.

With the Highlanders went Captain Frederick William Burroughs. Much later, General Burroughs became the most hated landlord in Orkney history, but his early career is far less well known. While the letters of some of his army contemporaries dismissed both the country and its people with an arrogance and disdain which go far to explain why the Mutiny happened, the letters of the young Captain Burroughs to David Balfour are full of fascinated detail, describing the landscape, architecture, people and customs of a country he enjoyed and often admired. His humorous descriptions of long and uncomfortable journeys across India, enthusiastic account of a furlough in Kashmir and vivid images of military life on the Frontier in the mid 19th century are a delight to read. We are also reminded of the terrible price that India exacted from Europeans. In sad letters to his mother and to David Balfour, Burroughs recounted the tragic toll that cholera took of his regiment and of his closest friends.

David learned more of the difficult and lonely conditions experienced by British officers stationed in remote parts of India from the letters of his brother-in-law, Bridgeman Rees, but light relief comes in the form of Bridgeman's excited description of the 'first-class tiger' he is sending to David as a present.

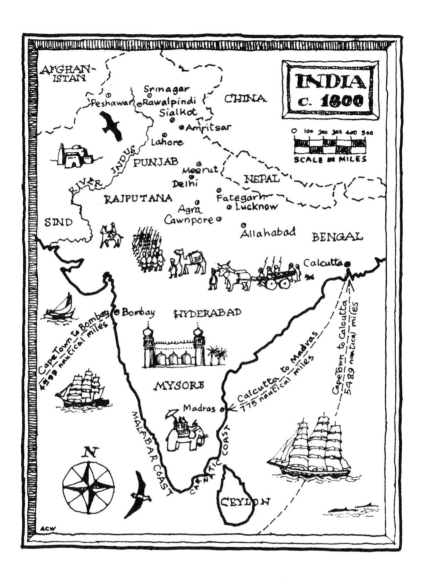

Figure 8.1

An Orkney Nabob

It is resolved I shall go to the East Indies and ... return in a short time a Nabob with a fortune of at least £5000, if my stars are kind much more.[2] With such high hopes did so many young men set out from Britain, to find the fabled wealth of India and to bring at least a little of it home in their own pockets. From the younger sons of aristocracy, who inherited high expectations but no cash to support them, to the totally impoverished who had nothing to lose in risking all on a bold adventure, the East India Company held out the lure of a distant and exotic land. There a young man could reinvent himself and the able and courageous make social and economic leaps that would be undreamt of at home.

The *Governor and Company of Merchants of London trading into the East Indies* received its Royal Charter from Queen Elizabeth in 1600 (70 years earlier than the founding of the Hudson's Bay Company). It was a joint-stock company, controlled by the wealthy merchants and aristocrats who owned its shares, and its charter gave it a sweeping monopoly to import goods from all the countries (known, guessed at and as yet undiscovered) east of the Cape of Good Hope and west of the Straits of Magellan. The first ships to survive the return voyage brought home valuable cargoes of spices from the islands of Indonesia, especially Java, but the Dutch East India Company was already well-established there and the English merchants were forced to look elsewhere for opportunities. Their ships docked at the busy trading port of Surat in Gujarat, north of Bombay (Mumbai)[3] on their way east and there they discovered the huge potential for trade in India. Exotic spices – imported to Surat from all over the subcontinent and South-East Asia – were a high-value commodity wanted by the Western rich to flavour their monotonous diet; saltpetre was in huge demand in arms-hungry Europe for making gunpowder. Far more important was the discovery that India was the world's greatest producer of cottons and silks.

In 1612 King James I instructed Sir Thomas Roe to negotiate a commercial treaty with the Mughal Emperor, Nuruddin Salim Jahangir, that would give the Company exclusive rights to reside in and build factories (warehouses) in Surat and other areas. Over the next few years it built trading posts not only in Surat but in Madras, Bombay and Calcutta (Kolkata);[4] by 1647 it owned 23 factories and had 90 employees in India. (From 1672 it was also trading with China – importing tea from it and exporting opium to it.) The Company opened up markets for Indian textiles not only all over Europe but also in North America and West Africa, exporting every quality from costly luxury silks to cheap cotton cloth. In the 17th century fabrics from Gujarat and the Mughal cities in the north were traded mainly from the west coast ports like Surat. Madras and the ports along the south-east coast (the Coromandel Coast) collected fabrics woven in the south for export and here the Company's trade was at its most lucrative. In the course of the 18th century, an increasing volume of trade from inland cities such as Delhi, Lucknow and Benares (Varanasi) was carried down the Ganges to its delta. Here, a small cluster of houses on the Hooghly river that had been acquired as a Company base in 1690, grew into Calcutta, and fifty years later was a multinational city of half a million people. In an astonishingly short time the Company's ships accounted for half the world's trade.

Even more astonishing was the Company's growth from a commercial trading concern to a major political power on the sub-continent. In the 1670s King Charles II felt quite entitled to grant it the rights to acquire territory and exercise both civil and criminal jurisdiction over the acquired areas, mint money, command fortresses and troops, form alliances with cooperative Indian states and make war on the non-cooperative. At the same time as the Company was growing in wealth and influence, the Mughal empire was gradually disintegrating into independent states. In 1636 the emperor Shah Jehan had begun a campaign of conquest over the sultanates of the Deccan; by the end of the 17th century his son Aurangzeb had extended his rule over the whole of north and central India, including present-day Pakistan, Bangladesh,

Afghanistan and Kashmir. The empire was too over-stretched to survive and, with its collapse, a power vacuum yawned in central India which ambitious Britons were anxious to fill. One after another, the sultans and maharajahs of the Indian states, looking for allies against their rivals, played into the avaricious hands of 'John Company'.

As the power and arrogance of the Company grew, so inevitably did Indian resentment. In 1756 the Nawab of Bengal inflicted a humiliating defeat on the British by capturing Calcutta, their most vital and wealthy trading base, and carrying off a huge treasure. At the same time France and Britain, locked in the Seven Years War in Europe, carried the conflict to India and (with Indian allies on both sides), fought each other for colonial supremacy. After Robert Clive's decisive victory at the Battle of Plassey in 1757, Calcutta was regained and the Company was left undisputed masters of a vast territory with no competition from other colonial powers. By the late 18th century the British had a significant military presence in India. As well as the Company armies – Indian troops officered by Europeans – there were King's Regiments of British troops and, as appears in some of the letters home, a snobbish rivalry between the two.

As the Company took over the government of Indian states, so the number of civilians it recruited to run its administration increased rapidly. By the 1790s the Directors in London were filling some 400 posts a year. *The offices that once had been the preserve of men from Central Asia, Iran and Afghanistan now belonged to Scotsmen, to Irishmen and to the younger sons of clergy and the lesser squirearchy in the English shires.*[5] The turn-over rate was high due to the appalling mortality rate, but posts were eagerly sought by the many young men, well-educated but sadly impecunious, who were allured by the prospect of returning home *a Nabob with a fortune.*

William Balfour of Trenaby, after years of hard work to re-establish his family in a sound financial position after its nadir in 1746, when he was a hunted fugitive, was desperately anxious to launch his sons into lucrative careers. Opportunities for positions of good status and prospects were virtually limited to the Army or Royal Navy, the Church and the Law. There was the possibility of obtaining a commission in the army for his eldest son but William thought that John had a *solid and substantial Genius for business* that would be wasted as a soldier. In 1769 he wrote to his wife Elizabeth: *I am pressed by one or two friends to try some time hence to see to get Jack recommended to the East India, the greatest Harvest for mony even now, that perhaps ever was in the World. People who went out with nothing return in five or six years with, 15, 20 or 30 thousand Pounds and if they stay 15 or 20 years, 80 and a 100 thousand is common.*[6]

Figure 8.2
John Balfour 1750-1842. A portrait probably made in Edinburgh shortly before he sailed for India in February 1772. (Photograph by D. Shearer of the painting formerly in Balfour Castle, OLA)

There was no system of interview or examination for a post with the Company. As with most career opportunities in the 18th century, everything depended on obtaining 'interest' or patronage and no doors were opened without a recommendation from someone of influence. *In those days India was a sealed book to all who could not command personal interest at the India Office.*[7] Fortunately for William, the fabulously wealthy Sir Lawrence Dundas was on the Company's Board of Directors. Dundas had bought the Earldom of Orkney estate in 1766 and William had done good services for him in Orkney and as his factor in Shetland. Thomas Dundas, Sir Lawrence's brother, wrote to William early in 1770: *Sir Lawrence is inquisitive about the age of your sons; I beg you'll let me know, that I may inform, if they have any inclination to try fortune in the East Indies – if you have not fixt upon any particular line for them I would think one of them may have a good chance to succeed there with Sir L's recommendation – many people of the highest rank here are trying to get their younger sons sent out; and I know one of yours will be taken care of by my Brother, and pushed forward by him there.*[8]

In 1771 John and his two brothers left Aberdeen University and in December he was writing from Edinburgh to his mother in Westray:

Dear Mamma
By last post I wrote that I had orders to set out for London and that I was appointed a writer to Madras. It is reckoned a healthier climate than Bengal and is second in regard to the lucrative views.[9]

Two months later, the 21-year-old John sailed on the *Duke of Albany*, an East Indiaman bound for Madras.

My dear Mother Two days ago I came on board at Gravesend. We have had fine weather hitherto so I have not yet been sick ... We have a large Ship of 1000 Tons mounting 24 twelve pounders – There are about 250 people on board in all – 22 eat in the Cabbin, 18 of whom are passengers so we are a little crowded – There are three Ladies – Captain Stewart is a very good natured man and I dare say wont fail to make everything as agreeable as possible ...
If anything could add to the pleasure I feel at seeing myself about to

be independent and in the world, it is that if I keep my health I will soon
be able to be of use to my friends who stand in need of my assistance.

Long before this comes to your hand I hope to have bid Britain adieu …
your ever dutiful son John Balfour.[10]

John does indeed emerge from his letters as a dutiful son. Born only four years after his father emerged from hiding in a cave in Westray to find his house burnt down and most of his property confiscated, from a little boy he would have been the 'man of the house' in his father's long absences, and aware how hard his parents worked in order to rebuild their impoverished estate and afford a good education for their sons. Conscientious, admirably dependable and a little dull, he is a totally different character from his younger brother Thomas, who was probably much jollier company than John but had little sense of duty to anything other than his own advantage. John was sincere in his wish. It took him a great deal longer than he had anticipated before he had the funds to assist his friends, but, as soon as he had them, he kept his promise.

By early May the *Duke of Albany* was anchored off Cape Town and John was able to send a short note to his uncle Thomas Balfour and his mother by a homeward bound Indiaman.

My dear Uncle
After a passage of 2 mos. and 20 [days] we came to an anchor here two days ago – I have kept my health very well and have met with very good treatment on board … The Dutch have a very good little town at Table Bay, it lies on the other side of the Cape exposed to the west and NW winds which blow hard about this season – here the vessels are screened from all winds from that quarter by the high mountains. There are only a few houses here, we are very well entertained.

My Dear Mamma, I have just time to tell you that I am very well with the Hottentots.[11]

John was fortunate with his health and good treatment. The voyage to Madras took at least four months, often six or eight, closely cramped with the other passengers in conditions that must have been a severe test of civility. Most of his fellow-travellers

would have been other young men making their first voyage east
as 'writers' or cadets in the Company's service; (John was relatively
old, it was usual for writers to be recruited at the age of 16). *In those
days there were no leave-rules ... Accordingly almost everyone stayed
at Madras till he retired or died, and few but embryo nabobs were to be
found on eastbound vessels.*[12] It is a shame that we know nothing of
what John was actually feeling about his big adventure. Excitement
and delight at being independent, certainly, but there must have
been some apprehension, some emotion at leaving home for an
indefinite period of years and not knowing when, or if ever, he
would see his parents and brothers and sisters again. Most young
men have a happy facility for believing themselves immortal, so he
probably did not worry over-much about the likelihood of dying
from disease, but he must have been aware of the risk. There was
a marginally better survival rate in his time than in the previous
generation, perhaps because there was slightly less conviction
that tropical diseases could best be avoided by imbibing copious
quantities of alcohol, but the mortality rate was still appalling.
Between 1736 and 1834 only some 10% of the East India Company's
officers survived to take the final voyage home and promotion was
usually a matter of stepping into dead men's shoes.

John's letters home were infrequent. (Of the few that have
survived in the Orkney Archive, most are copies, the originals were
probably circulated around the family). There were only occasional
opportunities to send letters back to Britain, they took at least eight
or nine months to reach Westray and some did not arrive at all – at
least one batch of letters was shipwrecked. However, his arrival at
Madras must have been very similar to that described by a later
'nabob'. *Then one morning ... you would see to port a long, low line of
land rising above the sullen troubled blue of the sea. That was the Coast of
Coromandel ... A line of yellow sand would appear beneath the dark green
of the palms, and beneath that again white lines of surf. Then the Fort
itself would emerge into view, with its close-built houses, with a dark,
low, huddled mass of buildings lying close to it on the north, and another
spire rising over the houses of a village farther away to the south ... The
ship's guns would begin to salute the fort, which would answer with little
puffs of smoke and tiny reports like the sound of toy cannon ... The ship
would be surrounded by those strange masula boats ... Into one of these*

you would jump at the peril of a soaking, and be rowed ashore ... and after passing through the surf with your heart in your mouth, you would be carried to dry land on the back of a wet and slippery fisherman, and make your way through the deep sand up to the Water Gate of Fort St George.[13]

Figure 8.3
Fort St George on the Coromandel Coast Belonging to the East India Company of England, by Jan Van Ryne (1712-60), coloured engraving 1754. (National Maritime Museum, Greenwich, London)

Thrown into his new life in Madras, it is hard to imagine that John o' Trenaby did not experience something of a culture shock. Even today, to arrive in India for the first time is to be overwhelmed by the heat, sounds and smells and by the sheer numbers of people. Something that John was probably not prepared for was the extent to which many of his compatriots had become 'Indianised'. In his 18 years of service he would see attitudes changing and much more rigid distinctions being made between the Indians and the Europeans, but, in the 1770s, many Company servants were still living a comfortably hybrid lifestyle. They adopted the native dress that was so much more suitable to the hot climate, ate Indian food while sitting on the floor, smoked hookahs and took Indian 'bibis' or female companions who educated them in their own culture. *At*

291

*a time when the British showed no particular enthusiasm for cleanliness,
Indian women for example introduced British men to the delights of
regular bathing.*[14]

Coming from the narrowly-defined Protestantism of 18th-
century Orkney, John was probably horrified to see British men not
just tolerating but actively participating in Hindu rituals, though
not many went as far as General 'Hindoo Stuart' (for whom John
later worked as attorney), who bathed and worshipped in the
Ganges every morning according to Hindu custom.[15] How would
his Presbyterian relatives have reacted had they known that, at
the salt warehouses at the mouth of the Ganges, the Company
employed a full-time Brahmin to say prayers to the goddess
Lakshmi, *to secure the Company's trade in salt against loss*?[16]

It seems that William and John were over-optimistic about
the length of time it took to make an Indian fortune. John's salary
of £50 a year did not cover expenses, and without money of his
own he could not take the opportunities for private trading which
were the only way that a young writer could increase his income.
While some did return home wealthy men, a great many more lost
heavily. *Very few managed to carry home a fortune with them. Men were
much more likely to die than go home even with a mere competence.*[17] Nor
had the 'Recommendations' which William had been promised for
his son provided John with anything more advantageous than a
few dinners. In February 1774 he wrote a long letter to his father to
answer some of his many queries about his progress.

My Dear Father
*I had the happiness of receiving your Letter of 26 Sept 1772 from mid Yell
in Zetland in August last* [11 months after posting] *and in October
wrote you a Letter by the Mercury packet which was a short one for the
reasons therein mentioned, viz that the vessel which would have been
dispatched from here in October was lost in her passage from Bengal, that
we did not expect the Mercury would have touched here and that from the
apprehension of bad weather incidental to that season she lay here only
twenty four hours ...*

*In your letter you complain of my not having informed you what
recommendations I carried to India ... You know of the letter I had to Mr
Sinclair. That one only has been truly useful to me ... Inhospitality and*

want of regard to strangers are the particular characteristics of the people here. Had I brought 20 times as many letters I would have at most got by them 20 times as many How d'ye dos.[18]

Almost the whole of his life John had lived in Westray or in Aberdeen, where hospitality to strangers was taken for granted, so it is not surprising he was stung by the coldness of his compatriots in India. In a later letter to William from Samuel Mitchelson, the Edinburgh lawyer who worked for several Orkney lairds, we learn that John had been disappointed in receiving no favours from Lord Pigot, the Governor of Madras, to whom Sir Lawrence had recommended him. *I am exceedingly vex'd and out of humour at the accounts which Jack gives of Lord Pigot's behaviour to him – It is truly wrong in the highest degree – because a little Friendship and countenance from him when he reach'd Fort St George would have done your Son's business.* Mitchelson, however, advised William not to complain to Dundas because it would hurt his pride to know he had no influence with Pigot and *it might put him out of temper with you and at present he has occasion for his whole stock of that Commodity!*[19]

John tried to describe his work as a writer, and asked for reference books to be sent to him which he found himself unable to borrow locally and could not afford to buy. *The Company's civil servants are the Judges in all matters civil and criminal. The Courts are a court of Requests, Mayors court and Quarter Sessions. It falls to the part of the youngest Servants to preside in the Court of Requests and to sit on Inquests, therefore a compendium of the laws of England ... with other more particular directions on the different Branches of it are absolutely necessary for me ... A Writer of tolerable capacity and behaviour is sure if he lives to rise to the highest and most important trusts: it is in expectation of this that he serves the Company and not for a present pitiful allowance which is never supposed adequate to the absolutely necessary Expences of the severest economist.*

William wanted a full description of the other Company servants, but it emerges that John does not know many people because he cannot afford to mingle socially with his better-off colleagues. *I know not from which it proceeds, pride or want of Assurance that I am not able as so many are, to push myself into Company where I cannot appear in all respects on a footing with others ... With respect to my prospects of making money soon ... you will conclude aright that they are not very sanguine. Without friends to countenance support and assist and without money to trade with, it is impossible for a young Servant to avoid getting into debt ...*

I hinted before something of endeavouring to procure a loan of a little money from home. If this has been or can be brought about, I probably will be soon able to assist you; at any rate it would enable me to live in a much more satisfactory manner here; for it is but disagreeable from the want of a little money.[20] To his mother John was more succinct. *I have my health in this country as well as I had at home. My situation & employments are easy enough but I get no money, have no pleasures, no great prospect at least for some time.*[21]

Although he would never have admitted it to his parents, John's first years in India must have been miserably lonely and his hopes of a loan from Orkney were dashed by the letters he received from his father, posted in May and October 1773. The 1770s were years of cold and stormy weather, repeated crop failure and famine among the poor. William, trying to balance hard business sense with benevolence to his starving tenants, had his hands full and no money to spare. It was September 1774 before John could send a reply.

My dear Father
The distresses you therein make mention of brought on the people of Great Britain in general by the failures of the trading people and consequent delay of credit, I had before been pretty well informed of, but the aggravation of those by other calamities particularly on the people in the North of Scotland I had not heard. Their misfortunes in general affect me much but those which fall heavier on you and my other friends I feel severely not on my own account for I assure you it is no disappointment to me that you could not spare me money.

... In my letter of 29th Oct which went by the Mercury Packet I mentioned my having met with a loss which put it out of my power to make a small remittance which I had intended, but that I hoped about this time to be able to do it. Since that though I have had no other loss yet having had no tolerable lucky adventure, I have scarce cleared the interest ... so that I am still as poor as ever which makes me so far only uneasy as it may occasion disappointment to you.[22]

By the same ship he wrote to his sisters Peggy, Betty and Mary. He summed up his life in India: *I should not much dislike this country provided the Pagodas* [coins] *would come in a little quicker than they do at present.*[23] While John was fond of his family and genuinely anxious to assist them, it is quite clear that he never wasted any emotion on homesickness for Orkney. *I am exceedingly sorry to hear of the necessities of my poor countrymen from Bad Crops and other calamities; and do not doubt but their hardships will induce them, spiritless as they are, to seek more clement habitation, and if they can only find themselves the means of removing themselves, the effect of their misfortunes will be happy for them, seeing that, without going northward, they will have bad luck indeed if they fall on a worse country for them than their own.*[24]

Figure 8.4
Gold star pagoda with a figure of Vishnu on one face and a star on the other. Minted in Madras 1740-1807. (Classical Numismatic Group, Inc., Wikimedia Commons)

Although money from home was not forthcoming, John found that there were plenty of people in the international finance community with pagodas to lend. Carefully preserved bonds show that from 1773 he was regularly borrowing money from English, Scots, Indian and Jewish merchants – five thousand or even ten thousand star pagodas at a time, at a hefty 10% interest – but, despite the loss he mentions in the letter of 1774, he must have had 'lucky adventures' with his private trading, for all the loans were eventually fully repaid.[25]

John's frustration at the slow accumulation of pagodas is understandable; he would have been well aware that many senior officials in the Company's service had indeed come home 'nabobs' with fortunes to spend on extravagant life-styles and on buying estates and seats in Parliament. The able but ruthless Robert Clive, who defeated the Mughal emperor Shah Alam and forced him to hand over the taxation rights in Bengal to the Company, returned to England the richest self-made man in Europe. William Dalrymple writes that one of Clive's British homes, Powis Castle, *is simply awash with loot from India, room after room of imperial plunder, extracted by the East India Company ... There are more Mughal artefacts stacked in this private house than are on display in any one place in India – even the National Museum in Delhi.*[26]

Was John also aware of how these fortunes were obtained? The East India Company (EIC) used its powers to plunder Bengal rather than govern it, shipping its great wealth to London for the enrichment of individual officials and the shareholders at home. With ruthless tax extortion, bribery, corruption and straightforward loot (a word taken from India, along with its substance), it totally impoverished the province. When drought in 1769 led to famine, the Company focused on raising its revenues and increasing its military budget and spent nothing on relief. Platoons of sepoys (Indian soldiers) were marched into the countryside to enforce payment of taxes from starving people. *The husbandmen sold their cattle ... they devoured their seed grain; they sold their sons and daughters ... they ate the leaves of the trees and the grass of the field ... the living were feeding off the dead.*[27] In 1770-71, at the height of the famine, the EIC sent a staggering profit to London, the equivalent of about £100 million sterling today.

It has been estimated that 1.2 million Bengalis, one-fifth of the population, died of starvation.[28] By the end of 1771, news of the death toll had reached Britain and there was loud public criticism of the inhumanity and corruption of the EIC and especially of Clive, 'the Vulture.' John Balfour was in Edinburgh and then in London at the time, waiting for his orders to take ship for India. It is inconceivable that he saw and heard nothing of the attacks in the press or the satires in the theatres. The famine lingered into 1773; is it possible that it was never spoken of in Company offices in Madras? Like the letters to Orkney from sons on the slave-worked plantations in the West Indies, it is what is not said that is interesting. Unpalatable truths about how money was earned were not subjects for letters to the parents at home.

Despite its extortions, by 1772 the EIC was in financial crisis; its chairman, Sir George Colebrooke, went bankrupt and many banks around Europe with investments in the EIC collapsed as it defaulted on its debts. The government bailed out the Company – too many MPs had shares in it to let it fail – but there was now too much criticism of corruption and abuse by its officials for it to remain independent. From 1773 Parliament appointed a governor-general of India with a governing council in Calcutta.[29]

With John settled, if struggling, in his career, William was tackling the problem of finding a situation for his more flamboyant and unreliable son Thomas, who had just graduated in medicine at Edinburgh but was showing no particular enthusiasm for that profession. Could John help him to a post in India? John spelt out the difficulties: *I was extremely happy this year by a letter from Tom, from which he appears to be himself sensible of the great levity and thoughtlessness which was but so conspicuous when I was in Edinburgh* ... John firmly discouraged Tom's idea of *a military plan*, but suggested instead that he should apply for a post of Surgeon with the East India Company ... *Everything should be tried to bring it about for Tom, and tho it will perhaps be attended with difficulties, a year or two hence when he has got a little more Gravity in his appearance it may be accomplished ... A knowledge of the eastern languages is by no means requisite ... I spent a good deal of money in endeavouring in Edinr to learn what was called Persian. I have often since wished that I had spent in what would have been called by many people a foolish and idle Expence, travelling thro my own or any other country.*[30]

It is interesting to see the sober and dutiful John giving way to this rather wistful regret that he had not had something of a gap year, or even gap few months. In the event, Thomas saved himself from the hardships of pursuing a career by making an advantageous marriage.

A Company employee who served in the cities of the interior was often the only European or one of very few, and some of them lived exactly like Indian gentlemen, or even princes. Sir David Ochterlony, for example, general of a Company army and Resident in Delhi from 1803 to 1825, travelled with a huge entourage and kept 13 wives who all promenaded round the Red Fort with him every evening, each one on her own elephant. Those who lived in the trading cities on the coast, however – Madras, Calcutta, Bombay, and the big cantonments in Bengal – were becoming more and more insulated from India in the late 18th century and it was quite possible to enjoy an English social life of theatres, balls, cricket and hunts and have little exposure to Indian culture. *18th-century Calcutta struck visitors as a dislocated outpost of Europe, as if Regency Bath had been relocated to the Bay of Bengal.*[31] John spent the entire 18 years of his service with the Company at Fort St George and, apart from a brief foray to Calcutta for his marriage, seems never to have ventured beyond Madras.

While William Balfour demanded details of his son's work, colleagues and prospects, Elizabeth was curious about the country itself. John had to admit that he had seen little of it, but this did not prevent him from expressing some vehement but interesting prejudices which almost certainly reflect the attitudes of most of his British contemporaries to Indians.

My dear Mother
... You desire me to write you concerning the manners and customs in this country – Confined to this one place I have hitherto had little opportunity of making any observation and that only on the people who from their more immediate connection and dependence on us, are as far as is consistent with their religious tenets obliged to conform to our manners ... The original inhabitants of the country called Gentoos[32] or Hindoos are an effeminate enervated quiet people easily submitting to any government which will allow them the unmolested enjoyment of their religion to which they are so much attached that any deviation from what it enjoins subjects the offender to an everlasting expulsion from the society of the people of his own Tribe or Cast and there are several instances of their chusing death as a smaller evil than to have life sustained by any forbidden food which they are taught to believe will pollute them ... I do not think they have much morality but their charity which their religion strongly inculcates is universal.

The invaders of this Country Persians Tartars and Arabs who conquered the greatest part of it go indiscriminately under the name of Moors and with their religion, Mohammedanism, also retain in general

*the customs of their respective countries but in a great measure assimilate
to the manners of the Gentoos. They soon lose in indolence the virtues
they profest which were only the worst of military ones and become as
effeminate as Gentoos, without acquiring their temperance, humanity and
charity. So they are the meanest, the most abject, profligate and perfidious
race under the sun.*

One wonders what had given John Balfour such a vehement
hostility towards Muslims, but much of the tragedy of the Mutiny
might have been averted if all other Europeans had taken on board
the fact that many Indians would rather *chuse death* than violate
their religious taboos.

*The Company's Servants being the principal people in the country,
from their influence live with much greater show and splender than people
of the same rank can do at home where they are of no such consequence.
One who here has his levee and is like a minister of State, upon his return
to England is only a private gentleman of a comparatively moderate
fortune and of little consequence but in the circles of his own acquaintance.
We have Balls, Assemblies, Concerts, Horse Races, Plays with all other
diversions fashionable at home.*

*Please to present my Compliments to all our friends and my love to
my dear Sisters – With earnest wishes for your health I remain with all
affection your ever Obedt Son J Balfour*[33]

The young man who set out for India with such high hopes
must have been bitterly disappointed as several years of
service slipped by and he was *still as poor as ever still unplaced
and unpensioned.*[34] By 1777, however, John's abilities must finally
have been noticed by his superiors for he was appointed as
coroner in the inquiry into the death of Lord Pigot, governor
of Madras, (the man who snubbed John when he first arrived).
There is no mention of this affair in John's letters though it
caused a major furore not only in Madras but in London at the
time. Pigot, who a contemporary described as a man *of excessive
vanity and overbearing despotism* had returned to Madras for a second
term in 1775 and immediately quarrelled with his own council.
A furious row erupted, Pigot suspended his opponents, Colonel

Stuart arrested Pigot who then, *to the embarrassment of all concerned, died in custody.*[35]

The case must have been a turning-point for John for soon afterwards he was promoted from writer to factor and the following year he was able to remit over £400 to his agent, his brother David, who was by then a lawyer in Edinburgh. After five years of struggling to keep out of debt on a paltry income, John was at last on his way to becoming a reputable merchant banker dealing with officials, traders and moneylenders and repaying bonds worth thousands of star pagodas.

Figure 8.5
Tipu Sultan, Sultan of Mysore, at the battle of Pollilur in 1780, defeating the British East India Company troops under Lt.Col Baillie. Copy of a mural painted on Tipu's palace at Seringapatam, gouache on paper. (Mary Evans/© Otto Money, photography by AIC Photographic Services)

John, conscientiously amassing his fortune in Madras, never alludes to the turmoil of the Anglo-Mysore wars which troubled southern India throughout his service. By making alliances with, or waging war on, prominent rulers, the British extended the territory under their control but they did not achieve this easily. When war was renewed between Britain and France in 1778, the kingdom of Mysore, under its highly capable sultans Haidar Ali and his son Tipu, sided with the French and inflicted humiliating defeats on the British. In 1780 a Company force of nearly 4000 men was wiped out at Pollilur, with 200 taken prisoner to Haidar's fort and palace, Seringapatam. The wars led to four years of famine, widespread devastation and disruption to trade, but Madras merchants were able to pocket huge profits by supplying transport and food and cash both to the army and to a supporting British naval squadron.[36]

The wealth that John Balfour brought home to Orkney, however, was made less from his astuteness as a merchant than from his marriage to a wealthy heiress, and to the misfortunes of the Rajah of Tanjore. The Rajah had borrowed vast sums from Europeans on the security of his revenues; one of his principal creditors being Lt. Colonel Alexander Maclellan, commander of the Company's garrison in Tanjore. When Maclellan died in 1780 his widow Harriet inherited his claims.[37] She seems to have been an attractive, cheerful personality and when she married John in November 1783 his love for her and his happiness tumble out of the usually rather formal and impersonal letters to his family.

Fort St George 22nd November 1783
My dear Father ...
I am married and so married, that I possess, at present, and assure myself of enjoying in the future, every happiness which an anxious affectionate parent can wish for his son. If I were to attempt a description of your Daughter, I might fail and not do her justice, while others would esteem it the exaggerated language of a man only Eight days married and now more a lover than ever – I shall therefore only say that she is all I ever wished, and more than I ever expected to find – that she possesses the most benevolent, generous soul and the kindest most affectionate Heart I ever knew.[38]

Apart from his personal happiness, the marriage provided John with influential relations among his in-laws, the Sullivan family, who were in the top-rung of East Indian politics and so in a position to support the claim on Tanjore, though it proved far from easy to obtain repayment of the loan from a war-torn country. He became an Auditor of the East India Company; he earned commission on grain he supplied to the army; as well as having expectations from Harriet's inheritance. *She is entitled to a pretty considerable fortune by the Will of her former husband, but the whole of his Estate having been*

301

outstanding at the time of his death, and the situation of the Country having since prevented the recovery of the Debts, little has been realised.[39] In fact it was 15 years after Sullivan's death before Harriet finally received full repayment of his loan and the interest but, with his prospects greatly improved, John was immediately thinking of how he could at last help his family. His thoughts turned to improving their home in Westray.

Fort St George 5th January 1784
My dear Mother ... I have become a husband ... It will give my dear mother sincere happiness to learn that in this greatest cast for happiness or misery in this life I have been most fortunate; and that the woman who providence has allotted to me possesses whatever can engage and most secure the affections and everything truly amiable in female character.

[My father] writes that the house at Trenaby stands in need of repairs, by all means let it be repaired and when the business is in hand, it should also if possible be enlarged or made more commodious, whether I shall ever again see it or not. The ground floor should be raised considerable above the level of the ground without and the Cellars, Kitchen and lodgings for servants should be detached.

I write by this conveyance a few lines to my sisters – I beg to be remembered to all our friends – my Nurse in particular. I some time ago desired that an allowance sufficient for a decent maintenance might be made her annually – I hope it has not been forgotten.[40]

The loyalty not only to their family but to tenants and old servants is an attractive theme that runs through the Balfour letters. However, in July 1787 John was writing to his mother that he still did not feel financially secure enough to leave India.

Some time ago I was in hopes that I should have left this country before now but my affairs not having turned out as well as I expected, I have been under the necessity of deferring my scheme from time to time ... it is my wish to acquire as much before I leave this country as will be sufficient to my necessary expense of living and to enable me to give that assistance, which it is my inclination as well as Duty to afford those of my Brothers and Sisters who have occasions for it ... Mrs Balfour requests to be affectionately remembered to you – her health is very poor and on her account more than on my own I am solicitous to be able to quit this country.[41]

In January 1790 the Balfours finally set sail from India and, as soon as they landed in England, John hastened north to stand for Parliament as member for Orkney and Shetland. When they had married, Harriet had written to her father-in-law with the wish that her *very cheerful disposition might contribute to render the Evening of your days pass away cheerily*[42] but, sadly, William died four years before he could meet her. Nor did he see his son not only succeed financially beyond his wildest dreams (Harriet's Tanjore claim eventually realised some £60,000), but also enter Parliament. John served two terms as MP for Orkney and Shetland, 1790-96 and 1820-26, but apart from visiting Kirkwall for the elections, he and Harriet lived in England for the rest of their lives. They both suffered from ill-health, which they blamed on the damp climate, and sent home for Orkney delicacies such as *smoked Geese & Tongues and a couple of Casks of the best Butter in the Country and some salted fish* to cheer them up.[43]

Figure 8.6
Balfour Castle in Shapinsay, designed by David Bryce for David Balfour, heir to John Balfour. (Purplebaron, Wikimedia Commons)

Despite his poor health, John lived until he was 92 and, as he and Harriet had no children, it was his great-nephew David Balfour who inherited his wealth. With the nabob's fortune, David transformed his grandfather's house Cliffdale into the vast and opulently-furnished Balfour Castle, purchased land all over Orkney and founded the Balfour hospital in Kirkwall.

The India that John and Harriet left in 1790 was changing rapidly into a very different country from that into which John had arrived 18 years earlier. Increasingly, the European community were importing wives, culure and prejudices 'from home' rather than adapting to their adopted country. There would be no room for 'Indianised' Britons like Ochterlony, with his harem on their elephants, or 'Hindoo Stuart' performing his morning puja, in the India that was emerging.

One of John's former colleagues wrote to him of the changes in Madras. *This Place is wonderfully increased in Houses, Inhabitants, Carriages and – on a late Enumeration … there were 110 Ladies at Madras exclusive of some Blue Skins and of Ladies who were here on a visit.*[44] 'Blue Skins', who could not be considered as 'Ladies' were Anglo-Indians (a word that was not in use at this time) who were increasingly being marginalised by racism. Traders became conquerors, and legislation drove an iron wedge between conqueror and conquered. When Lord Cornwallis arrived in India in 1786 to take up the governor-generalship, his humiliating defeat by George Washington five years earlier was still fresh in his mind.[45] He was determined to prevent a class of colonists emerging in India who would undermine British rule as they had in America. Laws were passed excluding Anglo-Indians from employment in the Company and the orphans of British soldiers were banned from travelling to England to be educated, in order to prevent them from qualifying for service in the Company army. (Colour prejudice was more extreme among the British in India than it was at home; in England a darker shade of skin was less of a social barrier than a Scots accent.)[46] In 1797 Lord Wellesley became governor-general of Bengal and head of the Supreme Government of India and he established that government on a foundation of British arrogance and racism.

Scandal and the Siege
of Seringapatam

John's connection with India was not completely severed when he and Harriet came home. His friend Chamier wrote to him from Madras, stirring a good dash of scandal and gossip about former Company colleagues into comments about the current political situation in India. In 1798 the British were preparing for a fourth war against the state of Mysore, which finally ended with Tipu Sultan's defeat and death the following year. Tipu, the 'Tiger of Mysore' was a formidable opponent, his French-trained troops as well-organised and well-armed as the British.

Fort St George 22 July 1798
My dear Balfour
We are now engaged in preparation for a War against Tipoo and I sincerely hope it may end in preparation for with an exhausted Treasury, an immense Bonded Debt and a sinking Credit our resources for carrying on a War cannot be considered flattering. I much fear that Lord Mornington,[47] is not aware of the very serious consequences which may ensue. Saunders is quite in his dotage and Fallowfield's attention is wholly engaged by low Company – He is quite a disgrace to his situation, frequently engaged in drunken parties and having entertainments of half cast People at his house where he manages to make the husbands drunk and then to cuckold them.

Lord Clive has been here upwards of a month but has mixed very little in Society; he does not seem fit for the arduous situation in which he is placed – He appears to know very little of what relates to the affairs of this Government and not to be disposed to labor for the purpose of obtaining information.[48]

15 Oct Charly Smart has killed himself by drinking. Mr Y--- and Mr W-- will soon follow. We are still preparing for War here. [49]

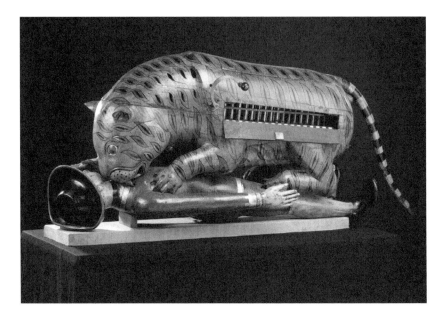

Figure 8.7
'Tipu's Tiger', an automaton created for Tipu Sultan, the 'Tiger of Mysore'; carved and painted wood representing a tiger savaging a European. A handle operated a bellows causing the man's hand to rise, a wailing sound come from his mouth and grunts from the mouth of the tiger. A flap in the side of the tiger folds down to reveal the keyboard of a small pipe organ. The tiger was discovered in the palace of Seringapatam when it was stormed by East India Company troops in 1799. Lord Mornington, the Governor-General, sent it to London for public display. (Victoria and Albert Museum)

Six months later Chamier started another letter to which he added over several months until an opportunity came to post it.

28th January 1799. We have felt in this part of the world very little of the effects of the War which has during the last 10 years agitated Europe, latterly there has been some bustle among us ...
Lord Mornington is here, busily employed in politicks and finance – the latter is no easy charge, when it is considered that the Military Establishment at present on this Coast requires for its monthly Expence, no less that 6 Lakhs of Pagodas – Lord M is borrowing in all quarters – Lord Clive seems averse to the fatigues of business and does very little ... Sydenham is restored to the honors of Corpulency and is doing well – his Wife just as usual and following her propensities ...

306

3rd March The Army is now on the Frontier quite close to Tippoos Country, it is much superior in equipment to the one commanded by Lord Cornwallis[50] for there are 40 battery Guns and a Field Train in proportion – I believe there are 20,000 effective fighting men – 4 General Officers beside the Commander in Chief.

21st April Our Army having experienced very little opposition encamped before Seringapatam on the 5th Inst and was joined by the Bombay army on the 8th. If therefore the C---v--y does not come down earlier than usual there can be no doubt of the capture of the Place but I fancy the Sultan will submit to the Terms imposed, however severe, rather than risk that dismemberment of Empire.

Sunday 12 May Seringapatam was taken the 4th inst by assault with very little opposition indeed this has been the case throughout – Tippoo was killed – so that this seems to be the conclusion to the War, and will enable Lord Mornington to indemnify the Company for the immense expence already incurred.

15 May Lord M is going to Seringapatam in order to arrange the affairs of the Country – it is said an enormous Treasure has been taken.
General Baird commanded the storming party which was only six minutes getting into the Fort from the Trenches so that the opposition was trifling – some officers (not more than 8 or 10) lost their lives in this war ... Some Promotion in the army will occur from the death of Col Sale, Lieut Col Parr and Lieut Co Murray of the Cavalry. Lady Strange died yesterday from the effects of her own imprudence in exposing herself to cold after lying in.[51]

Chamier's civilian view of the siege was written from the safe distance of Madras. In the eye-witness account of Lachlan Macquarrie, an officer in the Bombay army, both the Grand and the Bombay Army were in action at the siege from 10th April and encountered considerable opposition until the final assault, when most of the Fort's defences had been destroyed. *The final result of this glorious and memorable Day,* wrote Macquarrie, *was, that our Troops were in Complete Possession of Tippoo Sultaun's Fortress and Capital in less than an hour from the commencement of the assault; – the*

Sultaun himself, and a great many of his principal officers, killed in the Storm; – his sons and all his Family our Prisoners; and all his immense Riches and Treasures in our Possession ... Our own loss on this grand occasion – tho' comparatively very small in proportion to the magnitude of the object attained – is still very considerable; having had several very valuable officers – and great many gallant soldiers, killed and wounded in the Assault.[52]

The North-West Frontier

After John Balfour's retirement, there is a gap in the archives of letters between India and Orkney for a while, but it is impossible not to mention the most famous Orkney-India connection of all: the career of Sir John Login who became the guardian of Duleep Singh. Login was born in 1809 into a typically widely-travelled Stromness family. One grandfather had worked for the Hudson's Bay Company and the other commanded a merchantman trading to the West Indies. His father also sailed with the Merchant Navy until he came home to be a Stromness ship-owner. Aged 15, John went to Edinburgh to study medicine and he received his Diploma as a Licentiate of the Royal College of Surgeons in Edinburgh when he was only 19. A man of considerable ability, energy and charm, he was given introductions to 'men of influence' in India and sailed to Calcutta as a ship's surgeon in 1832. From then on his curriculum vitae, both as surgeon and soldier is astonishing. From the Horse Artillery at Dum Dum he moved to active service with the Nizam of Hyderabad. His next posting was Agra, as surgeon on the staff of Charles Metcalfe, (lieutenant-governor of the newly-created North-Western Provinces), where he organised famine relief and a hospital for the poor, and then Lucknow where he was both Acting Residency-Surgeon (again at a time of terrible famine) and Postmaster-General of Oude. The invasion of Afghanistan in 1838 saw him on active service again and employed on diplomatic missions to Kandahar and Herat and in 1841 he was stationed at Kabul.

Within three miles of the Residency and cantonment is a fine large lake, on which there are now two boats built by Lieut. Sinclair of H.M. 13th Light Infantry, a Caithness man from near Thurso, and considering that no Cabul carpenter had ever before seen a boat, they are certainly most creditable to Lieut. Sinclair as a boat-builder. Sinclair himself was, however, the only man that could manage them until I arrived and, as you may imagine, was not a little delighted to have an Orkney man to cope with. We have had many pleasant cruises on this same lake of Cabul; rather odd that an Orkney and Caithness man should be having races and matches in boat-sailing in such a place![53] There is something almost surreal, never mind odd, about this regatta interlude in what was about to become one of the most catastrophic and bloody bungles in British military history.

Login returned to Lucknow as Residency-Surgeon and there he met and married an equally fearless and adventurous Scottish girl, Lena Campbell. In 1848 he was back in the field at the outbreak of the 2nd Sikh war. The outbreaks of revolts among the Sikhs after the death of Ranjit Singh, leader of the Sikh empire, gave governor-general Lord Dalhousie the pretext for taking direct control over the entire Punjab. By the treaty of Bhyrowal, which ended the first Sikh war in 1846, British forces occupied Lahore. The seven-year-old Maharajah was taken into British guardianship, and the Punjab was placed under the dictatorship of the British Resident in Lahore. When a local mutiny broke out two years later, Dalhousie – in a move of such breathtaking hawkishness that even most of his contemporaries in India and Britain regarded it as wholly unjust – declared that the Punjab was now part of the British dominions of India. John Login was appointed as the guardian of the deposed Maharajah, Duleep Singh, *a very lovable, intelligent and handsome boy, of 12 years of age, who very speedily developed a great affection for his guardian.*[54]

Login was also Governor of the Citadel of Lahore and all the fabulous treasure of the Punjab within it. It was an Aladdin's cave of enormously valuable Cashmere tents and carpets, horse and elephant trappings, not to mention the prisoners and harems of the late Maharajahs and a Treasury filled with exotic and priceless gems. Most priceless of all, and always kept under strong guard, was the enormous diamond the Koh-i-noor which Lord Dalhousie also 'annexed' and sent to England as a present for Queen Victoria. In Lahore the Logins lived a life of oriental splendour and in the field could not move camp without an escort of no less than 200 servants, accompanied by their entire families. Lady Login's memoirs are a delight and convey a wonderful picture of their fairy-tale life in the Court of Oude.

Other presents sent by different Nawabs included a brace of baby elephants, gaily painted and adorned, with two negro boy-slaves ... two huge Persian cats, more like leopards, chained to charpoys and accustomed to kill and eat their food! These were sent as playmates for the children! ... at one time I remember fourteen pairs of carriage horses, with their equipages, in our lines, not including our own riding horses, and the elephants kept up for our private use by the King of Oude, and I found it quite an undertaking to make my daily round of the stables, with our old derogah, Alix Bux, in attendance, bearing a basket of sugar-cane.[55]

Figure 8.8
Duleep Singh, painting by Franz Xaver Winter-halter (1838-93), signed and dated 1854 (the year that Duleep was brought to England), Osborne House. Win-terhalter was the prin-cipal portrait painter at the court of Queen Victoria during the first half of her reign. (Roy-al Collection Trust/© Her Majesty Queen Elizabeth II 2020)

Duleep Singh was sent to England with the Logins in 1854 and, in the same year, John Login was knighted by the queen. Despite being deprived of his throne, his jewels and his revenues, the young Maharajah was on the best of terms with his guardian and Lady Login, and became a great favourite at court. He stayed with the royal family at Osborne House, where Queen Victoria sketched him playing with her children and the court artist Winterhalter painted his portrait. Most of the 'Black Prince's' teenage years were spent in Perthshire, (Lena Login's home) where first Castle Menzies and then the Grandtully estate were leased for him to enjoy the life of an upper-class sportsman. However, he was prevented from returning to India and, although the Logins did their best to persuade the India Office to settle sufficient money on him (out of his own revenues) for him to live in Britain as an English aristocrat, with an estate to hand on to his children, Duleep Singh's later life was soured by the parsimony of the British government. Increasingly bitter at the loss of his throne and country, he identified with the exiled Jacobites and collected Jacobite relics.[56] He ended up living abroad, renouncing his baptism and returning to the Sikh religion, and announcing that he was an ally of Russia and an 'implacable foe' of Britain.

A few of the more intelligent British officers and administrators in India could see the danger in pursuing policies of aggression and retaliation rather than conciliation in India. Sir John Lawrence wrote: *I myself am a strong advocate for some kind of amnesty. But few are of my way thinking. The general cry is for a war of extermination – No-one seems to count the cost ... Now we have all united in one common bond against us. We cannot run down and kill 40,000 or 50,000 such fellows without suffering ourselves.*[57] There were all too few Lawrences, before and after the bloodbath that exploded in northern India in 1857.

In the summer of that year, the 93rd Regiment of Foot, the Sutherland Highlanders, was part of a British force on its way to China to deal with political tensions there. On the voyage, the ships put in at the Cape of Good Hope, heard the horrifying news of the Sepoy Mutiny and were diverted to India. On board was a young officer of the 93rd, Frederick William Burroughs, a veteran of the Crimean War and a friend of David Balfour of Trenaby. By a sad irony, this man, whose name would become notorious and hated as that of a tyrannical landlord in Orkney, wrote the most interesting, appreciative and sympathetic letters about India.

Burroughs arrived in Orkney as the heir to George William Traill, owner of the Westness estate in Rousay. The tenuous link between these Orkney lairds was forged in India, both men owing their careers to their connection with the wealthy and powerful Colebrooke family. Sir George Colebrooke was a merchant banker who became chairman of the East India Company in 1769, a position which enabled him to provide careers for all his descendants. Colebrooke's son Henry came out to India in the relatively humble role of writer, like John Balfour, but became known as an exceptionally gifted judge, author and translator and the foremost Sanskrit scholar in Europe. Henry's sister Mary had a grand-daughter by her first marriage who married an Anglo-Irish officer in the Indian army, Frederick William Burroughs, (*a testy, touchy little man* according to his wife) and their son of the same name became the 'Little General' of Rousay notoriety. Mary's son by her second marriage, to William Traill, was George William Traill.

George William, well-supplied with the essential 'interest' in high places, arrived in India in 1810 and by the age of 24 – in that meteoric rise to power characteristic of young colonialists with ability and the right connections – was governor of Kumaon province, 11,000 square miles of mountainous territory in the far north of India. He was an energetic, capable and popular ruler, replacing the previous oppressive regime of the Gurkhas with one that was much better organised and just. After a splendid career in India he returned to Britain and purchased property in Rousay that had previously belonged to another branch of the Traill family. Here his popularity quickly soured. With the same efficiency that he had reorganised the administration of Kumaon, he ruthlessly cleared tenants from their lands in the name of agricultural improvements. George died childless in 1847 and his estate passed to his relative by marriage, the 16-year-old Frederick Burroughs, who would earn undying opprobrium in Orkney for his high-handed and even brutal treatment of the Rousay crofters. *It was the misfortune of all of this family that they were more likeable in India than they ever were at home.*[58]

The Burroughs and Traill Families

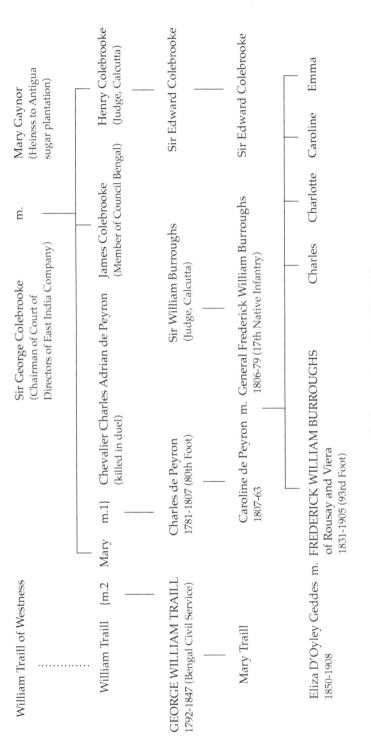

Figure 8.9: The Burroughs and Traill families.

Burroughs grew up in the military cantonment in Fatehgarh near Cawnpore until he was taken home by Traill for schooling in England and Switzerland. His cousin Mary Traill[59] wrote to him at Hofwyl with news of his parents, who were returning to India after settling their younger children, three little girls, in a school in Walthamstow.

My dear Fred
... Your Papa and Mama left our house at nine in the morning to proceed by Railroad to Portsmouth where they embarked on board the Queen for Calcutta ... she is a very large ship with a very long deck without a poop so that there will be plenty of room for dancing and as there are several young ladies on board your Papa will be in daily request for Polkas and waltzes ... Your Papa's cabin is very very small no larger than a bathing machine how they intended to stow away all their furniture and all their baggage in so small a space we could not imagine.
Grandmama and mama all unite with me in sending their love and in hoping that you are growing very tall, that we know to be your own wish.
yours affectionately Mary Traill. [60]

One has to feel sorry for the diminutive Frederick, whose friends regularly nagged him about his failure to grow. George William Traill put it down to sheer negligence, on a par with his poor spelling and geography.

Oriental Club, Hanover Square, London
My dear Fred ... Your knowledge of Indian geography does not appear to be very profound, Cawnpore is nearly five hundred miles distant from Ferozeshah[61] on the Sutlej near which the late Victories were gained over the Sikhs. Have you no map of Hindostan at Hofwyl ... your Father has been appointed aidedecamp to General Little [?] who commands the Left Wing of the Army and he will now enter the Punjarb in Company with the grand Army. Your Mother as a matter of course will remain with the regiment at Cawnpore as Ladies are not wanted in the Field in India. I have now sent in your name to the Duke of Wellington as a Candidate for a Commission in His Majesties Service and therefore beg that you will without further delay begin growing. There is as you justly observe no precedent of a Field Marshall under Five Feet in height. Sir

Edward [grandson of Sir Henry Colebrooke] *tells me that at Fifteen he was under 5 feet and now he is near 6 feet so you see what may be done with perseverance.*

... Yours affectionately Geo W Traill[62]

In 1848 Burroughs was commissioned – despite failing to reach five feet in height – into the 93rd Regiment of Foot and for the next six years he was stationed in Britain and regularly visited his Orkney estate on his leaves. His friend Arthur Lillie, who was already stationed in India, wrote to him from Cawnpore. The bored, contemptuous tone of the young officer was probably all too typical of his contemporaries.

Cawnpore Aug 31st /48
My dear Burroughs,
I am very glad to hear that you have got your commission and hope that you like your regiment; I must say myself that I would rather be in the Queen's service for some things, such as the feeling that you are not bound down to India all your life, and also in action you know that you are fighting with your own country men instead of a pack of these horrid niggers, I like India tolerably well for some things and for others I hate it, you can have very good fun out here sometimes when you are at a good station: balls, dinner parties, tiffin parties, cricket matches, shooting, fishing etc but since I have been out I have seen nothing but hot weather and seen little or no fun. I arrived in Calcutta in what was called the cold weather there, which consisted of damp foggy mornings, and hot daytimes ... and now I am at a miserably dull station where there is nothing going on; all our fellows are in debt and saving money to pay off their debts ...

... There is a force now marching against the Moulraj in Moultan and I suspect that they have cooked his goose by this time for him; we expect to form part of a force which it is rumoured that they are going to assemble in the cold weather to put the Punjab to rights ...[63]

Yours very sincerely, Arthur Lillie

With men like Lillie 'putting India to rights' it is hardly surprising that Indian anger and resentment boiled over in the Mutiny nine years later.

Burroughs' first foreign posting was the Crimea, where the 93rd was in the thick of the fighting, and he distinguished himself both for bravery and for an iron constitution that was never affected by the cholera, dysentery and fevers that killed so many others – a constitution that ensured his rapid promotion in India a few years later, when cholera similarly removed all the senior officers in his regiment. The news of the Mutiny that diverted the 93rd to India was horrific: not only had Company troops been defeated in battle, but gruesome massacres of civilians had taken place. In one of the worst incidents, the Cawnpore garrison that had been besieged and starving for three weeks in June was allowed to evacuate under treaty. The evacuees were attacked, all the men killed and over 200 women and children taken hostage. When the mutineers heard that a Company relief force was marching to Cawnpore, all the hostages were hacked to death and the dead and dying thrown into a well.

Not only were hundreds of lives lost at Cawnpore but it also brought the death of any hope of friendly and trusting relationships between Indians and Europeans. The brutal revenge taken on the mutineers created yet more bitterness among the Indians while attitudes hardened among the British and anti-Imperial and pro-Indian voices were drowned. The India that Frederick Burroughs led his Company through in 1857, making their painfully slow way by boat, rail, bullock

Figure 8.10
Captain Frederick William Burroughs. (OLA)

cart and foot from Calcutta, was a very different place from the India of his childhood. In Cawnpore they saw the bloodstained site of the massacre and, only a short distance away, Fatehgarh, where Burroughs visited the burnt-out remains of the cantonment bungalows where he had lived as a child.

The 93rd was part of the force that Sir Colin Campbell led to Lucknow, where another small British garrison was still holding out after a three months siege. The Resident, Sir Henry Lawrence (a good friend of John Login), had been murdered on the steps of his Residency. The Relief of Lucknow became one of the most celebrated episodes of the Mutiny, and the high-point of Burroughs' military career. For conspicuous bravery in the assault – he was the first, or one of the first, to leap through the breach into the Sikanderbagh, the garden surrounding the Residency – he was recommended for the Victoria Cross, but he was badly wounded in the action and had to be invalided home with a fractured leg. When he visited Orkney on his sick leave he was greeted as a military hero and given the Freedom of the Burgh of Kirkwall.[64]

Figure 8.11
The 93rd Highlanders Storming of the Secundra Bagh 16 November 1857, watercolour by Orlando Norie. (Image courtesy of the National Army Museum, London)

By 1859 Burroughs had recovered sufficiently from his wound to prepare to rejoin his regiment in India. A Caithness friend, William Donald Macdonald of Sandside, a disgruntled young officer stationed at Allahabad, tried to dissuade him in a long letter packed with discontent. As well as complaints about the weather and the boredom, his pay, and numerous injustices, his letter expresses the long-standing rivalry between the Queen's army and that of 'John Company' and between military and civilian, and the appalling toll that cholera and dysentery took of both. Three years later, Macdonald would die in Peshawar in yet another epidemic of cholera, aged 35.

Allahabad 17 July 1859
My dear Burroughs, Glad to get your letter and hear you are getting so much better but sorry to hear you are contemplating coming out to this infernal country not fit for Xtians [Christians], *where you lose in every way every day you remain in it ... I have been shabbily treated here ...*

This has been a most infernal season in Allahabad and I hear Cawnpore is the same Cholera has really been awful here – ditto the extreme heat producing sunstroke, dysentery and fever not only with the Europeans but also in the city of Allahabad. Since the beginning of April we have lost some 300 men dead here all who can have gone either home or to some hill station.

... Whoever is the strong minded man to put India in order, his task will be no light one – ... we are as matters are going now losing in prestige every day and the country is most discontented.

The grumpy Macdonald had worked out a system for taxing the native population. *I should if I was despotic ruler have a census – mark out and register all the fat people, taking all people who were above a certain weight and taking height into consideration because as a man (nigger) becomes wealthy he gets fat from extra sloth and good living, well a tax at so much a lb every lb he is beyond the proper weight of his height – same for the women – tax their horses and conveyances. Now my dear fellow I must close and hoping you will spend a day or two with my father at Sandside – and answer this*
very sincerely yours
W Macdonald[65]

Despite Macdonald's warnings, Burroughs returned to India, first to visit his father in Barrackpore and then to rejoin his regiment which had been posted to Peshawar in the Punjab. On his visits to Orkney he had struck up a friendship with David Balfour and he described his travels in a long letter to Balfour that is full of observation and detail. Frustratingly, he claimed that the journey to India was *such a hackneyed everyday occurrence now* that it was not worth writing about, but he filled in the stage from Marseilles to Ceylon (Sri Lanka) with entertaining portraits of his fellow passengers.

> *Rawal Pindee Punjarb*
> *July 22 1860*
> *My dear Mr Balfour*
> *... I travelled from Marseilles to Ceylon with the French General Montauban, 'Commandant en Chef de l'expedition Indo-Chine' and his brilliant staff. He was a very nice gentlemanly old man, but I should say had a peppery temper, which the climate of China is not calculated to improve ... [he] was one of the blood-thirsty French Colonels ... so his appointment therefore to act in concert with us to maintain the Entente Cordiale may be questionable.*

Frederick's overland journey to join his regiment in Peshawar was appallingly slow and uncomfortable but, for anyone familiar only with the irascible, belligerent General Burroughs of the Rousay landlord years, it is hard to believe that this letter is written by the same man. In contrast to the arrogance, boredom and racism shown in the letters from Lillie and Macdonald, the young Captain Burroughs seems to have thoroughly enjoyed the landscape, architecture and everything about the country he passed through and his descriptions are full of humour, appreciation and admiration. The spelling, as 'Uncle' Traill had gruffly pointed out, occasionally falters.

> *I was only allowed to remain two months and a half with my Father and then I had to start on my journey "up Country" to RawalPindi, almost on the frontier of the Punjarb and distant from Calcutta some 1400 miles. I accomplished this in about a month, partly by Rail, partly*

by Palanquin, but chiefly by posting, in a vehicle not unlike an Orkney Box bedstead on wheels and drawn by one horse. The grand trunk Road of India is the perfection of a carriage Road and over it I rattled at from 4 to 14 miles an hour. The pace depends much upon the quadruped, some of which are very obstreperous and won't move, but when one does move it is generally at a hand gallop.

Figure 8.12
The Taj Mahal, Agra, built 1632-58 by Shah Jehan as a mausoleum for his wife Mumtaz Mahal

He revelled in his sightseeing along the way, was thrilled with the Mughal architecture and always looked for comparisons with Orkney. *Agra is full of wonderful ruins and must once have been a mighty city ... I here saw some most beautiful ... perforated screens of old red sandstone, as like the stone of which Kirkwall Cathedral is built as one pea is like another pea ... In the Fort is a Palace some of the appartments of which are covered with most beautifully executed inlaying work, representing wreaths and garlands of flowers inlaid into the marble in bloodstone and agate, carnelian, gold-stone, turquoise and carbuncle. I am a bad hand at architectural description, being at a sad loss for the technical terms wherein to express my meaning and I often and often wished that you or Sir Henry Dryden or anybody who could thoroughly appreciate what I saw had been with me.*

As for so many millions of visitors before and since, the highlight of his journey was the Taj Mahal. *To see the Taj at Agra, I think would alone repay the making a journey to India. My reverence and respect for Shah Jehan increased at every new monument of his reign that I saw. This admiration reached its climax at the Taj which I think is one of the most perfect "Things" I have seen ... The impression left on my mind by the Taj was one of intense admiration at its grandeur, simplicity and solidity and elegance.* (It seems astonishing that the same man who so admired the simplicity and elegance of the Taj Mahal was later responsible for the *monstrous pile on a bare hillside* that is Trumland House, Burrough's later home on Rousay. [66] Possibly David Bryce's design was the choice of Lady Burroughs.)

I then went to Delhi ... The most wonderful Sight about Delhi I thought was the "Kootub Minar", the highest & almost oldest Pillar in the world. It was before History began ... It stands in the centre of wonderfully primitive looking old Ruins that must have flourished soon after the flood.[67] ... I left Delhi with the conviction that there is nothing new under the Sun; but still a considerable amount of vanity and much vexation of spirit. From Delhi I went to Umballa, [Ambela] and Amritsar, a charming little capital, the Paris of the Punjarb.[68] Its appearance is most gay and cheerful & one sees here representations of every Race in India. I then went to Lahore & at length arrived at my journey's end ...

I think India's future is promising & that the Mutinies will prove a great blessing to the Country ... I hope someday to hear from you of all your doings in Orkney. I am very glad to read about your Volunteer Compies, Roads & good prices for Cattle. Begging to be very kindly remembered to Mrs Balfour & to my friends in Orkney, I remain sincerely yours FW Burroughs[69]

Figure 8.13
One of India's most famous monuments, the Qutub Minar in Delhi was begun c.1198 AD, so not quite as old as Burroughs thought.

While Burroughs was stationed in India, he was also negotiating for the purchase of Westness House (which was not part of the estate he had inherited) and discussing with David Balfour his options for leaving the army and settling in Rousay.

> *Peshawar 23 April 1862*
> *My dear Mr Balfour*
> *... I am afraid however I shall not be able to return to Orkney to take possession of the house for two or three years to come ... Being so near a Lt Colonelcy I think it a pity to throw up my profession now, until I get it ... I have thought very seriously over the matter of coming Home and in every way I think it is better for me to remain a few years longer in India. They say a Master's Eye is a second Sun! and I do hope when I settle down in Rousay to follow in your footsteps and to endeavour to do some good.*

The sincerity of Burroughs' hopes for *doing good* as Rousay's laird make poignant reading. It is always clear that his island estate, and his keen interest in the archaeological sites that are being excavated in Orkney by Farrar and Petrie and others at this time, are never far from his mind. However, unlike Lillie and Macdonald and many other British officers, he enjoyed his life in India. One highlight was his tour of the Outposts and he conjures up a wonderful image of an Aberdeenshire huntin' shootin' fishin' squire on his North-West Frontier estate.

> *Since I last wrote to you I have been on a tour of the Outposts guarding our Frontier ... Col. Lumsden of Belhelvie in Aberdeenshire I found in command at the posts. He is a thorough Country gentleman with a fine red face, a burly person encased in Knickerbockers & shooting suit. He keeps Hounds & Horses & a perfect country establishment. I never saw Hawking in such perfection as here. Perhaps what added excitement to the sport was the garrisons of these Forts "menent une vie de Révolver". No British officer here ever stirs out without a Revolver in his belt or without an armed Orderly at his back. Out hawking of a morning we were accompanied by a Section of Irregular Cavalry thrown out in skirmishing Order thus serving as Beaters for the game and for our own protection at the same time. The neighbourhood of Peshawar is extremely unruly – Col Lumsdens Neighbors are of the wildest tribes in all Asia, yet he enlist*

them into his force (the Corps of Guides) & keeps them as quiet as sheep.

... Dost Mahomed King of Kabul is very ill. He has 40 sons all anxious to succeed him & it is expected that at his death anarchy will break out in Afghanistan. We may move to interfere.[70]

The last sentence is ominous, especially in the light of the results of British 'interference' in Afghanistan in the late 20th and early 21st centuries. When Burroughs was writing, it was only 20 years since the first Afghan war, when a spectacularly unjustified and ineptly conducted British 'interference' resulted in the deaths of some 4,500 soldiers, 12,000 camp followers and the virtual annihilation of an entire regiment. *A war begun with no wise purpose, carried on with a strange mixture of rashness and timidity, brought to a close after suffering and disaster, without much glory attached whether to the government which directed or the great body of troops which waged it and not one benefit, political or military, was acquired with this war.*[71] In the Second Afghan War of 1878-80 and the Third of 1919 the British achieved military victories but at the cost of much suffering and no lasting stable peace.

Six months later, the news from Peshawar was much grimmer. The dreaded cholera had struck the 93rd and the cantonment was full of the dead and dying. In October 1862 Burroughs wrote to his mother in Dresden from a field camp with family news – his father and sisters were still in India – and his own sad story. He had made up his mind to retire from the army when, within a few days, his senior officers had died and he had no option but to take over command of the remnants of his regiment.

Camp Jalozai near Peshawar
Oct.28. 1862
My dearest Mother
... I have been away on a 6 week tour of the Hills laying up a store of Health wherewith to withstand the sickly season of Peshawar ...

Another matter I have been employed in has been about the purchase of the House of Westness and my retirement from the Army either on Half pay or by the sale of my Commission. I had made up my mind to go and told Mr Scarth [his factor] he might expect me home in May 1863. However I had not returned to Peshawar a day when my Regt was driven out of cantonments by the scourge of cholera. We marched out of Peshawar on 15th Oct and have ever since been flying before Cholera. Between 19th and 25th Oct we lost by death 3 officers and 13 men. Our Sick Lists in Hospital swelled up to 240 men and nearly every man in the Regt was more or less affected by the sickness. Of the Officers Major Middleton commanding the Regt, Dr Hope and Ens. Drysdale are dead. Brevet Col. Macdonald is not expected to live and almost every officer has been more or less sick. By Major Middletons death and Col Macdonalds sickness I, as the next senior, am left in command of the Regt. We are now hurrying across the Hill towards the Indus River which we are to cross at Neelab. Sickness I am happy to say is considerably diminishing amongst us. Poor Dr Munro has been nearly worked to death. But thank God he has been spared. He is such a treasure that without his energy and judgement it might have even fared worse with us. I thank God for having watched over me. I have been well throughout all our troubles hitherto but no-one can say whose turn it may be next. The strongest and healthiest has been taken ill and in a few hours afterwards were dead. Perhaps there was no healthier man in the Regt than Major Middleton. On the morning of his death he had taken the Regt through a smart drill. He was taken ill after breakfast and was a corpse by 10 pm. Col Macdonald too is a tall strong man. He has held on and he has now been some 6 days ill, but I am much afraid of hearing of his death every minute. It has been a most sad sad time with us, but I pray God that the worse is now over.

Oct 31. I was not able to finish this the day I commenced it, nor have I been able to write a word of private correspondence since. I have had much to do and to think about in the last few days than perhaps I ever had to do or to think about before. Poor Colonel Macdonald I am pained to say died on the 29th.[72] Sickness however thank God is abating. The deaths of our comrades have thrown a gloom over all, but there is yet no desponding. You must not get alarmed and frightened on my account. In such sad times I have naturally much to cause me anxiety in the responsible position in which I find myself so suddenly placed, but I am in no alarm and with Christ's help I will do my duty and should I succumb pray for me that it may be for the best. I have not time to write more. I hope my next letter may be more cheerful. With kindest love to Charlotte, Charley and to Mrs Hawthorne,

I remain
My dearest Mother
your affectionate Son
F Burroughs.
PS I heard from Papa yesterday he and my sisters are all down Country and well.
The sickness appears to be confined to the Valley of Peshawar[73]

Burroughs repeats the ghastly story of the epidemic and his regiment's flight from it in a further letter to his mother, written a month later, and in one to David Balfour, as if trying to exorcise his personal anguish in the retelling. No military history or statistics convey a sense of the terrible price that India exacted from her conquerors as vividly as these letters, written when the 32-year-old officer had just watched death cut a swathe through his regiment and claim the lives of two of the comrades he had campaigned and 'chummed' with in Scotland, the Crimea and India for the last 14 years. By the time that the 93rd had crossed the Indus, nearly 100 of its men were dead and the cholera had put an abrupt end to Burroughs' plans for retiring from the army. Despite his grief and the huge responsibility so suddenly thrust upon him, there was time to be excited at the historical significance of his epic crossing of the Indus in the footsteps of Alexander the Great, and leading the first European army to pass that way since then.

Sialkate, [Sialkot] Punjab
Jan 12. 1863
My dear Mr Balfour
... We continued our march to the Indus rivers which we crossed in Boats a little below Attock at Neelab (anglicé blue water) & evidently the "Nanlike" of Arrian where he says Alexander the Gt crossed. We took 2 days crossing. We had only 8 boats & had to convey across the Regt, its Hospital its Baggage & Baggage Cattle. The Cattle consisting of some 20 Elephants & 600 Camels. We were the first British troops that had come this way ... I have obtained my promotion in a very sad way & would have gladly foregone it than have obtained it through the anguish & sorrow through which it has been obtained ... I had visited [Col Macdonald] several times at Sandside & after leaving the Army we were

both looking forward to frequently visiting one another as Neighbours in the North.

... I hope to be able to save some little money towards paying off debt & towards the erection of a Pier at Trumland (Rousay) or wherever may be found most convenient for the future North Isles steamers, which I hope soon to hear of as in existence.[74]

Figure 8.14

Fort Attock on the Indus River, seized by the British after the 2nd Sikh War 1848-49, guarded the passage of the Indus where it crossed the military and trade routes from the Khyber Pass. Here the river was crossed by Alexander the Great in 326 BC, and by Major Burroughs in 1863 AD with the remnants of the 93rd regiment and its 'baggage cattle' of 20 elephants and 600 camels. Photograph by Maj. M.C. Holmes of the 10/11th Sikh Regiment, 1919. (Image courtesy of the National Army Museum, London)

It would be another eight years before the 93rd, and Colonel Burroughs, returned to Britain for good. Meanwhile there was still hard campaigning on the North-West Frontier before him. In 1863 he was leading his regiment in the Umbeyla (Ambela) Campaign against tribes of the Yousafzai who were violently opposed to colonial rule. This proved to be no minor border skirmish but *a fiasco caused by bad planning and poor intelligence,* which led to heavy casualties on both sides.[75] Burroughs led one of the regiments of reinforcements, was mentioned in dispatches and promoted to Lt. Colonel.

In 1866 Burroughs wrote cheerfully to David Balfour from Sialkot. *The 93rd has been very fortunate in remaining so long here as it is one of the healthiest and prettiest Stations in India so that life with us has been much more enjoyable than it might have been. I have a very nice house and my sister takes great care of me.*

In 1870 the 93rd Regiment left India and Burroughs took up the command at Edinburgh Castle. Only a few months later he and his newly-acquired wife, Eliza D'Oyley Geddes, were given an elaborate welcome at Westness in Rousay. *At Westness House everything wore a holiday aspect. The flagstaffs were covered with flags ... on the road from the pier a triumphal arch had been erected bearing the appropriate motto 'Welcome' in large characters ... Directly the gallant colonel and his lady touched the island they were received with three hearty cheers.* There was, however, an only thinly veiled apprehension and warning in the welcome speech given by John Gibson of Langskaill: *No connection between man and man ought to be more carefully guarded than that betwixt landlord and tenant and every good man who loves his country should do what in him lies to cement that tie, and to continue what in troublous times has formed the strength of the nation – that union and co-obligation of classes which made a brotherhood of all claiming the same country – landlord and tenant, standing back to back and facing the enemy at all points. While you were fighting your country's enemies on the hills of Crimea and in the unhealthy jungles of India we, too, have been fighting against a rugged and uncertain climate, endeavouring to make two blades of grass grown where one, or rather none, grew before ...*[76]

In 1873 Burroughs retired after 25 years in the 93rd and came to live on Rousay. The islanders had reason to be apprehensive. Their previous laird, George William Traill, had cleared tenants off their lands in Quandale and reduced the settlement to a hillside of sheep and empty crofts. Farming's 'golden age' of the mid 19th century was now over and agricultural returns were diminishing, but Burroughs expected his estate not only to finance the lifestyle of himself and his wife, (Trumland House was built at £9,000 over the architect's quote), but also to pay off the enormous debts accumulated by his incompetent father and extravagant mother and sisters. David Balfour must have watched with sadness as his prophecy came true: *What I fear most is that if you delay long* [returning to Orkney] *your tastes and habits of thought will be so Indianised that you will not be happy among us when you do come – that the changes to our climate, scenery, customs and character may be so violent as to disgust you with a life in Orkney and you will not be able to judge fairly between conditions so contrasted.*[77]

Figure 8.15
Trumland House, Rousay, 1875, designed by David Bryce for General and Mrs Burroughs.

Burroughs could have adapted to changes in climate and scenery easily enough, but not to his change in role. Nothing in his upbringing or service life had prepared him for the transition from colonial army officer to Orkney laird. There was an impossible gulf between the rootlessness of both Frederick's and his wife's foreign service families and their tenants' deeply rooted attachment to the land of their ancestors; between the colonialist's habits of command and knowing what was best for 'the natives' and the natives' divergent views of their own needs. For so many years, through the hardships of India, Burroughs had nursed the idea of coming home as a benevolent landlord who would 'do good' to his estate and be appreciated for so doing. Instead, he found himself stubbornly opposed by tenants whom he could not thrash or shoot into submission, and that opposition was deeply wounding. Almost more embittering than the attitude of the tenants was that of the British government who, to his total incomprehension, in the Crofters Act of 1886 swept away altogether one of the most fundamental assumptions of the landed class: that a man's property was his own, to do as he wished with, and interference with that right was theft. In 1904, the year before he died, Burroughs was knighted and the occasion celebrated with due pomp on Rousay, but he had sadly failed all those sincere good intentions of his plans and dreams in India to *do good* as a laird. *He might own Rousay but he never belonged to it,* summed up William Thomson. *Money could buy ownership, but belonging – that close identification with a place and its people – was a more difficult matter.*[78]

Furlough in Kashmir

In the summer of 1861, Captain Burroughs spent his leave travelling in Kashmir with some friends. He wrote a long account of their trip to David Balfour in a letter which vividly conjures up both the place and the time and the writer's enthusiastic response to the country.

Rawal Pindi, Punjarb,
Sept 9th 1861
My dear Mr Balfour
I returned from Cashmere on the 20th August – I will endeavour to give you some account of my journey to this somewhat unfrequented part of the globe. My party consisting of a Mr Brennan, our Presbyterian Chaplain, a Major Brown [?] *and* myself *assembled at Murree, a Hill Station & the sanitorium of the Punjarb, on the 24th of August.*[79] *Accompanied by a following of some 50 Natives we started on our travels ... My baggage consisted of a small Tent & Portmanteau, Bath & Camp bed and some supplies in the way of Wine, Spirits, Sauces, Tea, Sugar etc & cooking utensils. My companions were similarly provided. I also took a Pony with me. Thus equipped we started & travelled for some 100 miles over the tops & along the sides of high Hills, across deep Valleys & rapid streams & over break neck roads until we crossed the Pass of Barramoula* [Baramula] *in the Valley of Cashmere ... As the roads are very rugged & as Engineering as an Art was unknown to those who constructed them, travelling under the hot sun of India, although at a considerable altitude, is indeed most laborious. The terraces are carefully & extensively cultivated with crops of Rice & Maize & it is on these Terraces that the Villages are usually situated ... At Barramoulla we left our "coolies" ... & shipped ourselves, our Baggage & our Servants into the Boats & paddled up the Jhelum river & through the Wulwur* [Wular] *lake to Siri Nugger* [Srinagar] *(the City of the Sun) the capital of Cashmere. The valley of Cashmere is entirely*

surrounded by high mountains from 10 to 17,000 ft high ... The Wulwar lake is some 30 miles long & perhaps 15 broad, but the lake is more than half covered with the Lotus plant ... The lotus flower is like a large pink tulip. The plants were in blossom when we sailed through & presented the effect of our sailing through beds of tulips. Our sail through the lake was very delightful. The thermometer was at 70 degrees a pleasant breeze swept over the Waters, the Mountains towards the North rose straight out of the Water to a great height & a heavy bank of clouds was resting on the Mountain tops, enclosing the Valley & appearing as if shutting out this lovely valley from the hot unpleasant plains of India beyond. Cashmere would be a lovely valley in any Country, but bursting as it does in all its freshness & coolness & beauty upon the feverish worn traveller from the burning plains of India, to him it indeed appears a paradise.

Siri Nugger the capital is beautifully situated at the foot of high hills, on the Banks of the Jhelum river. It is one of the most picturesque places I ever was in, but like all Eastern towns, when not under European supervision, it is extremely dirty. The Jelum forms the "Broad Street" of the Town & numerous riverlets & canals form other streets ... The houses are chiefly built of wood. They have not glass windows, but beautifully carved wooded screens instead ... The Canals are narrow & the Houses quaint looking & the effect is most picturesque ... On our arrival at Sirinugger the Maharajah's Vakul [Vakil, agent or representative] *met us & presented to each of us a Present from HH consisting of sheep & corn & flour & oil & sugar etc etc, enough to keep us alive for a week.*[80]

We moved into one of the Houses built by HH for European Visitors & set about seeing all that was to be seen ... I was fortunate in being present at a very magnificent Nautch given in the Shalimar Gardens by Colonel Seymour of the 2nd Dragoon Guards.[81] *These gardens are situated at the foot of a High range of Hills sloping down into the Lake of Idols. A rivulet from the Hills passes through the gardens forming numberless Pools, fountains & Cataracts ... All the fountains were playing & the gardens and cascades were illuminated. I have written in the Diary of my travels: "The dancing was accompanied by the music of the Dulcimer, Viol & Drum & by the Voices of the Danseuses. The black marble saracenic Columns & arches of the great open Hall, the illuminated Gardens & Cascades beyond, the quaint music, the bright dresses of the Danseuses &*

the intent turbaned Countenances of the Spectators presented a gorgeous Eastern spectacle such as I had never before seen."

Figure 8.16
Houses on a canal, Srinagar, Kashmir, engraving by Alfred Koechlin-Schwartz 1858.
(Mary Evans Picture Library)

... The Valley of Cashmere is one entire Orchard. We found every day growing wild in our Path: Figs, Grapes, Pomegranates, Mulberries, Peaches, Apricots etc etc. In the Hills I went day went after a Bear, but did not kill it. As roads are here scarce & our time was short we returned by the way we came having our enjoyed our trip very much.

Whilst writing this I had the pleasure of receiving yours of 22 July, which I have not here space to more than thank you for. I shall be delighted to hear if the Antiquaries open up Kolbein's Castle & Swein Drop [Swandro][82] *There is also a remarkable Pichts House between the Farms of Sockness & Farraclet which might repay a visit ... With my kind regards to Mrs Balfour, the family at Birstane & to all my friends in Orkney, I remain sincerely yours FW Burroughs*[83]

A First-Class Tiger

Through his friends in India David Balfour was able to embellish Balfour Castle with those essential accoutrements of the Victorian landed gentry: exotic hunting trophies. In June 1861 he was in Edinburgh when he heard a satisfactory report of his latest acquisition from James Drummond.

Sir,

I have left your Tiger Heads with Mr Sanderson 66 George Street, who I know will make a good job of them, if you should be passing that way it would be worth to see the Tiger's Head belonging to Mr David Kennedy, it was a celebrated one who had Killed 100 of the Natives. Sir David watched him for 8 days before he got him. The Head of this Tiger is very much inferior to either of yours and the teeth much smaller. Now this being a first class Tiger I consider that yours are Specimens that are not easily equalled. Mr Sanderson was not at home, but the man in his shop says they are the finest he has ever seen.

I am, Sir
Your Most Obdt Servt
James Drummond[84]

We do not know who shot or presented Balfour's first class tiger, but only six months later another fine prize was on his way to him from his brother-in-law Bridgeman Lees, an officer then stationed in Assam. Bridgeman had married David's sister Jeanette (or Jenny) who returned to India with him but died suddenly in August 1860. Bridgeman was deeply attached to David and his wife Eleanor and his sad letters convey his misery at Jenny's early death, his sense of the impossibility of the military task of keeping the peace in a vast and unsettled country with just a handful of troops, and his longing to retire to

336

Orkney. Somehow, he apparently also sent a live tiger to friends of the Baikie family.

22 Jan 1862
Dear David,
Write to Grindaly & Co 55 Parliament Street London and tell them to send you the Picture and Tiger Skin when they arrive. The latter is a beautiful thing, claws, whiskers, Eye Brows and all complete with the head and feet stuffed. You might get the eyes put in the head and then it will be a very handsome ornament. It is a beautifully marked skin and vandyked all round the edge with red cloth.

11/3/1862
Dear David,
A poor young man a Lt Suigen (?) has been beaten to death by these savages with sticks some 4 months ago and up to the present the ringleaders have not been apprehended. the only wonder is how we are in the Country at all, the French Nation with their Emperor ought to rule India – here am I put in orders to Comd the Troops in the D ... District Area of the district, three thousand square miles, and its population is about two hundred thousand souls. My force amounts to sixty six rank and file.

2/6/62 Fezpoor
Dear David ...
I have been very ill from dysentery and am only now recovering. All our Hill Tribes are in a very unsatisfied and unsettled state and I fear that there will be very heavy and responsible work for us all in that quarter in the ensuing Cold Season, there are no less than 11 different Tribes in my front and rear and one Chief has been the terror of both Natives and Europeans for years. I was out after him three years ago and kept him quiet ...

I am glad the Photograph and Tiger Skin reached you safe the latter was beautifully marked and you can very seldom secure them so perfect with the Claws, Whiskers and Eyebrows for the Natives extract them as Charms. I am proposing to send a magnificent Tiger (a live one) to William and Jessies friend (Mr Grote) the brother of the Historian he is a great friend of mine also ...[85]

Bridgeman's story was all too typical of the British in India. Losing his beloved young wife to a tropical fever, suffering chronic ill-health himself but hanging on to a demanding and responsible job because he could not afford to do otherwise, he never did get back to his family in Orkney or the *little cottage with 5 or 6 acres and a fishing boat* that he longed for. He died of cholera in October 1865 within a few weeks of retirement. *He was everything to me* wrote his brother, the brilliant linguist William Nasau Lees, *Ever cheerful, ever kind, generous and good hearted ... He had made everything ready to set sail for Home and the Orkneys and it seems hard that at the moment that he had completed his hard service and was about, as he thought, to enjoy a little repose – that he should be thus cut off. But it is the will of God – that such should be – and He wills nothing that is not for the best.*[86]

Chapter 8 Notes

1   In 1996 the Tamil Nadu government officially changed the name of Madras to Chennai. However, the name Madras is still used by people born before the 1990s.
2   Letter from John Balfour, Madras to his sister Betty Balfour, Westray 16/12/1771, OLA D2/8/16. 'Nabob' is an anglicisation of the Indian title Nawab, ruler.
3   In 1995 the Hindu nationalist party Shiv Sena officially changed the name of Bombay to Mumbai, the city's name in Marathi.
4   In 2001 the government of West Bengal officially changed the name of the capital city to Kolkata, to reflect the original Bengali pronunciation.
5   Johnson 140.
6   Letter from William Balfour to Elizabeth Balfour, Westray 8/9/1769, OLA D2/12/19.
7   Login 1890, 8.
8   Letter from Thomas Dundas of Fingask to William Balfour 15/2/1770, OLA D2/3/2.
9   Letter from John Balfour, Edinburgh to Elizabeth Balfour, Westray 16/12/1771, OLA D2/8/14.
10 Letter from John Balfour, on board ship for India, to Elizabeth Balfour, Westray 12/2/1772, OLA D2/8/4.
11 Letter from John Balfour, Cape Town to Thomas Balfour of Huip, Kirkwall and Elizabeth Balfour, Westray 12/5/1772, OLA D2/8/14.
12 Dodwell 3.
13 ibid 9-10.
14 Dalrymple 2003, 36.
15 ibid 42. It was normal at this time for Company attorneys to have no formal legal training, Dodwell 158-9.
16 Dalrymple 2003, 47n. Lakshmi, the wife of Vishnu, is the Hindu goddess of wealth and good fortune.
17 Dodwell 34.
18 Letter from John Balfour, Madras to William Balfour 6/2/1774, OLA D2/8/14.
19 Letter from Samuel Mitchelson, Edinburgh to William Balfour 23/9/1776, OLA D2/ADDL/15.
20 Letter from John Balfour, Madras to William Balfour 6/2/1774, OLA D2/2/14.
21 Letter from John Balfour, Madras to Elizabeth Balfour, Westray 6/2/1774, OLA D2/28/14.
22 Letter from John Balfour, Madras to William Balfour 30/9/1774, OLA D2/28/14.
23 The pagoda was a gold or half gold coin with Indian motifs, minted by the dynasties of southern India and by foreign traders. The most valuable coin was the gold star pagoda, which was struck by the East India Company 1740-1807 and circulated in the Company's Madras Presidency. There was a mint in Fort St George.
24 Letter from John Balfour, Madras to his sisters, Westray 30/9/1774, OLA D2/8/16.
25 Bonds of John Balfour, merchant Madras, to various merchants in Madras and Calcutta, OLA D2/23/9.
26 Dalrymple 2019, Introduction.
27 Dalrymple 2019, ch.6, *Racked by Famine*, quoting Sir William Hunter.
28 Dalrymple 2019, ch.6.
29 The first governor-general was Warren Hastings, followed in 1786 by Lord Cornwallis.
30 Letter from John Balfour, Madras to William Balfour 6/2/1774, OLA D2/28/14.
31 Dalrymple 2003, 33.
32 The word 'Gentoo' (possibly derived from Portugese) was used by Europeans for the indigenous peoples of India, before the word 'Hindu' was used to distinguish people of one religion from Muslims and other religious groups. In 1776, (the year after this letter was written) the EIC financed the translation

from Persian of *The Gentoo Code*, a digest of Hindu law originally written in Sanskrit.

33   Letter from John Balfour, Madras to Elizabeth Balfour, Westray 25/1/1775, OLA D2/28/14.
34   Letter from John Balfour, Madras to Elizabeth Balfour, Westray 28/2/1776, OLA D2/28/14.
35   Fereday 1990, 82. The territory of the Rajah of Tandore had been seized and transferred to the Nawab of the Carnatic. In 1776 Pigot announced the restoration of the rajah. Some of the councillors had lent large sums of money to the Nawab which they stood to lose when he was removed from Tandore and so demanded repayment; Pigot refused to allow their claims.
36   Madras merchants benefited from Bills drawn on the Commissioners of the Navy in London to pay the costs of victualling Admiral Hughes' squadron which arrived in 1780 to support the British troops.
37   MacLellan had loaned the Rajah of Tandore 72,000 star pagodas.
38   Copy letter from John Balfour to William Balfour 22/11/1783, (wrongly dated 1784 in copy), OLA D2/8/15.
39   ibid.
40   Letter from John Balfour, Madras to Elizabeth Balfour, Westray 5/1/1784, OLA D2/28/14.
41   Letter from John Balfour, Madras to Elizabeth Balfour, Westray 30/7/1787, OLA D2/28/14.
42   Copy letter from Mrs Jack Balfour, Madras to William Balfour 22/11/1783, OLA D2/8/15.
43   Letter from John Balfour, London to Elizabeth Balfour, Westray 30/10/1790, OLA D2/28/14.
44   Letter from J. Chamier, Madras to John Balfour, London 28/1/1799-15/5 /1799, OLA D2/4/ 5.
45   In 1781 Cornwallis was defeated by combined American and French forces at Yorktown in Virginia. Escape was blocked by a French fleet and he was forced to surrender his entire army; some 7,000 men were taken prisoner.
46   This is perhaps less surprising than it seems at first sight, for anti-Scots prejudice in 18th-century England, especially after the Jacobite rebellions, was extreme and fostered by scurrilous 'histories', pamphlets, cartoons etc depicting Highlanders as barbarians and cannibals.
47   Richard Wellesley, Earl of Mornington was governor of Madras and governor-general of Bengal 1797-1805. His younger brother Arthur Wellesley (later the first Duke of Wellington) fought at Seringapatam.
48   Edward, Lord Clive was the son of the much more able Robert 'Clive of India'. William Dalrymple described him as 'the notably unintelligent Governor of Madras' (Dalrymple 2019, Dramatis Personae 1) so Chamier's criticism is probably justified.
49   Letter from J. Chamier, Madras to John Balfour, London 22/7/1798, OLA D2/4/5.
50   Cornwallis commanded the British troops in the 3rd Mysore War 1790-92, which ended in the defeat of Tipu Sultan and the Treaty of Seringapatam, by which Tipu had to surrender half his territory to the British East India Company and its allies.
51   Letter from J. Chamier, Madras to John Balfour, London 28/1/1799-15/5/1799, OLA D2/4/5. From the mid 18th century the EIC maintained three distinct armies: the Bengal, Madras and Bombay armies.
52   Lachlan Macquarie Journal 4 Feb 1799-5 May 1799, original held in the Mitchell Library, Sydney A 769-A, pp.27-38; mq.edu.au/Macquarie-archive/lema/1799.
53   Login 1890, 62.
54   Login 1916, 73.
55   ibid, 44.
56   Duleep Singh's collection of Jacobite and Stuart relics was donated to the Inverness Museum by his son Prince Frederick Duleep Singh. It included a portrait of Oliver Cromwell which 'Prince Freddy' hung upside-down in his lavatory at his house Blo'Norton.

57   Login 1916, 67-8, quoting letter from Sir John Lawrence 1858.
58   Thomson 1981, 14.
59   Mary Traill was an illegitimate daughter of George William Traill, and co-heir of his estate with Burroughs.
60   Letter from Mary Traill to F.W. Burroughs, n.d., OLA D19/8/6.
61   The British were almost defeated in a battle at Ferozeshah in the 1st Sikh War in 1846, but it ended in a British victory.
62   Letter from George William Traill to F.W. Burroughs 24/2/1846, OLA D19/8/6.
63   Letter from Arthur Lillie, Cawnpore to F.W. Burroughs, Fort George 31/8/1848, OLA D19/8/6. The Moulraj surrendered the city of Moultan in the Punjab to a British force in February 1849. Astonishingly for a British army officer, Lillie became a Buddhist while in India and wrote a series of books on the influence of Buddhism on primitive Christianity. Reviewed as 'a wide reader without great powers of mental digestion', his most successful work was a rule book for a Scottish croquet tournament.
64   Minutes of Kirkwall Town Council 13/9/1859, OLA K1/1/12.
65   Letter from Maj. William Macdonald (son of Capt. Donald Macdonald of Sandside, Caithness) to F.W. Burroughs 17/7/1859, OLA D19/8/7/3.
66   Thomson 1981, 115.
67   The 240 foot tall Qutub Minar was built by Qutub-ud-Din Aibak, the founder of the Delhi Sultanate, as a victory tower after the defeat of Delhi's last Hindu kingdom. At its base is the Quwwat-ul Islam mosque, the first mosque in India, built with pillars plundered from 27 Hindu temples.
68   Amritsar, famous for the Golden Temple, the Centre of the Sikh faith.
69   Letter from F.W. Burroughs, Rawalpindi to David Balfour, Orkney 22/7/1860, OLA D2/21/11.
70   Letter from F.W. Burroughs, Rawalpindi to David Balfour, Orkney 23/4/1862, OLA D2/21/13. Col. (later Lt. Gen. Sir) Harry Burnet Lumsden was *one of the ablest and best military officers in the service* according to Sir John Lawrence. He was also renowned for his passion for hunting expeditions throughout the Punjab.
71   Chaplain G.R. Gleig, one of the very few survivors of the First Afghan War 1839-42.
72   Macdonald's grave at Jalozai reads: *Sacred to the memory of Lt Col Wm Macdonald, Deputy Lieutenant and Justice of the Peace of the county of Caithness, Scotland, who died of cholera whilst commanding the 93rd Sutherland Highlanders at Camp Jalozai on 29th October 1862 aged 35 years.* Macdonald had married Emma Lindsay in 1860 and had a baby son. His younger brother, Maj. Henry Macdonald, served in the Mutiny and was murdered in India in 1873.
73   Letter from F.W. Burroughs, Camp Jalozai to Caroline Burroughs, Dresden 28/10/1862, OLA D19/8/8/1. Burroughs' parents were separated by this time.
74   Letter from F.W. Burroughs, Sialkot to David Balfour, Orkney 12/1/1863, OLA D2/21/14.
75   Tim Willasey-Wilsey, www.victorianweb.org. The people described as 'Hindustani fanatics' in the contemporary press were in fact a militant Islamic sect akin to Al-Qa'ida whose leader declared a Jihad against the British.
76   The Orkney Herald 2/8/1870.
77   Thomson 1981, 15 quoting letter from David Balfour to F.W. Burroughs 16/6/1866.
78   ibid, 211-12.
79   Murree was a new town when Burroughs visited; it was developed by Sir Henry Lawrence as a sanatorium for British troops, construction starting in 1851. It was the HQ of the colonial Punjab government until 1876.
80   Kashmir did not join the Mutiny in 1857.
81   Nautch, a style of popular dancing performed by nautch girls as an entertainment, originally in the Mughal courts but became popular in the palaces of the Nawabs and also (as here) in the households of the senior officers of the East India Company and the British army.
82   The chambered cairn at Swandro on the west side of Rousay was re-excavated in 2015 and subsequent seasons.

341

83   Letter from F.W. Burroughs, Rawalpindi to David Balfour, Orkney 9/9/1861, OLA D2/21/12. David's brother, William Balfour, built Birstane House outside Kirkwall, also designed by David Bryce.
84   Letter from James Drummond, Edinburgh to David Balfour, Shapinsay 6/6/1861, OLA D2/21/12.
85   Letters from Bridgeman Lees, India to David Balfour, Shapinsay 22/1/1862, 11/3/1862, 2/6/1862, OLA D2/21/13.
86   Letter from William Nasau Lees to David Balfour 22/9/1865, OLA D2/21/14. W.N. Lees was a Persian and Arabic scholar, the principal of the madrasah in Calcutta and for some years the owner of *The Times* of India.

From the Other Side

Prologue

I cannot resist concluding these stories of long-dead Orkney men and women with the story of one who died but refused to lie quietly in his grave. One of the most intriguing letters in the Balfour Archive concerns the ghost of James Stewart of Brugh,[1] who returned to Westray on a winter's day in 1863, five years after his death.

The sight of the laird caused all the consternation one might expect amongst those who saw him but, when the Reverend James Brotchie heard about the apparition, he was thrown into such paroxysms of terror that he had to have three men staying in the house with him every night. Marcus Calder, David Balfour's factor, gleefully related the story in a letter to Balfour which he wrote just a few days after the event.

The Stewarts of Brugh

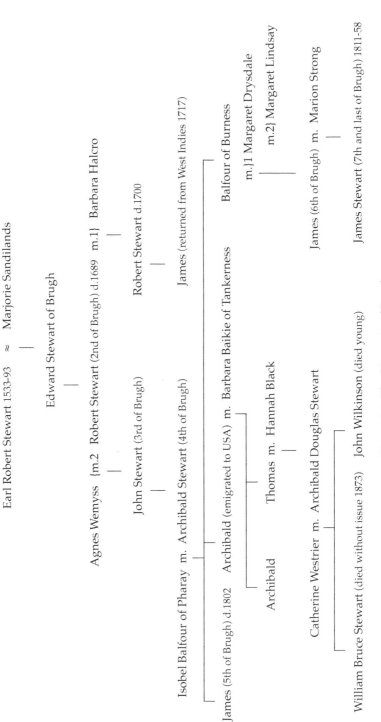

Figure 9.1: *The Stewarts of Brugh.*

A Westray Ghost Story

In absence of better I'll tell you a Westray story, quite new and exciting
... your tenant in Ouseness David Manson got the old doors of the isle
[aisle] where J Stewart of Brugh was buried (you know the place) from
Mr Brotchie [the minister], the doorway being built up. Well, the poor
man made a Barn door of it.

About ten days ago [22nd November 1863] Manson's wife was
going about and chancing to look into the Barn, what should she see
sitting in the doors inside the Barn, but the Laird o Brough! She screamed
and fainted. Her daughter (a great big woman) hearing the noise, came
running out to see what was the matter. She saw the same sight and
followed the mother's example. A boy seeing his mother and sister, as he
thought dead, ran down to the shore where his father was working at the
ware and told him that their mother and sister were "lying in the Close".
Of course David hurried home and saw the Laird still sitting in the door.
After picking up the two women, he hurried off to Cocklehouse and told
Mr. Brotchie. When the latter heard the story he was in a [illegible] and
ordered David to go immediately and put the door back to the Old Kirk.
Well, David got the door in his cart and took off with it to the North
Kirk. As he was coming near it he met some men who spoke to him, and
who, after a minute, said "The Guid preserve us, there's the Laird of
Brough sitting in your cart." David in a fit of desperation couped the cart
and cleared himself of the presence of the Laird and the haunted doors.
Brotchie requires two men to sleep with him now and a third to watch in
the interim.[2]

The story of the laird and the minister is a mysterious whodunnit
which is still waiting to be fully unravelled by a Hercule Poirot
of the archives. Why was the minister, who never saw the ghost,
put into such a fright that he needed three men to guard him at
night? Significantly, Calder has no need to make any explanation
to Balfour about Brotchie's reaction, so it must have been common

knowledge that the minister had some sinister reason for fearing the deceased laird's reappearance. In Westray and Papay, half-remembered scraps of rumour and of a poem still linger, pointing accusing fingers at the minister, and sometimes also at two of his elders, as being responsible for Stewart's death. Yet neither Balfour (a prime pillar of Orkney society) nor anyone else brought any charges against Brotchie, who administered the Brough estate as sole trustee until his own death 14 years later. There are so many questions that cannot be answered, but at least some of the background to this wonderful story can be reconstructed.

Figure 9.2
St Mary's, the old parish kirk in Pierowall, Westray. The chancel at the east end became a burial aisle for the Stewart family after the Reformation.

James Stewart of Brugh died in Westray on the 25th of June 1858. He was buried in St Mary's, the old kirk beside the sea in Pierowall where his ancestors had appropriated the chancel for a family burial aisle after the Reformation. The nave was used as a parish kirk into the 19th century but, by the time of James' death, a new kirk had been built in the centre of the island and the medieval building allowed to fall into ruin. The doorway between the Stewart aisle and the rest of the kirk was being built up and the wooden doors were redundant. Or so they had seemed to the minister.

Stewart was just 47 years old, an only son and a bachelor. He was the seventh generation directly descended from Robert Stewart, Earl of Orkney, who was an illegitimate son of King James V. Earl Robert's son Edward Stewart was holding the lands of Brugh in South Ronaldsay in 1617 and, with every generation, the estate grew larger through judicious marriage alliances. Cleat and other lands in Westray came to Edward when his son Robert married the heiress Barbara Halcro in 1638, and their grandson Archibald acquired the island of Pharay by marrying Isobel Balfour in 1724. Archibald also purchased the Fair Isle and, later, the lands of Burness in Firth and Campston in St Andrews on the Mainland were added to the extensive Stewart estate.

However, like several of the other great families that dominated Orkney politics in the 17th and 18th centuries, (such as the Traills, Baikies, Feas) the dynasty quietly fizzled out in the 19th century for lack of male heirs. When James, the fifth laird of Brugh, died childless in 1802, the estate passed to his nephew, also James, who himself died young in 1811, shortly after his son was born. This son James (the ghost in this story) was the last of the Stewarts to live in Westray. When he died in 1858 the estate passed back to the line of a great-uncle, another Archibald, who had emigrated to America with his wife Barbara Baikie of Tankerness. The only legal heirs to Brugh were thus Archibald's American great-grandsons, the children of Archibald Douglas Stewart, a cooper in Louisiana. Two older sons had already died young, leaving nine-year-old William Bruce and his brother John Wilkinson.

Long before he died, James had taken careful thought for the disposal of his estate and instructed his lawyer to search for claimants in America. Assuming that the little boys would come to Orkney to enjoy their inheritance, he left them his mansion house of Cleat with all its contents. His family had repaired and extended the old house after it was burnt by government troops in

1746 but, a century later, it was neither comfortable nor fashionable and Stewart had started to build a smaller modern house close by. When he wrote his will, he intended that the house would be finished after his death so that the heirs could use it, and they were also to receive rental income from the estate until they came of age. It was stipulated that they would become British: the estate was to be entailed on the heirs of William Bruce and, failing them, of John Wilkinson, *born in this country after their fathers shall have qualified as British subjects.*

Figure 9.3
James Stewart of Brough (1811-58) as a child, painted by John Watson Gordon.
(Orkney Museums)

If there were no heirs the whole estate was to be conveyed to the Reverend James Brotchie as sole trustee, the income to be divided as: one-quarter to be given to the hospital in Kirkwall, one-quarter to missionary societies (even-handedly divided between Church of Scotland and Church of England missions) and the remaining half to be administered by the North Isles Presbytery to fund itinerating ministers. Brotchie was nominated as trustee for life, earning a salary for the post of £70 a year (equivalent to more than £5,000 in 2020),[3] to be succeeded by four lawyers and ministers nominated by Stewart.

What James could hardly have imagined was the ill-fortune that dogged the Stewart line. John Wilkinson died in his early teens in 1863. The following year William Bruce was duly brought to Scotland, after difficulties and delays owing to the American Civil War, and sent to a Scottish school to be educated 'according to the wishes' of James Stewart. It can only have been a traumatic transition for the young boy from Louisiana. In 1869 William married Anne Dowling-Smith, the daughter of an Edinburgh doctor. Perhaps the marriage was as organised for him as the other major events in his life had been; it ended in divorce two years later. A baby son had died and Anne died not long after. In August 1872 William remarried. He had now qualified as a natural born British subject and was drawing the income of the trust-estate, but there is no record of him ever coming to Orkney to see, let alone live in, his inheritance. On the 22nd of January 1873 the 24-year-old heir died, leaving an 18-year-old widow. *The last of the Stewarts of Brugh rests in Norwood cemetery* wrote William Peacock, one of the Trustees, to Sheriff James Robertson. *Poor boy, his life and experiences have been sad indeed.*[4]

Three days after James Stewart died, the Orcadian reported briefly in the Deaths columns the demise of James Stuart Esq. of Brugh *at his residence* in Westray. A week later, a polite correction was inserted into the Letters to the Editor, pointing out that the melancholy event had in fact befallen the late lamented Brugh at *the Manse of Westray, where he happened to be taken ill.*[5] This would seem a totally insignificant correction if it were not for the fact that rumours had connected the Reverend James Brotchie with the premature death of the laird of Brugh. Someone (the letter is signed

B.D.S) was anxious that it was known that Stewart died in the manse, not at his home, and the inference is that it was a sudden and unexpected death. The letter does sound as if the writer is trying discreetly to make a point.

It was inevitable that Stewart's early death and the unusual appointment of a single trustee should spark comment, but there is plenty more that is odd, at least. On the death certificate the Westray doctor, William Rendall, stated the cause of death as Purpura Haemorrhagica, a rare form of internal haemorrhaging normally associated with horses (commonly known as strangles), but not with humans. Given that this seems to be a most unusual cause of death, it is a little strange that there was apparently no follow-up enquiry or investigation. A line of a lost poem: *the laird he drank the poisoned cup* filtered down through Papay memory, and a Papay tradition stated that Brotchie had quarrelled with Stewart and he and two of his elders had murdered the laird. The deed was said to have brought down a curse on the men and their families, which was still bringing multiple misfortunes to their descendants in the 1960s.[6] However, Brotchie retained and acted in his position of trust as Stewart's executor for the rest of his days, so there was never any public accusation made against him.

As Stewart had inherited Brugh when he was a few weeks old, the estate was managed by a Trust and this continued even after the laird had come of age in 1832. What is rather surprising is to find that it is the Reverend James Brotchie who is acting as the estate factor, writing all the letters regarding the leasing of farms, the shipping of kelp and so on from the Westray manse. Admittedly, Brotchie's role as minister of the Church of Scotland left him with a great deal of time on his hands. Many of his flock in Westray and virtually the entire population of Papay defected to the Free Church in 1843 – the minister found the door of the brand-new kirk in Papay firmly locked and no-one apparently able to find the key. Virtually redundant, Brotchie had *some release from clerical duties* ...[7] Nonetheless, it is understandable if contemporaries regarded his influence over the laird as excessive and unhealthy. Ten years before Stewart's death, Sheriff Robertson had recorded in his journal having dinner with Brotchie. *He has got James Stewart of Brugh in a curious state of vassalage to him, and so has he young*

Gordon of Burgher – and the whole Presbytery of the North Isles as well. He is a sleak oily man of God, meek and plausible, and I believe honest, tho somewhat bilious. He ... sounded me as to becoming one of a set of Trustees for Stewart but I declined at once.[8]

So, long before there were any unsavoury rumours circulating linking the minister with Stewart's death, the Sheriff (and presumably others as well) were commenting on the strange way in which he appeared to be manipulating the laird to the advantage of himself and the North Isles Presbytery. It is also interesting that Robertson wanted nothing to do with the Trust. To be fair to Brotchie, Robertson did *believe* [him] *honest,* and in all the complications which arose from interpreting and administering Stewart's wishes, he was seeking legal advice as to what he could or could not do, so he cannot be accused of acting underhandedly. Could he let out the farm and old house of Cleat to a tenant, for example; should he spend estate money on completing the new house, or suspend the work?[9] Although it may have annoyed people that he attempted to challenge the codicil to the will which Stewart added just two weeks before his death, altering or cancelling some of the annuities he had left to his father's relations, the attempt was made through legal channels and not secretly.

In fact the lands of Brugh were so scattered and extensive, and Stewart's will so complex, that it was 1882 before the estate was finally transferred to the North Isles Presbytery. Before this, it had been realised that some of it was so encumbered with debts that it was costing more to administer it than the income was worth. In 1866 Brotchie sold the Fair Isle. The Trustees continued conscientiously to administer what was now known as the Stewart Endowment, but after the First World War the properties became even more unprofitable. The lands in Firth and St Andrews were sold, leaving those in Westray and Pharay and, in the late 1970s, virtually all the land in Westray was sold too. Only the island of Pharay, dotted with abandoned houses, remained, its green fields let for grazing to a Westray sheep farmer. In 2018 Pharay was sold, to the Orkney Islands Council. It will now support neither families nor sheep but only wind turbines. With its sale went the last thread that for almost 400 years had connected Westray to the Stewarts of Brugh.

And as for the ghost? Maddeningly, Calder writes no sequel to his story – or none has survived, leaving all the questions unanswered. Did the ghost appear again, or was it appeased once the doors had been returned to the kirk? For how long did Brotchie require three men to stay in his house at night for fear of being haunted? Most of all, just what had the minister done that warranted such a terrible fear of the laird's revenge?

Chapter 9

1   The spellings Stuart and Brough were also in use by contemporaries. The older spelling is invariably Brugh, but from the mid 19th century Brough is more common.
2   Letter from Marcus Calder, Westray to David Balfour, Shapinsay 2/12/1863, OLA D2/21/14.
3   www.nationalarchives.gov.uk/currency converter equates £70 in 1850 with £5,613 in 2020, however it quotes its purchasing power as 4 horses or 13 cows, which would cost much more today.
4   Letter from William Peacock SSC, Edinburgh to Sheriff James Robertson, Kirkwall 29/1/1873, OLA, bound volume of letters: Westray Manse Case, p.1.
5   *The Orcadian* 28/6/1858, p.4; *The Orcadian* 12/7/1858, p.4.
6   Tom Muir (letter to Lucy Gibbon, Orkney Archives 19/1/2015) quoting J.D. Mackay from Papay.
7   Brugh Trust Letter Book vol.2, 29/6/1851, OLA D34/B1.
8   Journal of Sheriff James Robertson 15/5/1848, OLA D99/1/2.
9   In 1869 Bruce petitioned for the house to be completed so that he could live in it. In 1873, after Bruce's death, it was exchanged for the old manse and glebe. For some years it was the Church of Scotland manse, conveniently situated close to the new church that had replaced the old Westside church (at Tuquoy) and the Northside church (at Pierowall).

Postscript

If Orkney is a small dot on the map of the globe, there were few places on that map where Orkney farstraers did not venture in their search for riches, adventure, or simply survival. I am aware that many of their stories are only half-told here, the next instalment in a letter which I never found – perhaps lost forever in a shipwrecked mailbag, or still waiting to be discovered in the formidable depths of the Balfour Archive. The careers of prominent Orcadians are sometimes well documented but so many other individuals enter history only briefly and disappear again, their stories left hanging in the air. I often wondered What Happened Next?

I wanted to know what happened to ten-year-old Peter Petrie and the other children who fled poverty in Orkney only to be caught up in a brutal civil war in America. Were they shot in skirmishes like young Baikie Harvey, or did they survive to become prosperous citizens of the newly-minted United States? Did Hugh Mowat, dispatched half way across the world in his teens to find a livelihood on a plantation in Grenada, end up a wealthy 'planter' or succumb, like his brother Robert and so many thousands of young men, to tropical fever? Where was Isobel Gunn, in the 30 years in which she disappeared from official sight in Orkney? Most of all, I wanted to know if the Reverend James Brotchie killed the laird of Brugh ...

Many of these stories are sad, emerging from a poverty-stricken Orkney so different from the one we know today, and from a life which most people knew only as one of hardship and lack of opportunity. For the few who came home to enjoy an affluent retirement, like Captain William Balfour or William Manson, there were many more who died on Britain's innumerable battlefields, or in the frozen Arctic or the disease-ridden tropics. Families were desperate to dispatch their teenage sons into any 'situation' that offered itself, gambling on the slim chance that they would survive and prosper. The Traills of Tirlet were typical in seeing the probability of their son dying on a man-o-war or of fever in the West Indies as less of a risk than staying at home in Westray and marrying a girl with no tocher.

Women were often forced into unfeminine roles by the absence of men, and successfully ran farms and businesses, but severe penalties awaited any who dared to cross the uncompromising boundaries set by Kirk and culture and society. In the 16th and 17th centuries, women whose skills or behaviour alerted the fear, superstition or sheer malice and jealousy of their neighbours, met ghastly deaths on Gallowhill. Two centuries later, society was still unforgiving to those who did not conform. Isobel Gunn, the most courageous, capable and adventurous woman in these pages, spent her last 50 years of life as a pauper and vagrant and social outcast.

However, I also found much that was intriguing and entertaining in the lives I researched. Enticing doors were always opening into side-alleys I longed to explore, though they stretched the Orkney connection impossibly thin. The embassy of the Yamacraw chief, Tomochichi, to London in 1743 (to ratify a treaty with George II) must be a story in itself. Other fascinating characters made brief appearances in the letters I read. Captain Burrough's description of a hunting expedition in the Punjab with the knickerbockered Colonel Lumsden of Belhelvie introduces one of the brilliant and eccentric 'soldier-sahibs' of the North-West Frontier who became legends in their own lifetime. Closer to home, how could one not want to know more of the scandalous life of Penelope Pitt?

While war, famine, shipwreck and loneliness are dark shadows in the background throughout the pages of this book, there is a bright counterpoint in the courage and enterprise shown by the farstraers, both men and women. In their very different ways, they all added to the story of both Orkney and the far-flung destinations of their voyages and their resilience to adversity remains an inspiration.

Glossary

Assize trial by jury

bent bent grass (marram grass), coarse grass growing in dunes, used for making baskets, tethers, simmons (rope for thatching) etc.

bere a type of barley, probably introduced by the Norse, grown in Scotland from the 8th century and formerly a staple food in Orkney.

bere multures a proportion of the grain brought to the mill to be ground into beremeal, paid to the miller as his fee.

curche woman's head-covering, kerchief.

Episcopalian system of church government by a hierarchy of clergy under direction of bishops; one belonging to or supporting Episcopal Church.

Established Church church 'established' by Act of Parliament in 1560 as the state Church, the Church of Scotland.

feu tenure of land in perpetuity in return for fixed annual payment (feu duty) to the overlord (feudal superior). In Orkney, the superior was the owner of the earldom: the Earls of Morton from the 17th century until 1766, when it was purchased by Sir Lawrence Dundas.

habeas corpus law that states that a person cannot be kept in prison unless they have first been brought before a court of law.

kelp the fused slag produced by burning dried tangles (seaweed), valued as a source of alkali used in soap- and glass-making and, later, as a source of iodine. Kelp brought significant wealth to Orkney lairds in the late 18th and early 19th centuries.

ley land left uncultivated, fallow.

teind tithe, tax to the Church.

township community farming land in common, eg sharing common grazings or cultivating arable land in *runrig* – intermingled strips of land periodically redistributed.

Presbyterian system of church government by elders or presbyters, developed by John Calvin in Geneva and John Knox in Scotland; a member of this church.

privateer privately owned ship or person given commission from sovereign in time of war to harass and attack enemy shipping, take prizes etc. A thin line divided privateers from pirates, and they often turned to piracy in peacetime when their commission ceased.

	EVENTS IN ORKNEY	EVENTS IN BRITAIN	EVENTS OVERSEAS
1560		Scottish Reformation – Kirk of Scotland Established	
1563		Act anent Witchcrafts (Scotland)	
1597		24 'witches' burnt in Aberdeen	
1600		East India Company (EIC) founded	
1603		James VI of Scotland crowned James I of England	
1607			1st permanent British colony in N.America, Jamestown
1610			Henry Hudson maps Hudson Bay
1614-19	Robert Stewart's rebellion 1614		Sir Thomas Roe negotiating trade deals for EIC at Mughal court
1615	Jonet Drever and Katherine Bigland burnt	Earl Patrick Stewart executed	
1624	Marable Couper and Annie Taylor burnt		
1638		National Covenant signed in Edinburgh	
1642		Beginning of English Civil War	
1643	Katherine Craigie and Jonet Reid burnt		
1649		Execution of King Charles I	
1650	Montrose raising royalist army	Montrose defeated at Carbisdale and executed	
1650-58	Occupation by Cromwell's troops	Commonwealth under Oliver Cromwell	
1660		Restoration of Charles II	

	EVENTS IN ORKNEY	EVENTS IN BRITAIN	EVENTS OVERSEAS
1668			*Nonsuch* sails to Hudson Bay, returns with cargo of furs
1670		Hudson's Bay Company founded (HBC)	
1679	*The Crown* wrecked off Deerness	Covenanters defeated at battle of Bothwell Brig	Covenanter POWs transported in 1670s and 1680s
1688		'Glorious Revolution', accession of William and Mary	
1707		Union of Scottish and and English Parliaments	
1714		Accesssion of George I, 1st Hanoverian king	
1715	'James VIII' proclaimed in Kirkwall	Jacobite rising defeated	Jacobite POWs transported to plantations
1732			Colony of Georgia founded by James Oglethorpe
1745		Jacobite rising	
1746	Jacobite lairds in hiding in Westray. Trenaby burnt	Jacobites defeated at Culloden, severe reprisals	Jacobite POWs transported to plantations
1756-63	Pressgangs active	Pressgangs active	Seven Years War in Europe and India
1757			Battle of Plassey, British under Clive defeat French in India
1766	John and Thomas Balfour to University	Sir Lawrence Dundas buys earldom of Orkney	
1766-69			Voyages of *Flora* of Whitby to Archangel, Carolina etc
1772		James Somerset case	
1773			Boston Tea Party

	EVENTS IN ORKNEY	EVENTS IN BRITAIN	EVENTS OVERSEAS
1774-75	Emigrant ships in Kirkwall		Manson family and Orkney emigrants sail to Georgia
1775		Thomas Balfour marries Frances Ligonier in London	1st battles of American Revolution
1776			American Declaration of Independence
1777	Thomas Balfour recruiting troops for America		Gen. Burgoyne defeated at Saratoga, surrendered army
1778	Balfours take lease of Bu in Burray, Mary born	Joseph Knight case	
1779			Grenada and St Lucia captured by French
1780	Edward Balfour born		
1781	William Balfour born	William Manson and family return to Britain	Gen. Cornwallis defeated at Yorktown, surrendered army
1783	Thomas Balfour buys estate of Sound		Treaty of Paris recognises independence of United States
1787	Thomas Balfour builds Cliffdale in Shapinsay	Peggy Balfour presented at court of George III	
1787	William Manson marries Elizabeth Balfour	Society for Effecting the Abolition of the Slave Trade	
1793	Orkney and Shetland Fencibles raised		French Revolutionary War begins
1795			Billy Manson dies in Antigua
1795-96		Col. Balfour and North Lowland Fencibles to Ireland	Sandy Watt in Gen. Abercromby's expedition to Caribbean

Year	EVENTS IN ORKNEY	EVENTS IN BRITAIN	EVENTS OVERSEAS
1796		French prevented by storms from landing in Bantry Bay	
1797		French attempt to land at Fishguard	William Balfour in naval battle of Cape St Vincent
1798		Irish Rebellion. French invasion forces defeated	
1799		Thomas Balfour dies in Bath	Edward Balfour dies in battle of Alkmaar
1800		Act of Union created United Kingdom of Great Britain and Ireland. End of Irish Parliament	William Leith prisoner in Russia
1805			James Leith in naval battle of Trafalgar
1806	Capt William Balfour marries Mary Manson		Isobel Gunn sails for Hudson Bay as 'John Fubbister'
1807		Act for the Abolition of the Slave Trade	James Scarth, son of Isobel Gunn, born at HBC Fort Pembina
1809	Isobel Gunn and son return to Stromness		
1812			Red River settlement founded
1813	Frances Balfour dies in Kirkwall	Emigrants from Kildonan set out for Red River	
1815			Napoleon defeated at battle of Waterloo
1821			Hudson's Bay and North-West Companies merge
1832		Reform Act widened franchise	Dr John Login arrives in India
1833		Slave Emancipation Act	

EVENTS IN ORKNEY	EVENTS IN BRITAIN	EVENTS OVERSEAS
1836-37 Surviving ice-bound whalers return to Stromness in spring with remnants of crews		
	1837 Accession of Queen Victoria	
		1839-42 1st Afghan War
1847 Balfour Castle built on Shapinsay		
		1848-49 2nd Anglo-Sikh War - annexation of Punjab
	1853-56 Duleep Singh brought to England 1854	Crimean War
		1857 The Mutiny. Cawnpore massacre etc, Siege of Lucknow.
		1870 Red River joined Confederation of Canada as Manitoba province
		1870 HBC transferred its charter to Canadian government
1873 Gen. Burroughs retired to Rousay		
1886 Crofters Act (Scotland)		

Bibliography

AM = Abbotsford Miscellany, see Maidment, J. and W. Turnbull

Barry, G., 1805 *History of the Orkney Islands* (facs. repr. Edinburgh 1975)

Basker, J.G., ed. 2002 *Amazing Grace, An Anthology of Poems about Slavery 1660-1810* (Yale University)

Beattie, J.H. and H.M. Buss, 2003 *Undelivered Letters to Hudsons Bay Company Men on the Northwest Coast of America 1830-57* (Vancouver)

Ben, Jo, c.1529 *Descriptio Insularum Orchadiarum* (repr. The Orkney Herald, Kirkwall 1922)

Bolus, M., 1971 (Winter), *The son of I. Gunn,* The Beaver 23-26

Brand, Rev. J., 1701 *A Brief Description of Orkney, Zetland, Pightland-Firth and Caithness* (repr. Edinburgh 1883)

Brunton, M., 1820 *Emmeline* (Edinburgh)

CPR = Minutes of Cairston Presbytery meetings, OLA, OCR/2

Cashlin, E.J., 1999 *The Kings Ranger. Thomas Brown and the American Revolution on the Southern Frontiers* (NewYork)

Chambers D.B., ed., 2013 *Runaway Slaves in Jamaica* (University of Southern Mississipi, online)

Clouston, J.S., 1928 *The Orkney Parishes, containing the Statistical Account of Orkney 1795-1798, drawn up from the Communications of the Ministers of the Different Parishes by Sir John Sinclair, Bart.* (Kirkwall)

Craven, Rev. J.B., 1897 *History of the Church in Orkney 1558-1662* (Kirkwall)

— 1911 *Church Notes from South Ronaldsay and Burray* (Kirkwall)

— 1912 *History of the Episcopal Church in Orkney 1688-1912* (Kirkwall)

Cuthbert, O., ed., 2001 *Low's History of Orkney* (Orkney Heritage Society)

Dalrymple, W., 2003 *White Mughals* (London)

— 2019 *The Anarchy, The Relentless Rise of the East India Company* (London)

Dalyell, J.G., 1835 *The Darker Superstitions of Scotland* (Glasgow)

Davis, R. S., Junior., 1982 *Scottish and English Immigrants to the Georgia Frontier 1774-5*, (bound typescript in Kirkwall Library)

— 1983 *The Last Colony, William Manson and the Friendsborough Settlement* (bound typescript in Kirkwall Library)

Devine, T.M., ed., 2015 *Recovering Scotland's Slavery Past, The Caribbean Connection* (Edinburgh)

Dobson, D., 1989 *The Original Scots Colonists of early America 1612-1783* (Baltimore)

Dodwell, H., 1926 *The Nabobs of Madras* (London)

Elliott, M., 1989 *Wolfe Tone, Prophet of Irish Independence* (New Haven and London)

Fenton, A., 1978 *The Northern Isles: Orkney and Shetland* (Edinburgh)

Fereday, R., 1980 *Orkney Feuds and the '45* (Kirkwall)

— 1990 *The Orkney Balfours 1747-99* (Oxford)

— ed., 2000 *The Autobiography of Samuel Laing of Papdale 1780-1868* (Kirkwall)

Goodare, J., 1998 *Women and the witch-hunt in Scotland*, Social History 23, 288-308

Gorrie, D., 1868 *Summers and Winters in the Orkneys* (London and Kirkwall)

HBCA = Hudson's Bay Company Archives, Manitoba

Hewison, W.S., 2001 *Not Born to be Drowned, An Orkney soldier in the Napoleonic wars* (Kirkwall)

Hossack, B.H., 1900 *Kirkwall in the Orkneys* (facs.repr. The Kirkwall Press 1986)

Innis, H.A., 1970 *The Fur Trade in Canada* (University of Toronto Press, orig. ed. 1930)

Johnson, G., 1995 *Cultural Atlas of India* (Oxford)

Larner, C., 1981 *Enemies of God, the Witch-hunt in Scotland* (London)

— 1984 *Witchcraft and Religion, The Politics of Popular Belief* (Oxford)

Leask, J.T. Smith, 1931 *A Peculiar People and Other Orkney Tales* (Kirkwall)

Login, Lady L.C., 1890 *Sir John Login and Duleep Singh* (London)

Login, Lady L.C. and E.D. Login, 1916 *Lady Login's Recollections, Court Life and Camp Life 1820-1904* (London)

Low, Rev. G., 1773 *Description of Orkney*, POAS 1923

MacGillivray, E., ed., 1956 *Letters of Thomas Balfour to William Watt 1784-87*, Orkney Miscellany 3, 68-79

MacInnes, M., 2008 *Alias Isobel, an Orkney narrative* (Stromness)

Mackintosh, W.R., 1892 *Curious Incidents from the Ancient Records of Kirkwall* (Kirkwall)

Maidment, J. and W. Turnbull, eds, 1837 *Trials for Witchcraft, Sorcery and Superstition in Orkney*, Abbotsford Miscellany vol.I, 135-85 (Edinburgh)

Marwick, E., 1991 *Northern Witches* in J.D.M. Robertson, ed., An Orkney Anthology: The Selected Works of Ernest Walker Marwick (Edinburgh)

Maxwell-Stuart, P.G., 2011 *Witch Beliefs and Witch Trials in the Middle Ages, Documents and Readings* (London)

Mooney, H.L., 1954 *The Wreck of the "Crown" and the Covenanters in Orkney*, Orkney Miscellany 2, 1-8

NSA = *New Statistical Account* 1842, *The Statistical Account of the Orkney Islands by the Ministers of the Respective Parishes* (Edinburgh)

NIPR = Minutes of North Isles Presbytery meetings, OLA, OCR 3

OCR = Orkney Church Records, OLA

OLA = Orkney Library and Archives

OP = Minutes of Orkney Presbytery meetings 1639-1646, OLA, OCR 4/1

OSA = *Old Statistical Account*, see Storer Clouston, J., 1928

POAS = Proceedings of the Orkney Antiquarian Society

PRO = Public Record Office

Peterkin, A., 1820 *Rentals of the Ancient Earldom and Bishoprick of Orkney* (Edinburgh)

Pogue, the Rev. V.C., 1954 *Church Life in Orphir 200 Years Ago*, Orkney Miscellany 2, 24-33

— 1956, *Schools in the Cairston Presbytery in the 18th Century*, Orkney Miscellany 3, 47-67

Rich, E., 1968 *The Fur Trade and the Northwest to 1857* (Oxford University Press)

Rigg, S., 2011 *Men of Spirit and Enterprise. Scots and Orkneymen in the Hudson's Bay Company 1780-1821* (Edinburgh)

Ritchie, E., 2009 *A Collected History of the Traill/Trail Family* (privately printed)

Robertson, D. J., 1924 *Orkney Folkore,* POAS II, 37-47

Robertson, J.D.M., 2011 *The Pressgang in Orkney and Shetland* (Kirkwall)

Scott, H., 1928 *Fasti Ecclesiae Scoticanae* vol. VII (Edinburgh)

Stuart, J., ed., 1841 *Extracts from the accounts of the Burgh of Aberdeen,* Miscellany of the Spalding Club Vol.5 (Aberdeen)

Thoms, G.H.M., *Copy of documents relating to Orkney; Originals deposited in the General Register House Edinburgh by G.H.M .Thoms Esq Sheriff of Orkney and Shetland,* OLA, SC11/79/1

Thomson, W.P.L., 1981 *The Little General and the Rousay Crofters* (Edinburgh)

— 2001 *The New History of Orkney* (Edinburgh)

Troup, J.A., ed., 1987 *The Ice-Bound Whalers* (Kirkwall)

Uglow, J., 2015 *In these Times, Living in Britain through Napoleon's Wars 1793-1815* (London)

Van Kirk, S., 1980 Many Tender Ties, Women in Fur-Trade Society 1670-1870 (University of Oklahoma Press, Norman and London)

Wenham, S., 1996-7 *Margaret Vedder, Orkney 1788: her Household Goods and Body Clothes,* Review of Scottish Culture 10, 128-131

— 2001 *A More Enterprising Spirit, The Parish and People of Holm in 18th Century Orkney*

Wheelwright, J., 1989 *Amazons and Military Maids: women who dressed as men in pursuit of life, liberty and happiness* (London)

Wilson, B., 2013 *Stromness, A History* (Kirkwall)

Index

Married women are generally indexed under their marital surname, cross-referenced under maiden name, except when they appear in the text only under their maiden name.

Abercromby, Gen. Ralph 1734-1801, 90, 102, 115, 218, 364
Aberdeen University, 154, 185, 273, 288
Aberdeen, Burgh of, ix, x, 4, 28-9, 64, 127, 167, 204, 293, 362, 370; Aberdeenshire 38, 324
Ackworth School, xi, 195-7, 205
Adams, John 1735-1826, 2nd president of U.S., 70
Afghanistan, 3, 286, 309, 325
Africa, 20, 93, 102-3, 117, 171-2, 209, 285
Agra, India, 321-2
agriculture, 18, 66, 156, 237
Aitkin, the Revd James, 44
Alaska, 274, 277
Alexander the Great, 327-8
Alfieri, Count Vittorio Amadeo, Italian dramatist 1749-1803, 163
Allahabad, India, 319
Ambela, India, 322; Ambela Campaign, 328
America (North), 4, 59, 61-85, 96, 131, 171, 193-4, 232, 262, 266, 268-9, 285, 340, 349
American Revolution, also American Rebellion/War of Independence, 4, 7, 54, 62-83, 97, 117, 154, 209, 211-12, 229-30, 351, 357
Americans, Native, 71, 76, 193-4
Amritsar, India, 322, 341
Anglo-Mysore wars, 300
Antigua, West Indies, 94, 97, 100-01, 184, 202-3, 205, 314, 364
Anti-Slavery movement, 106, 131
Archangel (Arkhangelsk), xii, 53, 57-8, 121, 169, 363

Assiniboia (Red River), xii, 263, 270
Assiniboine people, 235, 263
Attock, Fort, Indus River, xii, 327-8
Augusta, Georgia, U.S, 69, 71, 73, 75-6, 80, 85
Bahamas, West Indies, 80
Baikie, James of Tankerness d.1675, 32
Baikie, Robert of Tankerness 1738-1817, 139, 189, 220, 222
Baikie, the Revd Thomas, 46
Baikie, Thomas of Burness, 65, 82, 84-5, 97, 106
Balfour archive, 11, 165, 193, 345, 357
Balfour Castle, xi, x, ii, 11, 142, 214, 287, 303-4, 336, 366
Balfour, Alison, accused of witchcraft, burnt 1594, 31
Balfour (Huip), Ann 1763-?, see Ann de Monti
Balfour, David (1) 1754-1813, 139, 150, 153, 155-6, 165, 178-9, 185-7, 189, 204, 219, 222, 300
Balfour, David (2) 5th of Trenaby 1811-87, xii, 6, 139, 282, 303, 312, 320, 327, 329-30, 332, 336-7, 341, 342, 345, 355
Balfour, (John) Edward Ligonier 1780-99, 38, 157, 160, 162, 186, 189, 204, 209, 215, 218, 221, 262, 364-5
Balfour, Elizabeth (Betty) née Covingtrie d.1796, x, xi, 8, 131, 137, 140-5, 151, 178-9, 183, 185, 188, 204, 222, 287, 298, 339, 340
Balfour (Huip), Elizabeth 1758-?, 139, 188, 189, 204
Balfour, Frances, née Ligonier 1742-1813, x, xi, 5, 7, 41, 49, 137-40, 144, 147-52, 154-65, 178-9, 186-7, 189, 191, 204, 211, 218-20, 222, 364-5
Balfour, Henrietta (Harriet), née Sullivan c.1747-1844, 139, 301-4
Balfour, John 1st of Trenaby, 139
Balfour, John 3rd of Trenaby 1750-1842,

371

372